The United States, Israel, and the Search for International Order

How do emerging states become full, functioning members of the international system? In this book, Cameron G. Thies argues that new and emerging states are subject to socialization efforts by current member states, which guide them in locating their position in the international system.

Thies develops a theoretical approach to understanding how states socialize each other into and out of different roles in the international system, such as regional power, ally, and peacekeeper. The concept of state socialization is developed using role theory, a middle-range theory developed in the interdisciplinary field of social psychology. This middle-range theory helps to flesh out the theoretical mechanisms often missing in grand theories like neorealism and constructivism. The result is a structural theory of international politics that also allows for the explanation of actual foreign policy behavior by states. The foreign policy histories of the United States and Israel are analyzed using this theoretical approach to show how international social pressure has affected the kinds of roles they have adopted throughout their histories, as well as the kinds of roles that they have not been allowed to adopt. By considering the effects of international socialization attempts on their foreign policy behavior, Thies shows the well-known cases of the United States and Israel in a new light.

The United States, Israel, and the Search for International Order argues that the process by which states learn their appropriate roles and behaviors in the international social order is crucial to understanding international conflict and cooperation, which will be significant for those studying both theory and method in international relations, foreign policy, and diplomatic history.

Cameron G. Thies is Professor, Harlan E. McGregor Faculty Fellow, and Chair of the Department of Political Science at the University of Iowa. His research focuses on International Relations theory through the contributions of role theory, as well as state building in the developing world. He has published widely in journals such as *World Politics*, *European Journal of International Relations*, *British Journal of Political Science*, and *International Studies Quarterly*.

Role Theory and International Relations

Edited by Cameron G. Thies, University of Iowa, and Juliet Kaarbo, University of Edinburgh

The *Role Theory and International Relations Series* aspires to attract and publish the latest and best research integrating knowledge in the field of International Relations with role theory. This aspiration cuts across a wide swath of subfields, including foreign policy analysis, peace and security studies, international political economy, diplomatic studies, and international organization. While each of these subfields of study is presently organized as an "island of theory," this series intends to integrate their signature phenomena within a system of knowledge, a "theory complex" or an alliance among different subfields. This series showcases the ability of role theory to generate useful theoretical insights on its own or in combination with existing theories across these traditional subfields. Role theory's conceptual repertoire, plus its ability to span multiple levels of analyses and the major meta-theoretical divides in the discipline, position it to be an important integrative force in the study of International Relations.

The United States, Israel, and the Search for International Order

Socializing States

Cameron G. Thies

Routledge
Taylor & Francis Group

NEW YORK AND LONDON

First published 2013
by Routledge
711 Third Avenue, New York, NY 10017

Simultaneously published in the UK
by Routledge
2 Park Square, Milton Park, Abingdon, Oxon OX14 4RN

*Routledge is an imprint of the Taylor & Francis Group,
an informa business*

Library of Congress Cataloging-in-Publication Data

Thies, Cameron G.
  The United States, Israel and the search for international order :
socializing states / Cameron G. Thies.
      pages ; cm. — (Role theory and international relations ; 2)
  1. International relations—Philosophy.   2. International organization.
3. Newly independent states.   4. United States—Foreign relations.
5. Israel—Foreign relations.   I. Title.
    JZ1242.T53 2013
    327.101—dc23
    2012045361

ISBN: 978-0-415-81847-6 (hbk)
ISBN: 978-0-203-58124-7 (ebk)

Typeset in Sabon
by Apex CoVantage, LLC

For Steve Walker—an exceptionally gifted mentor and friend.

Contents

Figures

Table

Preface

This book has been a long time in the making. The first version was produced as my Ph.D. dissertation under the direction of Stephen G. Walker. Steve was an incredibly patient advisor who allowed me to try out a number of potential topics in the Fall Semester of 1998 before settling on the idea of using role theory to flesh out the concept of state socialization. I was heavily influenced at the time both by structural theorizing in Kenneth Waltz's and Alexander Wendt's work, and the more agent-oriented work carried out by my advisor. Walker's own previous work on role theory had provided a number of ways to think about incorporating role theory into existing international relations theory. The agent-structure debate had been in full swing for a while at that point in the discipline, and constructivism as we have come to know it was just beginning to find adherents. The idea that states could be socialized into or out of certain roles and associated behaviors seemed to me the ideal solution to marrying international relations theory and foreign policy analysis, as well as the agent-structure debate. Steve encouraged me to pursue this line of thinking and provided such fast turnaround commentary on my draft chapters that I was able to complete the dissertation by August of 1999 in time for the start of my first academic position.

The intellectual milieu at Arizona State provided exactly the right mix of ideas and tools to complete the dissertation. Carolyn Warner introduced me to institutional theory and associated methodological approaches, like the analytic narrative, that were essential in developing the socialization game and carrying out the case studies of the United States and Israel. Colin Elman and Miriam Fendius Elman both lent their interest in realist theory to the project, helping me to think through the possibilities and limits of fleshing out the socialization concept already contained in Waltzian neorealism. Colin and Mimi also brought their developing focus on improving the rigor of qualitative methods to the project. Sheldon Simon grounded my analysis through his traditional national security focus. In addition to my actual committee members, I owe an intellectual debt to Pat McGowan, Richard Ashley, and Roxanne Doty, each of whom influenced my thinking about structural theorizing in his or her own way.

After I began my first job as an assistant professor, I began to shop around a revised version of the dissertation as a book manuscript. Steve was very helpful in determining how to revise and repackage the dissertation into a book. As luck would have it, Alexander Wendt's landmark book, *Social Theory of International Relations*, was out in time for the American Political Science Association annual meeting in 1999. I quickly read Wendt's book with both trepidation and excitement. In my view, Wendt's book was largely about meta-theory and stylized examples, while my own project involved the development of specific theory and empirical case studies. Unfortunately, editors at the time could or would not distinguish the two. The most common response I received to my book proposal was: Hasn't Wendt already done this? Almost nothing could be more discouraging to a new assistant professor than to hear that you have been beaten to the punch by someone else, even if is not entirely true. As a result, I began to spin off pieces of the dissertation into articles that were tangentially related to the core argument.

It was not until I was awarded an International Studies Association Workshop Grant to host a small workshop on role theory in 2010 did the idea resurface to publish the dissertation as a book. In the process of assembling workshop members, we discovered that there were people all over the world using role theory. Rather than emanating from within the foreign policy analysis tradition in the United States, scholars elsewhere became attuned to role theory due to its affinity with constructivism. Through the workshop, I renewed and started new intellectual relationships with scholars like Marijke Breuning, Sebastian Harnisch, Julie Kaarbo, and Paul Kowert. The resulting workshop was a great success resulting in the publication of a special issue of *Foreign Policy Analysis* that included an article I extracted from the dissertation concerning Israel. The positive reception of this work then prompted a series of discussions between Steve, myself, and others that ultimately led to the launch of the book series with Routledge. My much-revised dissertation is now the book you have before you as one of the initial contributions to that series.

There is a great deal of path dependence built into a book that has taken fourteen years to see the light of publication. I have chosen to retain the original theoretical framework, despite having developed alternative approaches in other published work. If I had started this work from scratch today, I would probably be less beholden to the neorealist framework. As my thinking about international politics has evolved over time, I have become much less enamored of the "isms." I do think the book makes an important contribution in showing that even working within neorealism, one can create space for international society. I have also purposely chosen for this book not to be primarily a contribution to meta-theory; so extensive discussion about the relationship between neorealist ontological and epistemological underpinnings and that of role theory do not occupy a great deal of space in the following chapters. I expect that this will prompt plenty of discussion among those who are more inclined to such meta-theoretical debates. Finally, if my formal skills were more developed, I would try to convert the socialization game into an actual game theoretic model, rather than the heuristic model it currently is in the book. Steve has repeatedly shown in his work that game theory can be fruitfully combined with cognitive and social theories, including role theory.

I hope this brief intellectual history of the project helps to set the stage for what I believe to be an interesting theoretical and empirical contribution to the literature. In this book, I show how role theory can be combined with neorealism to develop a theory of how state socialization operates in the international system. The theory articulates how mechanisms of socialization and competition interact to create four master statuses, or the kinds of states it is possible to be in the system. States can then attempt to achieve a variety of other auxiliary roles consistent with their master status as they endure in the system. Socialization activities both ratify acceptable roles and attempt to end the adoption and enactment of unacceptable roles. This role location, or socialization, process is therefore the heart of the foreign policy process. The cases of the United States and Israel from emergence to the end of the twentieth century are then examined for evidence that socialization has occurred in a manner expected by the socialization game. The net result is a more social version of neorealist theory that finds a variety of types of states interacting with each other via socialization and competition to produce foreign policy outcomes and the larger contemporary international order.

Cameron G. Thies
Professor and Harlan E. McGregor Faculty Fellow
Iowa City, Iowa

1 Improving Structural Theories of International Politics

In the real world of events, we know that new states often emerge during very tumultuous times, such as at the close of world wars and the collapse of empires. States that form under these circumstances may be unstable at best. We need only recall the collapse of the Soviet Union and the new states that were formed in its wake. The Baltic Republics were welcomed back into the "family" of nations and even sought a role in the evolving European Union. Ukraine and Belarus, which started their international lives as nuclear powers, were gently stripped of that role by the international community due to the gap between their general capabilities and the possession of nuclear weapons. The specter of a continent-sized, nuclear power falling into chaos induced the international community to give Russia "complimentary" great power status by inviting her to meetings of the G-7, while at the same time the International Monetary Fund (IMF) and individual states like Germany tried to bail her out economically. Or consider the US response to the September 11, 2001, attacks, which ultimately led to war with the "rogue" states of Afghanistan and Iraq. These targets of the War on Terror demonstrate that the socialization of states is an ongoing process that great powers use to alter the behavior and very identity of states of lesser status in the international system. The crux of the matter is that the way members of the international system, and particularly great powers, socialize new states into the system affects the possibilities for both cooperation and conflict among states.

I argue in this book that all states undergo a process of socialization, which largely determines their success or failure as members of the international system. The socialization process begins as states emerge as independent actors, and it continues throughout their tenure in the system. A focus on socialization requires an examination of agents, their interactions, and the enduring structure of the international system. States (agents) are the initiators and subjects of socialization efforts. These activities occur through interstate interaction within the confines of an international system. An enduring structure of the system demands conformity from the agents to ensure its reproduction— hence the need for socialization efforts to maintain that conformity.

Previous attempts to incorporate socialization into the study of international relations have pushed our knowledge of this phenomenon forward, but it still remains incomplete. Waltz's (1979) *Theory of International Politics*, one of the most influential pieces of scholarship in modern international relations theory, assigns a special role for socialization. Along with competition, socialization is thought to be one of the two methods through which the international structure affects state behavior. Despite the centrality of socialization to his argument, Waltz provides only anecdotal evidence about the operation of socialization. Indeed, although socialization is often referenced in the literature as the means by which structure works its effects, few have delved beyond a superficial exploration of this concept for the anarchic international system as a whole. Constructivists such as Wendt (1999) discuss socialization, but their lack of application to specific cases results in abstract and incomplete models of the process. Scholars of the European Union and NATO explore socialization of member states but within the context of already highly institutionalized environments (e.g., Schimmelfennig 2000; Checkel 2005). This literature has generally failed to produce a generalizable model of the socialization process. In this book, I build upon Waltz's (1979) *Theory of International Politics* and offer several mechanisms that may theoretically account for the operation of the competition and socialization processes identified in Waltz's theory.

Since the study of socialization is relatively new—not only to Waltz, but also to international relations generally—this book embodies an interdisciplinary approach to the subject, drawing upon concepts and theories developed in economics, political science, psychology, social psychology, and sociology. In particular, this research fleshes out Waltz's spare structural theory by incorporating concepts from role theory. The focus on foreign policy roles as the subject of international socialization bridges the study of foreign policy and international relations. Unfortunately, these areas of study often proceed as if domestic-level factors and system-level factors were only distantly related. Waltz has advocated and repeatedly defended his position that neorealism cannot serve as a theory of foreign policy, despite strong counterarguments from Fearon (1998) and Elman (1996). The book concurs with the latter scholars by demonstrating how the structure of the international system and the domestic choices that lead to the adoption of state identity are linked through foreign policy roles. This theme fits quite nicely with the resurgence in the use of foreign policy role theory as a way to bridge agency and structure (e.g., Harnisch et al. 2011; Thies and Breuning 2012).

Roles in this book become the contents of socialization in the international system. Roles have the advantage of incorporating other possible contents of socialization, including norms, principles, beliefs, and rules. Role theory also provides us with an understanding of how roles are enacted; the kinds of normative expectations that are attached to roles; and, most importantly, the role location process. The role location process occurs when an actor attempts to achieve a role for itself in the system. Every role requires a partner to properly complete its enactment. For example, a regional protector role requires a regional protectee, a bloc leader requires allies to follow it, and so on. This role location process is essentially a role bargaining process, in which ego and alter ego interact to determine an appropriate role. The role bargaining process is the heart of socialization. Socialization is analyzed in this book as a role bargaining process between socializer and socializee.

The empirical research in this book is guided by a socialization "game"— really more of a visual metaphor that models the interaction between a state attempting to pursue a role in the system and its primary socializer. The socialization game incorporates insights from both role theory and dissonance theory. This game imposes a theoretical structure on the socialization process that is absent from previous discussions of socialization in the international relations literature. The socialization game models the role location process for the foreign policy roles that states may pursue in the system.

States pursue these foreign policy roles while occupying one of four master statuses in the international system: novice states, small member states, major member states, and great powers. These master statuses are produced by the interaction of the competition and socialization mechanisms. Hence, Waltz's (1979) insistence on the functional *un*differentiation of states is replaced by the differentiation of states into four major categories. This is due to the fact that the incorporation of socialization logically demands that states perform different functions in the system. At the least, some states socialize on behalf of structure, while others are socialized.

I argue that structure exerts its effects on the agents through the constraints imposed by the master statuses on the types of auxiliary foreign policy roles they might adopt. If an auxiliary foreign policy role is consistent with the master status, then it is likely to be accepted by the audience of interested states and the primary socializer. However, if a state chooses a foreign policy role that is inconsistent with its structurally derived master status, then it can expect to have that role rejected by its socializer and the audience of states. This process of socialization at the level of master statuses and auxiliary foreign policy roles works on behalf of structure to maintain conformity and continuity in the international system.

However, the role location process also opens up the possibility for the transformation of structure. The role location process for seeking change in a state's master status typically occurs in the critical juncture brought on by an international crisis. These crises usually produce a war that often leaves the system in flux. In systemic wars, the distribution of capabilities may change, thus altering the structure of the system. Further, socializers may fail in their attempts to ensure conformity on behalf of structure. Rogue states that refuse to conform during the role location process may indeed challenge the very structure of the system. While the notion of revisionist or challenger states is not unknown to classical or postclassical realists, it has not previously been theoretically incorporated into Waltzian neorealism.

The analytic narrative methodology employed in this research to examine these concepts and theories is also interdisciplinary by nature, with roots in economics, history, political science, and sociology. I employ the socialization game as a theoretical searchlight to examine the diplomatic history of the

United States and Israel. The history of these states is selectively examined in light of the model. I examine numerous auxiliary foreign policy role location processes within the four master statuses occupied by the United States and the three occupied by Israel during their tenure in the international system.

The analysis uncovers a number of similarities between the two states. As emerging states, both had to force the role of the sovereign state on their primary socializers. As novice states, both sought variations of the neutral role in their international relations. These neutral roles were ultimately rejected by their socializers. Great powers and major members attempted to cast both the United States and Israel in regional roles when they were still relatively new members of the system. The United States was allowed to offer a regional role at a young age, despite its inability to enact the role until it achieved its major member status. Israel was socialized out of its regional role during the Suez Crisis by the United States, and the United States attempted to prevent a regional role for Israel even when it reached the appropriate major member status.

The analysis of the United States as it attains great power status also reveals some interesting findings regarding socialization. As a great power in a multipolar system, the United States was still subject to socialization attempts from other great powers, such as Britain and Germany. The United States twice attempted to enact a neutral role before each of the World Wars, which was inappropriate given its master status. Britain and Germany successfully socialized the United States out of that role on both occasions. At the conclusion of World War II, the United States became one of only two great powers in the bipolar international system. After that point, the United States adopted a number of roles, issued in the form of presidential doctrines, that did not subject it to socialization attempts by the other great power.

The findings from this research make a significant contribution to our understanding of the operation of socialization in the international system. They also begin to bridge the gap between theories of international politics and theories of foreign policy. By transforming Waltz's structural model into a genuine systemic theory, I am able to show the extent to which structure constrains foreign policy choices by agents. The most telling case for this claim is the United States, whose range of roles is shaped by different systemic constraints over time. It offered mostly regional roles as a great power in a multipolar system, yet as it entered the bipolar system, it began to offer a truly global role. The US case also demonstrates the constraints of bipolarity, as the same set of roles (what I term "the roles of bipolarity") is offered by US presidents almost without exception. As the United States emerges into a unipolar system, the main role offered is that of a global leader, with some variations on how to enact that role. The United States has greater freedom of action in enacting its global leader role, as long as it is able to prevent other states from perceiving a threat from its leadership.

In addition to US experience as a great power, we see conformity in the auxiliary foreign policy roles offered by the United States and Israel within their respective master statuses. For example, as major members, both states attempt regional protector and leader roles. As novice states, both attempt to remove themselves from balance of power politics by adopting neutral roles. In both the US and Israeli cases, we see a general match between power status and social status in their role location processes. This reflects the fact that both states have been successfully socialized to the international system—or the "club of nations" (Maoz 1989).

Finally, in this book I examine the interplay of identity and interest in inter-state relations. I demonstrate that the socialization process allows us to bridge the gap between constructivists, who emphasize that identity drives state behavior, and rationalists, who argue that interests are the prime motivators for states. The master statuses for states, produced by the interaction of competition and socialization, are identities that shape their subsequent interests in the system. In fact, socializers perform their tasks on behalf of structure to maintain or alter those master identities. The master identities also shape the identities implied in the adoption of auxiliary foreign policy roles.

However, rational interests will often drive the initial adoption of these foreign policy roles, and only later do these roles become enduring parts of a state's social identity. Those roles may then subsequently shape interests as well. For example, the United States adopted the role of regional protector with the issuance of the Monroe Doctrine. One could argue that the adoption of this role was largely shaped by US security and economic interests in the Western Hemisphere; however, over time the regional protector role became an ingrained part of American state social identity. In part, it may explain the affective impact of the crisis triggered by the discovery of missiles in Cuba and later action by Johnson and Reagan to prevent "another Cuba" in the region when the threats to US security were far less serious.

To sum up, I shall try in the following pages to show that an understanding of the socialization process is critical to a more complete understanding of international relations for several reasons. The socialization process lies at the heart of the agent-structure debate. It also sheds light on the current constructivist-rationalist debate. Further, it incorporates a notion of process in a discipline that has long been focused on structure and outcomes. Finally, socialization provides a theoretical link between theories of international politics and theories of foreign policy, which have too often proceeded as separate academic enterprises.

THE CONCEPT OF SOCIALIZATION IN INTERNATIONAL RELATIONS THEORY

The concept of socialization is a relative newcomer to international relations theory, despite its central importance to social theory and most other social science disciplines. Waltz (1979) was one of the first scholars to recognize the importance of socialization in his structural *Theory of International Politics*.

This is not surprising, since a focus on socialization demands an emphasis on structure, and Waltz was the first international relations scholar to devise a structural theory of international politics.

Waltz's familiar definition of structure has three components: an ordering principle, the functional differentiation of units, and the distribution of capabilities across the units. In a system characterized by an anarchic order, the units of the system will not be differentiated by the functions they perform. This "sameness" effect is due to the formal equality that all states share in a competitive system. Finally, the distribution of capabilities across the units gives us a positional picture of the international system. From this definition of structure, Waltz argues that balances of power will form in the system as a result of the self-interested actions of states attempting to ensure their survival by preventing any one state's drive for universal domination.

Waltz (1979: 74) views the international political structure as a set of constraining conditions. The structure acts as a selector by rewarding some behaviors and punishing others. In this manner, structure limits the kind and quality of outcomes produced by agents in the system despite the varying goals and efforts of those agents. However, structures do not directly produce effects in the system. Structures affect behavior only indirectly through two activities: competition and socialization.

Waltz (1979: 127–128) gives anecdotal evidence for both the competition and socialization propositions. As an example of the effects of competition, Waltz points to the Prussian victories over Austria in 1866 and France in 1870 that then led the great powers to imitate the Prussian military staff system.[1] As an example of socialization, Waltz indicates that the Bolsheviks had no intentions of conforming to the conventions of diplomacy once they gained power in Russia. Trotsky evidently felt that there would be no need for an ongoing, active foreign ministry. However, as we know, the Bolsheviks did indeed begin to conform to traditional diplomatic practice.

Despite the evident centrality of socialization to Waltz's theory, neither he, nor other neorealists that followed in this research tradition paid much attention to its operation. Neorealists have generally focused on competition as the structural feature that encourages conformity.[2] Undoubtedly this is because neorealism's primary interest is in structure and not process, and because a focus on unit-level interaction would be seen as reductionist. Competition can be described without examining unit-level interaction based on analogic reasoning from microeconomics. Competition can be described as a situation in which the units find themselves, such as monopolistic, oligopolistic, or perfect competition. The situation of perfect competition generated by the anarchical structure is the standard explanation of why all the units appear and behave similarly in the system.

Whether by necessity or benign neglect, socialization has been absent from neorealist accounts of international politics. However, other rationalists have explicitly excluded socialization as an explanatory concept for international relations. Stein (1990: 26) maintains that socialization is important in understanding individuals within domestic society. In domestic society, beliefs and practices are clearly defined, formalized, and backed by organizations, such as schools, that perform the socialization of individuals as their central function. However, "such a sociological view of institutions cannot be sustained for the international system . . . the ways in which international structure peculiarly socializes nations is quite unspecified. Moreover, . . . the constitutive structures for states are amorphous and not substantiated."

Morrow (1988: 89) is similarly dismissive of socialization, particularly within Waltz's (1979) theory. Morrow argues that structure, acting through socialization, does not determine actor preferences. States in similar structural positions often adopt different preferences. Thus, socialization cannot explain why Finland conformed to great power expectations during the Cold War, while Albania flouted them. Further, Morrow argues that strategic misrepresentation might hide a state's true preferences. Thus, a state that appears to have been successfully socialized by observing its actions may in fact hold inconsistent underlying preferences. However, Morrow suggests that structure may indeed determine preferences, but Waltz has not yet established a sufficient argument to defend this claim.

Ikenberry and Kupchan (1990) attempt to salvage a rational version of socialization by focusing on its operation under hegemonic conditions—a purported hierarchical structure as opposed to the anarchical structure that Waltz maintains has never been overturned. Ikenberry and Kupchan also maintain the emphasis on material capabilities found in Waltz's neorealism. The key to socialization under hegemony is that "elites in secondary states buy into and internalize norms that are articulated by the hegemon, and therefore pursue policies consistent with the hegemon's notion of international order" (Ikenberry and Kupchan 1990: 283). Socialization occurs through material incentives and the exercise of coercive power when secondary states fail to conform. Socialization thus serves the interest of the hegemon because it makes hegemony "more durable and less costly than the exercise of coercive power alone" (Ikenberry and Kupchan 1990: 292–293).

The rise of social constructivism in international relations theory beginning in the early 1990s brought further interest in sociological theories favorable to the socialization concept (Ruggie 1998a, 1998b). Checkel (1998: 326–327) describes constructivism as an approach to inquiry based on two assumptions: "(1) the environment in which agents/states take action is social as well as material; and (2) this setting can provide agents/states with understandings of their interests (it can constitute them)." Social constructivism is an umbrella label that applies to conventional, critical, and postmodern sociological approaches to international relations (Katzenstein, Keohane, and Krasner 1998: 674–678).

Conventional constructivism, also previously known early in the literature as sociological institutionalism, suggests that sociological perspectives offer a general theoretical orientation and specific research programs that may complement rationalist approaches. This approach insists on an analysis of the social processes by which norms, rules, and roles evolve, and on how identities are constructed. Further, conventional constructivists argue that agents and structures are mutually constitutive. Thus, although conventional constructivists may differ in ontology from rationalists, they are similar in their epistemological and methodological approaches.

Sociological institutionalists such as Finnemore and Sikkink (1998) have focused attention on the concept of socialization and its operation. Finnemore and Sikkink (1998: 902–903) argue that socialization is the dominant mechanism whereby norm leaders persuade others to adopt a norm. A norm cascade occurs when a critical mass of states has endorsed a new norm, thus redefining appropriate behavior for all states. If elites fashion their identity as a state in relation to the international community, then a type of peer socialization occurs, resulting in legitimacy, conformity, and esteem for the state and its leaders.

Finnemore (1996a, 1996b) has documented the emergence of norms among the developed states, such as the Geneva conventions on warfare and the evolution of humanitarian intervention. Finnemore (1996c) has also documented norm diffusion through socialization in the case of bureaucratic structures in developing countries. Risse, Ropp, and Sikkink (1999) develop a "spiral model" that attempts to describe the extent to which states adopt human rights norms accounting for both domestic and international pressure. In a similar effort, Flockhart (2006) incorporates social identity theory into a "complex socialization" model to account for the adoption of liberal democratic norms in Central and Eastern European states. This research is related to growing literature in sociology that examines an emerging world culture, in which the practices and trappings of the modern state have become homogenized across cultures and geographic regions (Meyer 1980; Meyer et al. 1997; Thomas et al. 1987).

The research tradition that has grown up around the work of March and Olsen (1984, 1989, 1995) and DiMaggio and Powell (1991) also recognizes the importance of the socialization process for providing for the proper enactment of roles and the sanctioning of those who fail to do so. The socialization process is also expressly described as applicable to corporate actors such as the nation-state (March and Olsen 1998). Thus, the claim by English School theorists, such as Bull (1977), that states exist in an institutionalized normative social order, which requires maintenance through socialization, is now part of mainstream international relations theory.

International organizations are thought to act as socialization agents maintaining this "anarchical society." International organizations "impose definitions of member characteristics and purposes upon the governments of member states" (McNeely 1995: 33). Further, according to Finnemore's research, they teach states the appropriate norms for international and domestic action. International organizations are described as the source of legitimation for international behavior and are charged with ensuring adherence to international norms (Barnett 1995, 1997). Finally, the socializing impact of international organizations on postcommunist states in transition has been examined by Campbell (1995, 1996).

The socialization concept has also been applied to the study of revolutionary states. Armstrong (1993: 8) adopts the concept to explain the "pressures experienced by revolutionary states to behave 'responsibly,' to accept rules and norms that are acknowledged by other states, and in short to *be* states rather than revolutionary movements. . . ." Walt (1996: 43) also discusses socialization as the process by which revolutionary and counterrevolutionary states acquire greater information about the balance of power, the intentions of others, and the probability of contagion or counterrevolution. Walt finds that revolutionary regimes tend to modify their behavior so that their relations with other states become increasingly "normal."

The fact that Armstrong, an adherent of the English School, and Walt, a neorealist, both view socialization as an important process in international relations lends credence to Wendt's (1992: 403) statement that socialization is "a ubiquitous feature of interaction in terms of which all identities and interests get produced and reproduced." The concept of socialization should not be viewed as the exclusive domain of either constructivists or rationalists. In fact, constructivists have discovered, with some chagrin, that rationality is more important to the socialization process than they had previously imagined (Checkel 1997).

Armstrong (1993: 243) concludes that socialization involves "the avoidance of 'punishment' in the form of international censure and sanctions including the possible use of force, and the receipt of 'rewards' including international legitimacy and access to participation in the international discourse." Finnemore and Sikkink (1998: 909) also conclude that "the extensive body of empirical research on norms reveals an intimate relationship between norms and rationality." They determine that there is nothing about rational choice that requires a materialist ontology to determine utilities. The utilities of actors could just as easily be specified in terms of social or ideational values. The point is that both identity-based, constructivist approaches and interest-based, rationalist approaches to international politics can offer theoretical and methodological assistance to developing an understanding of socialization. This book attempts to blend aspects of both approaches into a model of the socialization process.

A SYSTEMIC APPROACH TO SOCIALIZATION

Despite the fact that both rationalists and constructivists have pointed to socialization as an important feature of the international system, no scholar has developed a generalizable model of this process at the level of the state system—Stein (1990) was correct in asserting that the way international structure socializes states is underspecified. The operation of socialization is thus a black box waiting to be opened for inspection in this book. I intend to build upon Waltz (1979) by fully incorporating socialization and its ramifications into his structural theory of international politics.

Despite the fact that Waltz views socialization and competition as the main methods by which structure influences behavior in the system, he gives little more than anecdotal evidence about how these two processes work. As I stated previously, this is because his primary interest is in structure and not process and because a focus on unit-level interaction would be seen as reductionist. However, if Waltz's theory is correct, then we should be able to elucidate the mechanisms behind the operation of both socialization and competition among the units. Even Waltz (1979: 128) acknowledges that his conjectures about socialization and competition are testable as hypotheses.

I concur with Buzan et al. (1993) and Dessler (1989) that Waltz's enduring impact upon the field of international relations makes it more sensible to try and improve upon his model to produce a better structural theory than to build a new one from scratch. Additionally, Waltz is one of only a few scholars with a well-developed theory that assigns a role to socialization. However, Waltz's model must be expanded if we are to explore the unit-level interactions that comprise competition and socialization.

One notable attempt to expand Waltz's structural theory to include unit level interactions is found in Buzan et al. (1993). These scholars correctly note that Waltz conflates system and structure throughout his *Theory of International Politics*. Waltz's main concern is with the effects of structure on the units. Waltz fails to discuss the other important aspect of a true system, unit-level interaction. Buzan et al. account for this problem by maintaining Waltz's two levels of analysis (structure and unit) and adding an interaction level of analysis that measures the interaction capacity of the system. The interaction capacity refers to the absolute quality of technological and societal capabilities across the system. Technological and societal capabilities are thought to transcend the unit level of analysis but are not properly located at the structural level. Buzan et al. refer to these capabilities as systemic, yet in schizophrenic fashion, they shy away from constructing an international *systems* theory.

Buzan et al. argue that any extension of Waltz's model is best served by a structurationist approach rather than a systems approach.[3] Buzan et al. (1993: 156) base this claim on the fact that, for Waltz, agents are constrained by structure to act in a way that reproduces the structure. According to these scholars, this is problematic for systems theorists. Their argument is as follows: first, by reviewing Wendt's (1987: 341–342) analysis of the agent-structure problem in international relations, they revisit the argument that Waltz develops an "individualist definition of the structure of the international system as reducible to the properties of states" (Buzan et al. 1993: 156) and thus creates an agent-centric solution to the agent-structure problem. However, it is still a solution, though not the ideal solution that most constructivist theorists would like to see, in which agents and structures mutually constitute and instantiate each other.[4]

Second, by citing one example of a systems theorist who argues that "change in any of the components, or in the interactions among them, produces change throughout the system, or its breakdown," Buzan et al. argue that systems theories ignore structure. Buzan et al. thus argue that a structurationist approach to improving Waltz's model is more appropriate than a systems approach. The task for their structurationist approach becomes to show how agents reproduce structure and how structures produce agents.

However, no matter how Buzan et al. try to slice the levels of analysis, they are introducing the notion of unit interaction in a system. So why not make a true systems theorist out of Waltz? One reason Waltz probably did not do so himself was that he was reacting to an earlier generation of systems theorists like Kaplan (1957) and Rosecrance (1963). General Systems Theory has fallen by the wayside for many reasons, but new approaches to systems overcome many of its shortcomings.[5] A systems theory of international relations can incorporate units, their interactions, and an underlying structure, despite Buzan et al.'s claims to the contrary. Furthermore, a systems approach is not incompatible with attempts at resolving the agent-structure problem. In fact, a systems theory may more fully explain how unit interaction reproduces or transforms structures. Finally, it seems much simpler theoretically to posit the existence of a system, rather than dance around it by creating endless levels of analyses.[6]

According to Jervis (1998: 6), "[W]e are dealing with a system when (a) a set of units or elements is interconnected so that changes in some elements or their relations produce changes in other parts of the system, and (b) the entire system exhibits properties and behaviors that are different from those of the parts." A systems approach has strong microfoundations in unit behavior but rejects any form of *reductionism* that claims the system is nothing but the behaviors of individuals (Jervis 1998: 16). This type of systems theory should be compatible with Waltz's concerns about reductionism in international relations theory. It also should allay Buzan et al.'s concerns about the use of systems theory to expand Waltz's model instead of a structurationist approach.

This definition of the system obviously includes the units and their interactions, but where does structure come into play? As mentioned previously, Waltz's solution to the agent-structure problem gives causal priority to agents. The structure of the international system emerges only from the coaction of states. States are therefore ontologically prior to the existence of the system and the system's structure. The formation of the structure is due to the unintentional actions of states engaged in a competitive, self-help struggle for survival. Once created, the structure is resistant to change. In fact, what Buzan et al. (1993), Ruggie (1986), and others have referred to as the "deep" structure—the organizing principle and the functional differentiation of the units—has never changed, according to Waltz. Only the distribution of capabilities across the system changes, albeit somewhat infrequently.[7]

The reason the structural element of the distribution of capabilities does change is that it is an emergent property of the system (Cederman 1997). The distribution of capabilities only has meaning because of the relational aspect of capabilities generated at the unit level. The distribution of capabilities, although considered a structural characteristic by Waltz, only attains meaning in a system of interacting units. If the units fail to interact in the confines of a system, then the distribution of characteristics is as unimportant as the functional (un)differentiation of states is to Waltz. This seems to be the point that Buzan et al. (1993) make when they discuss the interaction capacity of the system. When the interaction capacity of the system is low, it is difficult even to think of the units being engaged in a system. Of the three structural components, only anarchy would matter in a "system" with low interaction, and even so, would only describe the positional relation among states. Systems with high levels of interaction capacity are much more constrained by the effects of anarchy and the distribution of capabilities, and, as I will argue later, the functional differentiation of states.

Jervis (1998: 98) remarks that the crucial theoretical question for systems theorists is: what aspects of the system should be considered vital? How would you know if one system was replaced by another system? For Waltz, the vital aspect of the system is the distribution of capabilities. As the distribution of capabilities changes, so does the system. However, as Buzan et al. (1993: 53) note, changes in the distribution of capability may be of low consequence to the system. For example, if the number of great powers changes from seven to six, the international system may remain largely unaffected, although regional subsystem(s) may be affected. However, for Waltz (1979: 163), it appears that changes between one and four great powers are significant enough to be called structural changes (once again conflating structure and system). The most significant shift would be from bipolarity to unipolarity. According to this logic, we should definitely be able to classify changes between one and four great powers as changes in the international system. Changes in multipolar systems with more than four members may have a slight effect on the surface structure, but not on the essential nature of the international system.

Thus far, I have expanded Waltz's model of neorealism, based on two levels of analysis, into a systems theory based on three levels. How does this transformation into a systems theory affect the causal priority given to structure in Waltz's model? According to Waltz, structures work their effects indirectly on the units through competition and socialization. However, the actual mechanisms that account for competition and socialization are unexplored in Waltz. I will account for the operation of the mechanisms and demonstrate that, in particular, the process of socialization can only occur in a system. Indeed, Waltz offers an implicit systems theory, albeit an incomplete one. I will argue that the socialization mechanisms are incompatible with previous versions of Waltzian neorealism. The task is then to explain how competition and socialization work on behalf of structure to maintain or degrade the stability of the system through the processes of unit interaction.

MECHANISMS

The model developed in this book focuses on the causal mechanisms underlying Waltz's socialization and competition conjectures. A mechanism, according to Stinchcombe (1998: 267), is the representation of a causal process that has some actual or possible empirical support separate from the larger theory in which it is a mechanism, and that generates increased precision, power, or elegance in the large-scale theories. Mechanisms tend to be "bits of theory" about entities at a different level than the main entities being studied, such as a mechanism that describes an aspect of individual state behavior in an interstate system (Stinchcombe 1991: 367).

Hedstrom and Swedberg (1998: 21–23) identify three types of mechanisms. Type 1 is the situational mechanism, where an individual actor is exposed to a specific social situation, such as the state exposed to the international system. Type 2 is the action-formation mechanism, in which the individual generates a specific action based on how the individual assimilates the impact of being exposed to the situation. Type 3 is the transformational mechanism, which shows how the actions and interactions of individuals are transformed into a collective outcome.

This typology is based on Coleman's (1986) macro-micro-macro model for collective social action. Type 1 are macro-micro mechanisms, Type 2 are micro-micro mechanisms, and Type 3 are micro-macro mechanisms. Waltz's (1979) main concern is obviously with Type 1 mechanisms. His interest is in how the structure affects the units. His answer is that the structure encourages conformity among the units with regard to their internal characteristics and external behavior. However, the socialization and competition propositions are really the purview of Type 2 mechanisms. Competitive behavior occurs in unit interactions and has internal repercussions for the unit. Socialization is an adjustment process between the units, as well as within the units. Type 3 mechanisms are beyond Waltz's theory. The inability of Waltz's theory to deal with the consequences of unit-level interactions has been pointed out numerous times (Ruggie 1986; Milner 1991); it contributed to the birth of neoliberalism (e.g., Baldwin 1993; Kegley 1995), spawned research projects dedicated to demonstrating the transformative effects of unit-level interactions (Axelrod 1984, 1997; Oye 1986), and virtually ignored preexisting research programs dealing with this subject (Coleman 1964; Granovetter 1978; Schelling 1978).

In fact, the three dominant approaches to international relations theory today—neorealism, neoliberalism, and constructivism—each attempt to explain one of these mechanisms. Neorealism is largely interested in Type 1 mechanisms, although one can extend its logic to unit interactions (as Waltz conjectures, and as I will try to test). Neoliberalism presents an alternate portrayal of Type 2 mechanisms that demonstrates that neorealist predictions of unit-level behavior may be inadequate by drawing on neorealist Type 1 mechanisms. Finally, constructivism focuses largely on Type 3 mechanisms, which show how state interaction may transform the nature of the system— "anarchy is what states make of it," according to Wendt (1992). A fully-specified systems theory of international relations would account for all three types of mechanisms and demonstrate that each of the major approaches to international relations theory is really only one piece of the same puzzle.

This book is primarily concerned with explaining Type 2 mechanisms within the context of an expanded Waltzian neorealist theory. I will accept Waltz's (1979: 121) assertion that "balance-of-power politics prevail wherever two, and only two, requirements are met: that the order be anarchic and that it be populated by units wishing to survive." An examination of the net effects of Type 2 mechanisms of socialization and competition should support Waltz's version of balance of power politics. If the net effect of these mechanisms is to support balancing, then the idea of transformation of the system is replaced by reproduction of the system. However, we know that systems do change, so the source of the change may lie within the competition and socialization mechanisms. Competition and socialization may indeed provide positive feedback that induces change, as well negative feedback, which serves to keep the system in equilibrium (Jervis 1998: 96–97). Jervis (1998: 104–105) expresses doubt about the ability of some states to be "tamed," or socialized, such as Hitler's Germany. Indeed, revisionist, internally driven states may be the cause of system transformation if they cannot be socialized.[8]

What are the Type 2 mechanisms that underlie competition and socialization? I would propose that competition in Waltz's system is regulated by two mechanisms: organizational competency and rational imitation.[9] Socialization is also regulated by two mechanisms: the social proof heuristic and dissonance reduction. I expect that these four mechanisms will interact with each other, sometimes in mutually reinforcing ways, and at other times in a contradictory fashion. This type of interaction among mechanisms that produces sometimes uncertain or indeterminate effects is what Gambetta (1998: 105) refers to as "concatenations" of mechanisms.

Mechanisms of Competition

First, what do I mean by competition? For Waltz, competition is a *situation* within which units find themselves. The structural condition of anarchy means that no higher authority exists to regulate the actions of states other than the states themselves. Thus, all units conditioned by anarchy must potentially interact with others for power, prestige, and security. The situation of competition pushes all units to adopt a similar form and internal organization—whatever appears to be most efficient at securing power, prestige, and security. Competition as a situation does not say *how* the units will go about securing these things in the system. How they go about these tasks will largely be the result of socialization. The type of socialization that occurs in a given system may result in the pursuit of either (or both) absolute or relative gains (see Baldwin 1993).

Let us discuss the mechanisms of competition. Competition affects both new members of a system and existing members. Waltz is clear that competition should encourage the sameness effect among the units. Competitive mechanisms can create the sameness effect in two ways: sameness in form and sameness in function. Sameness in form refers to the fact that states are the key actors in world politics. The form that the units of the system have taken has become remarkably homogeneous given the fact that the state has not always been the dominant actor on the international scene. Stinchcombe (1998) has proposed a mechanism that has at its core the notion of appropriation of going-concern value due to organizational competency that can account for this aspect of sameness due to competition.

Stinchcombe bases his argument on the notion that states are engaged in monopolistic competition. This is a slightly different take on the type of competition thought to characterize the international system. Waltz (1979) seems to discuss the system as the result of perfect competition among the units when he is emphasizing the effects of anarchy. However, when Waltz discusses the distribution of capabilities, his arguments tend to favor a system of oligopolistic competition, hence his focus on great powers. Milner (1991) also argues that Waltz's model should be one of oligopolistic competition. However, Stinchcombe (1998: 268) characterizes states as engaging in monopolistic competition because each state dominates a unique territory despite the fact that there are close substitutes that make them subject to competitive pressure.

States have developed certain organizational competencies that enable them to appropriate benefits from certain legitimate activities, such as trade, and to be free of liability for whatever damage is caused in the legitimate pursuit of those benefits. The flow of benefits that the state monopolizes is used to maintain its status or rank in the system. That rank or status derived from such appropriation is precarious since one's own appropriation may be inhibited by the appropriation activities of others who are also not liable for damages. Essentially, states dominate the international political landscape because they have developed the types of organizational competencies that prevent other forms of organization from adequately competing with them. This argument is quite similar to Spruyt's (1994), who also argues that the sovereign territorial state was better able at organizing itself to take advantage of trade and commerce than its competitors, including city-states and city-leagues.

Stinchcombe and Spruyt suggest the mechanism by which the form and internal organization of the modern territorial state prevailed over its competitors. These scholars explain the sameness of form that is inherent to the international system. Stinchcombe also explains why the form, in terms of internal organization, of the modern state remains similar. Thus, organizational developments that might reap competitive advantage are quickly adopted by other states in order to maintain their rank in the system. That is why the composition of great powers has not changed much over time.[10]

Sameness in function, or functional undifferentiation, refers to the fact that all states face similar tasks, including raising revenue, establishing internal order, and defending themselves from other states. Hedstrom (1998) proposes a mechanism of rational imitation that can account for this type of sameness. Rational imitation does not arise from any notion of the need to adhere to social conformity. Rather, imitation is seen as a useful strategy for arriving at better decisions in the pursuit of resources or position. Imitation is also seen as a strategy for organizations to achieve legitimacy. When organizations imitate already existing and accepted models, they reduce the risk of being called into question by individuals and institutional actors, and they thereby increase their chances of survival. Thus, once the state-as-organizer of territory and population is seen as legitimate, then other corporate groups also adopt the state and its form of organization as legitimate. This mechanism of rational imitation seems to be what Waltz believes to be operating in the system.

Stinchcombe's and Hedstrom's mechanisms seem to account for the enduring qualities of the modern state, including both its form and function. Waltz does not have much to say about the form of the state since states exist *a priori* to his model. However, new states have emerged quite frequently in the last century and all have adopted a similar form due to competition. Waltz's main concern is with the types of activities that states undertake, such as the organization of military force, for example, which become similar due to the mechanism of rational imitation.[11] Emerging states should organize their activities very similarly to other states in their competitive field.

The competitive mechanisms are not the main thrust of this book. These mechanisms seem logically to support Waltz's notion of the sameness effect. As such, these mechanisms are primarily concerned with the internal features of states. The units in an anarchic system tend to adopt the same form and organizational features. However, these competition mechanisms do not have a direct link to conflict as most neorealists would argue. The character of the unit interactions, whether conflictual or cooperative, will be determined by the interaction of competition with the socialization mechanisms. While competition affects the internal adjustments of states to the structure of the system, socialization affects the state's external adjustment to the structure and the other units through interaction in the system.

If Waltz's conjectures are correct, the socialization mechanisms should also encourage the sameness effect in the units and lead to the reproduction of the system in a virtually identical state in time 1 as compared to time 0. However, socialization of units may also be the key to change in the system. Socialization is most felt by new members of the system. How those members react to socializing pressures determines the character of continuity in the system or introduces the possibility for rejection of existing norms and roles, thus introducing an element of change. In addition to emerging states, all states may need to be resocialized when the system changes, depending upon the magnitude of change in the number of poles.

Mechanisms of Socialization

What do I mean by socialization? According to Wentworth (1980: 85), "socialization is the activity that confronts and lends structure to the entry of nonmembers into an already existing world or a sector of that world." Socializing activity establishes a tension between the "member" and the "novice." This tension has several implications. First, there are relative differences in power, status, and prestige between the member and the novice. Second, the novice is within the sphere of influence of the member. Third, a variety of "others" may intervene in the socialization of the novice. Fourth, there is a varying degree of asymmetry between the member's and the novice's view of reality. Fifth, an ongoing historical institution, consisting of structure and roles, precedes a new generation of potential members.

The tension between members and novices in the international system requires a bit more explanation. Who are the members? The members are those states that are established in their roles in a given system. Who are the novices? The novices are states that emerge during a period in which the system is stable. What happens when the system changes? In a new system, all states are novices in a sense. However, due to the peculiarities of the international system, some states, namely great powers, are always "members." Great powers, due to their "organizational competency" as outlined in Stinchcombe (1998), retain their status and primary role(s) from system to system. The great powers will be the dominant socializers in any international system. However, small states should be considered "novices" when the system changes, just as emerging states are also considered "novices" at whatever point in history they enter the system.

Great powers have traditionally held sway over states within their spheres of interest. The great power who dominates a particular sphere of influence will socialize the novice states of that region; or, if a great power no longer holds sway, then a regional power will assume the role of member *vis-a-vis* the novice. The regional power itself may be a novice *vis-a-vis* a great power member of the international system. Thus, a novice may be subject to socialization pressure from a great power and a regional power. However, "others," such as local peer states, may also intervene in the socialization process (Harris 1998). This is the point where the "social proof heuristic" (as described further on) may become crucial.

The asymmetry between members' and novices' views of reality are important to the second type of socialization mechanism discussed further on: the dissonance reduction mechanism. The member largely structures the reality within which the novice must operate. However, entry into the system is a process of mutual accommodation and negotiation. Novice states, and particularly emerging novice states, are in the process of constructing their identity. Identity formation is partially the result of internal processes, but it is also conditioned by interaction with the "other," according to Social Identity Theory.[12] Thus, socialization is crucial to the construction of identity in the international system.

Finally, the ongoing historical institution that I discuss in the context of international relations is the existence of an international system. The deep structure that forms the base of all systems is regarded as constant by Waltz. The surface-level component of structure—the distribution of capabilities—changes to give rise to a new system. Certain roles are also part of the ongoing historical institution. Waltz acknowledges the special role that great powers play in the international system. This should not preclude the existence of other roles in the system. Members (largely great powers) must socialize emerging states and resocialize existing states to the new reality. Thus, the main elements of continuity of the international system are the deep structure and the socializing role of the great powers.

During the socialization process, the novice undergoes assimilation, which makes the novice more similar to the members. However, the novice also exerts influence on the members, thus necessitating accommodation on the part of members (Moreland 1985: 1174). This process fits well with the neorealist conception of the international system as an environment of mutual adaptation and adjustment. The speed with which novices are socialized depends on the following: the level of commitment of the novice to the member group and particular relationships within the group, the extent of the differences between the novice and members, and the number of novices that join the member group at any one time (Moreland 1985: 1174).

Stryker and Statham (1985: 334) list several processes found to be responsible for socialization in the literature: direct instruction, imitation or modeling, and altercasting. However, for my purposes these processes can be collapsed into two general socialization processes: those that involve the direct internalization of communicated normative expectations and those that involve the indirect assimilation of norms through a process of identification with socialization agents who exemplify the norms. Socialization should occur indirectly through imitation or modeling and directly through instruction and altercasting.

I postulate two mechanisms for socialization in Waltz's system. Socialization mechanisms should primarily affect the external behavior of states, with some requisite adjustments in internal organization. The first such mechanism is the "social proof heuristic" (Cialdini 1984) as elaborated upon by Hedstrom (1998). This is the socialization mechanism most likely to reinforce existing norms and roles in the system. The social proof heuristic states, essentially: when you are not sure what to do, look around to the actions of others for possible clues as to what your own behavior should be (Hedstrom 1998: 314). This mechanism is essentially one of imitation or modeling. The social proof heuristic is a pervasive mechanism found in all sorts of environmental settings.

The social proof heuristic should be most evident in emerging states as they seek to understand the role of the sovereign state itself. Other possible occasions for the operation of this mechanism include that of learning the role of an ally, or of a seeker of international aid. In general, the social proof mechanism should operate when there is little question about the appropriateness of the state's own role conception. The main question that the social proof mechanism helps to answer is how to properly enact that role in conformity with others' expectations (Biddle 1986: 78). The social proof heuristic works on external behavior in tandem with rational imitation working on form and internal function to produce Waltz's sameness effect.

To the extent that the social proof heuristic predominates in a system, we should see a fairly stable system in which the units engage in its reproduction. The range of acceptable behaviors in the system should be fairly constrained. However, work by Schelling (1978) on "tipping points," suggests that if a rogue state were able to engage in novel behavior with impunity, and other states adopted that behavior via the social proof heuristic, then, after a certain number of states adopted the behavior, the entire system would accept that behavior as normal and/or standard.[13] The nonaligned movement during the Cold War is an example of the normalization of socially deviant behavior in the context of a bipolar system.

Competition could provide the impetus for novel behavior. Just as firms in a competitive market often try to fill niches in the market structure by differentiating the products they supply, states may too find a niche for themselves in the international system by supplying different "products" and "services." Switzerland, for example, has long avoided entanglements in political and security alliances in favor of neutrality that allows it to serve as an entrepôt for wealth, people, and information in the European system.

However, innovations in roles, norms, or their behavioral manifestations are usually met with skepticism by the relevant others in any social system (Stryker and Statham 1985: 353). Deviance from expectations is permissible in the short run as actors engage in "aligning actions" to bring their behavior in line with standards, but in the long run, such behavior would be punished (Stokes and Hewitt 1976). The only exception to this rule is that social deviance could persist in a situation of structural failure (Stryker and Statham 1985: 365). In the case of the state system, structural failure would characterize certain regions where interaction capacity is low, such that it is difficult to even think of a system whose members could constrain agent behavior. The social proof heuristic could transmit innovative roles or norms from state to state by diffusion in such a low-interaction system only if states were actively seeking models for their own behavior, and this could eventually lead to their acceptance as standard.

The second socialization mechanism is dissonance reduction (Festinger 1957), as discussed by Jervis (1976), Elster (1998), and Kuran (1998). According to dissonance theory, inconsistency among cognitions causes a motivational state called dissonance (or "cognitive strain" in Sarbin and Allen 1968: 541). Dissonance leads to an aversive state of arousal. The aversive state of arousal leads to attempts to reduce the arousal/discomfort. Dissonance theory may seem oddly applied to socialization in the international system, yet dissonance reduction is a very general mechanism. Individuals within domestic society often feel dissonance with regard to the roles they wish to adopt for themselves in their environments leading to cognitive or behavioral efforts to reduce that dissonance. Leaders of states may similarly be greeted with skepticism or rejection based on the roles they choose for their state by leaders of other states. The leaders may often be forced to revise their stated roles or face punishment by other members of the system.

Dissonance reduction may also be thought of as a social process, rather than a purely cognitive mechanism. Agreement upon the operation of certain roles and norms is essential in order for any social system to remain stable. If a state challenges the roles assigned to it in a stable system, the result may be a balancing of other states against it to prevent the enactment of the nonsanctioned role. Balancing can thus be conceived of as a dissonance reduction mechanism in an interstate system. States that are content with the current distribution of great power roles are expected to thwart attempts by minor powers to break into the ranks of the great powers and to prevent a current great power from establishing a hegemonic role for itself. Any moves in these directions to destabilize a system will produce "dissonance" and attempts at its reduction. Hence, the mechanism of dissonance reduction is general enough to operate in the international system.

The dissonance reduction mechanism operates in those situations where there is the potential for disagreement over the appropriate choice of role(s) for a state. The socialization game described in Chapter 2 will highlight the role of dissonance reduction in the context of a state's role location process. Dissonance reduction in the socialization game may be the result of direct instruction or altercasting on the part of socializing states, both of which involve a socializing state's providing cues to a novice state as to its proper role in the system.

SOCIAL SCIENCE AND THE INTERNATIONAL SYSTEM

Conceptualizing the international system as a true system presents several methodological challenges to this investigation. First, causality is difficult to assess in such an environment. The traditional social science approach suggests that we identify a number of independent variables and a dependent variable to assess patterns in their covariation. A system confounds the traditional requirements of causality: association, direction of influence, and nonspuriousness. Unfortunately, in a system, there are no variables that are once-and-for-all simply independent or dependent. What is a dependent variable in one instance is an independent variable in the next. This is due to the self-contained nature of a system and the feedback effects that occur as one variable causes an effect in another, which in turn may affect the original causal variable over time.

Second, outcomes become less important than process in a true system. Outcomes are the traditional standard by which we judge social science explanations. Can we predict? In a system, we may be able to predict certain outcomes in the short term, but over long periods of time, predictions based on simple linear logic are bound to fail. A system is always in motion. Thus, understanding the process of the production, reproduction, and possible transformation is the key to understanding any system. Socialization is a process, not an outcome. If it is viewed as an outcome, then most states conform to expectations most of the time. This is not particularly interesting. What is interesting is *how* and *why* states conform.

Third, if we had to label the independent variable and dependent variable in this study, then the independent variable is actually the system structure, and the dependent variable is conformity (or similarity, or the sameness effect). According to Waltz (1979), socialization is one of the methods by which the anarchical structure produces like units in the system. The separate and similar units then reinforce the anarchical structure in a positive feedback loop. This is accomplished, for Waltz, through balancing. Others have investigated whether states do indeed balance, but I am interested in explaining the front end of the process that translates structural pressure into conformity. Since this process occurs between the independent and dependent variables, I am interested in identifying the causal mechanisms that produce the effect in the dependent variable. As Little (1991: 25) states, "inductive regularities are useful for identifying possible causal relations, but investigation of underlying causal processes is necessary before we can conclude that a causal relation exists."

Fourth, in the cases I will examine, it is actually the causal process that varies in each case, rather than the independent and dependent variables. This too should seem strange to traditional social science, but in a system, we should expect that variables may be related in different ways, yet produce similar outcomes. In Waltz's international system, the ultimate independent variable—the anarchic structure—has never changed. And most states seem to conform most of the time (the dependent variable). Yet, as previously discussed, the impact of structure may be uneven throughout the system, based on the level of interaction capacity. Additionally, some states do not conform. But I am interested in those states that are strongly affected by structure and that do become normalized members of the system because these are the majority of the states in the system.

Table 1.1 describes the possible range of cases that could be analyzed for evidence of the socialization process. States are categorized based upon the impact of structure in their region and their conformity. My interest, as is Waltz's, is in those states, heavily conditioned by structure, which conform to its dictates. These states inhabit what Maoz (1989) calls the "club of nations." I want to know how these states were successfully socialized into the system. How do these states in a highly structured environment learn to adapt the appropriate roles in the system?

As you can see, other possible cases exist to examine socialization. Rogue states are those that exist in a highly structured environment but that fail to

Table 1.1 Typology of Possible Cases

| | | Impact of Structure | |
		High	Low
Conformity Level	High	Club of Nations	Joiners
	Low	Rogue States	Quasi States

conform. These states would include Iraq (prior to the second Gulf War), Iran, North Korea, Cuba, or Germany before the wars. Quasi-states do not conform, yet they are not really impacted much by socialization efforts on behalf of the structure. Many African states fall into this category. Some states, which I might call "joiners," will also be quite conformist, despite the lack of impact from structure. These might include some of the successor states of the Soviet Union, or perhaps Eastern European states seeking membership in the EU or NATO.

CASE SELECTION

The cases I examine for evidence of the socialization process are the United States since its inception in 1776 and Israel since 1948 through the close of the twentieth century. Why the United States and Israel? Both cases are states that clearly fall within the "club of nations." These are the states that Waltz would expect to be socialized to the system. I will trace the socialization process from the time both states emerge to the present. The United States moves through all four of the master roles in the system, while Israel moves through three of the four. By following these two states through the critical junctures that lead to changes in master roles, I essentially expand the number of cases in this study from two to seven. This is one of the methods elaborated upon by King, Keohane, and Verba (1994: 227) to increase the number of observations in a study.

There are interesting differences between these two states that may affect the socialization process. First, these two states emerge in different international systems. The United States emerges in a multipolar system, while Israel emerges in a bipolar system. The United States actually becomes one of Israel's dominant socializers during its tenure in the system. Second, these states emerge in different geographical subsystems with very different security environments. Third, the United States ends up as the dominant power in the world after the collapse of bipolarity. Was this inevitable because of its capabilities, or was it socialized into that role?

Fourth, Israel is an interesting case theoretically because we should expect its socialization process to be fraught with difficulty given its emergence with a number of other states in the same time frame and its lack of similarity and commitment to these states on so many levels (Moreland 1985). One might also ask why Israel is not considered a great power, even though it has nuclear weapons, which are considered a symbol of great power status.

Fifth, both countries are identified as parties to protracted conflicts (Azar et al. 1978; Brecher 1984; Brecher and Wilkenfeld 1997), and enduring rivalries (Goertz and Diehl 1992, 1993). Bennett (1998) identifies the United States as a rival of Haiti, Mexico, Ecuador, the UK, Spain, the Soviet Union, China, Cuba, Peru, and North Korea. Israel is considered a rival of Jordan, Iraq, Egypt, Syria, Lebanon, and Saudi Arabia. Might socialization attempts have something to do with the serial nature of conflict between the states in these rivalries (Thies 2001)?

AN INSTITUTIONALIST APPROACH TO ANALYZING STRUCTURE

The type of explanation I offer for the operation of socialization in the international system is known as a causal structural explanation (Little 1991: 103–106). Such an explanation assumes that societies are complex systems incorporating a variety of social structures. Further, particular aspects of these structures cause patterns of stable organization and processes of change within society. And, finally, the causal powers of structure are found in particular causal mechanisms mediated by agent action. Causal structural explanations emphasize the impact of structure on agency, but they do not exclude the possibility that agency can affect structure. Agents are important in my analysis, as interpreters, enforcers, and resistors of structural imperatives. In fact, there are several levels of agency and structure within my analysis. Agents within the structure of the state debate and choose a role for their state. The state as an agent then negotiates that role within the structure of the international system. Or, the process may be initiated at the level of the international system and work downward.

The type of causal structural explanation I employ is grounded in institutional analysis. I argue that the international system is an ongoing historical institution, consisting of a structure that induces many rules, norms, and roles for interaction, as well as the arrangement of agents within the system. Historical institutionalism is a broad approach to social science that has at its core the notion that social phenomena must be understood in light of historical process (Steinmo, Thelen, and Longstreth 1992; Hall and Taylor 1996). This approach is an excellent fit with the study of socialization in a system.

Much of the existing literature on international institutions seeks to analyze formal institutions created by states to foster cooperation in particular issue areas (Martin and Simmons 1998). The key difference between liberal intergovernmentalism (Moravcsik 1993), neoliberal institutionalism (Keohane 1984), and other rationalist approaches to institutions, versus historical institutionalism, is that the former approaches view institutions as voluntaristic, intentional creations which have consequences that can be fully anticipated at the time of their creation, while historical institutionalism does not.

Historical institutionalism, in contrast, emphasizes the role of "unintended consequences." These consequences are the result of feedback loops and interaction effects generated in situations with large numbers of actors or high issue density (Pierson 1996: 136–137; Ikenberry 1988: 225–226). Central to historical institutionalist interpretation is the fact that participants in institutional design, such as governments and interest groups, are unable to know how an institution will function in the long run given the complex social processes involved in institutional evolution. One need only recall the unpredictable collapse of bipolarity in 1989 for evidence that this is the case.

Historical institutionalism emphasizes the path-dependent nature of institutions (Collier and Collier 1991). Once created, institutions shape and constrain the behavior of agents within them. Further, institutions are resistant to change. Institutional change is "sticky" and episodic, rather than continuous and incremental. This is due to the fact that institutional arrangements privilege agents who work to perpetuate those arrangements, such as the militaries of rival states. Finally, the costs of uncertainty act as a countervailing force against institutional change (Ikenberry 1988: 223–224). Thus, for example, states balance against each other with the result that anarchy is maintained and hierarchy prevented (Waltz 1979).

Historical institutionalism stresses the role of crisis in disrupting long periods of stability in institutional arrangements. Due to the "sticky," path-dependent nature of institutions, institutional change is most likely to be successful during times of crisis. According to Ikenberry (1988: 224), "political or economic crises act as a solvent, throwing into relief discontinuities between underlying social forces and existing institutions." We should expect a pattern of long periods of institutional stability, during which pressure for change builds, only to be released in sudden, infrequent fits of institutional change, or in what Gould's version of evolutionary biology labels "punctuated equilibrium" (Krasner 1988).

The concept of punctuated equilibrium is not only appropriate for describing the international system as an institution, but also for describing the state as an institution. The master roles negotiated by states should also fit this pattern. States will be altercast into, or achieve, a master role that should endure until such time as a crisis forces a change to a new master role (see Figure 2.2). These moments of historic change are known as critical junctures.

Collier and Collier (1991: 29) define a critical juncture as "a period of significant change, which typically occurs in distinct ways in different countries (or in other units of analysis) and which is hypothesized to produce distinct legacies." The major modification I will make to the Colliers' definition is that it is possible to analyze critical junctures from a "within-case" approach to explanation in addition to comparative case analysis.

A critical juncture must be preceded by a crisis that sets in motion the forces that produce a discontinuity, or punctuation, in the previous equilibrium.[14] I use the definition of "international crisis" developed by Brecher (1993: 29–42) and Brecher and Wilkenfeld (1997: 4–5). An international crisis is defined by: (1) an increase in the intensity of disruptive interactions between two or more states with an increased probability of military hostilities; and (2) the result of these interactions destabilizes the states' relationship and challenges the structure of the system, whether international or regional. Essentially, international crises lead to wars, which lead to changes in the structure of the regional or international system. A change in these systems will often require a change in the states' master roles.

Within periods of relative stability between international crises that lead to war, states also experience foreign policy crises. The distinction between a foreign policy crisis and an international crisis is that the former does not challenge the structure of the system (Hermann 1972: 9). Foreign policy crises lead states to adjust their auxiliary roles within the boundaries established by their master status. In order to label these auxiliary roles, I adopt the national role conceptions employed in Holsti (1970). Holsti's list of role conceptions, while not exhaustive, describes the vast majority of the roles adopted by the United States and Israel during their foreign policy crises. These roles will be explained further as they emerge in the narrative.

The specific form of institutional analysis I employ is the analytic narrative (Bates et al. 1998). This approach is analytic because it employs the use of formalized logic. It is narrative because it takes account of the historical record and context. This approach combines methods employed in economics, political science, sociology, and history. As Levy (1997: 27) observes, narratives are compatible with nearly any theoretical orientation. The critical junctures in a state's foreign policy are expected to promote changes in the state's master role, which is deduced from role theory and the socialization and competition mechanisms. The socialization game provides the formalized expectations of the role bargaining process. These analytic features provide the searchlight for an examination of the historical record, which is presented in narrative fashion.

The analytic narrative method is similar to George and McKeown's (1985) process-tracing procedure (see also George and Bennett 2004), which Collier and Collier (1991: 5) also advocate for the within-country portion of their analysis. Process tracing seeks to explain the stream of events in a process by which various initial conditions are translated into outcomes. It involves an attempt to reconstruct agents' definitions of the situation and their resulting action. The framework within which agents' perceptions and actions are described is given by the researcher, not by the agents themselves. The process of creating such an explanation is similar to the construction of a web or network, with the researcher assembling bits and pieces of evidence into a pattern. The process-tracing approach attempts to uncover what stimuli create agents' interests; how interests are translated into behavior; and the effects of various institutional arrangements on agents' behavior (George and McKeown 1985: 34–37). I believe that the process-tracing procedure applies not only to individual actors within domestic political systems, but also to collective actors in regional or international systems.

An important qualification to the type of analysis proposed here is to indicate the conditions for its falsifiability. Or, perhaps more precisely, how would I know if I was wrong? Bates et al. (1998: 14–18) list five criteria for evaluating a narrative. First, do the assumptions of the model correspond to what is known? I have argued that the socialization game is based on theoretical expectations from role theory and dissonance theory. Second, do conclusions follow from premises? This involves assessing the empirical content of the narrative, as well as the logical structure of the model. Third, do the model's implications find confirmation in the data? This involves checking the empirical content of the narrative against the logic of the model. Fourth, how well does the theory stand up to competing explanations? Finally, how generalizable is the explanation? These questions are addressed in the case studies and conclusion.

OVERVIEW OF THE BOOK

Chapter 2 defends a focus on roles as the appropriate content of socialization. While norms, beliefs, rules, and principles are also contenders, roles are argued to be particularly salient to studies of socialization, the realist tradition, and as a link between the study of foreign policy and international politics. A socialization "game" is created as a heuristic model of the process whereby states learn their appropriate roles in the international system. This game demonstrates how roles that states adopt such as "regional leader," "neutral," or "defender of the faith" are chosen by states. The chapter provides expectations for the types of roles states will pursue with reference to the socialization and competition mechanisms, which are argued to interact with each other to produce four master statuses or roles: novice, minor member, major member, and great power. Each master status is reviewed for the number and types of roles that a state occupying that status is likely to adopt, as well as the likelihood of success in having members of the international community accept those roles. Ultimately, the chapter argues that states are constrained in their choice of roles by the material power they have to support that choice. Hence, instead of ideas versus material capabilities as the debate between neorealists and constructivists is often framed, the book argues that the two are inseparable.

Chapter 3 applies the socialization model to the United States. After briefly reviewing the historiography of US diplomatic history and determining the periods in which the United States occupies the aforementioned master statuses, the chapter applies the model to attempts by the dominant socializers (Britain and France at various points) to socialize the United States into appropriate roles. The chapter interprets diplomatic history through the socialization lens to explain how these roles were selected and how they were received by the international community.

Chapter 4 analyzes the transition of the United States to great power status. The socialization game is still applicable to the early years of this master status, since the United States was uncertain about occupying this role. The United States seeks few roles during the first half of the twentieth century, with most having to do with regional leadership, and it attempts to reclaim its longstanding neutral role in the face of pressure to join global wars. The chapter concludes with some reflections on the Cold War period and beyond, as the United States is no longer subject to socialization pressure because it has assumed the role of dominant global socializer.

Chapter 5 applies the socialization model to Israel from its birth through the end of the twentieth century. After briefly reviewing the historiography of Israeli diplomatic history and determining the periods in which Israel occupies the aforementioned master statuses, the chapter applies the model to attempts by the dominant socializers (Britain, France, and the United States at various points) to socialize Israel into appropriate roles. The chapter interprets diplomatic history through the socialization lens to explain how these roles were selected and how they were received by the international community. The chapter concludes with a discussion of the dissension raised in the international system when the dominant socializer approves of a role for Israel that the international community in general does not accept.

Chapter 6 concludes with a comparison of the socialization experiences of the United States and Israel during their occupation of the four master statuses. It highlights the importance of roles in connecting the study of foreign policy and international relations. It reinforces the importance of socialization in fleshing out structural theories of international politics— even theories like neorealism that claim to eschew ideational factors and identity. The key theoretical claim is that neorealism can accommodate both material interests and identity as understood in terms of roles. Finally, the chapter concludes with a discussion of the applicability of the socialization model to other contemporary states.

2 Socializing States in the International System

AN ARGUMENT FOR ROLES

In his review of Waltz (1979), Dessler (1989: 460) asks the critical question: "what are the units socialized *to*, if not (at a minimum) understandings of conventions?"[1] Dessler's own project was to build a "transformational" model of international politics based on the existence of constitutive rules of the international system. He further argues that "if Waltz's theory did not presume the existence of a set of rules constitutive of 'the system' to which nations are socialized, it could not explain how state behavior is constrained by structure" (Dessler 1989: 460).

While rules figure prominently in Dessler's approach to building a structural model of international politics, they are not the only conceivable contents of socialization activities. Norms, principles, beliefs, and roles are also good candidates for the study of socialization. The contents of socialization that are the focus of this research are the roles adopted in the system. The obvious question at this point is: why roles? Why not study how norms, rules, or principles are instilled in states through socialization efforts?

Prior to the revival of norms, rules, and principles in the international relations literature on international regimes (Krasner 1983), these concepts were largely the domain of scholars of international law, and their utility for explaining international outcomes was largely rejected by the dominant realist tradition. However, principles and beliefs, in the form of "ideas" have received some attention in recent years (e.g., Goldstein and Keohane 1993). Further, the causal impact of norms has been explored by Axelrod's (1984, 1997) research tradition. Indeed, most of the current published research has focused on norms and their transmission through socialization (e.g., Finnemore 1996c).

Norms, principles, and beliefs are incorporated into role theory in terms of role expectations, conceptions, and demands, as well as social identity (Biddle 1986: 69; Sampson and Walker 1987; Walker 1992: 23). Norms operating on the role expectations and demands of relevant others refer to the regulative content of international politics, while norms operating on an actor's own role conceptions refer to the regulative accounts of actors themselves or their identity (Kowert and Legro 1996: 453; Wendt 1987; Dessler 1989).

Roles, therefore, incorporate all of the alternative contents of socialization in some fashion. Wendt (1987: 418–422) uses roles for this reason to explain how a competitive security system can be transformed into a cooperative one. March and Olsen (1998) also feature roles in their institutionalist explanation of the persistence and transformation of international political orders. Yet roles have not generally been studied by scholars engaged in the constructivist turn in international relations. Ultimately, this is in part due to the general neglect of roles and role theory in international relations theory.

Although various theorists like Holsti (1970), Jervis (1976), Walker (1987) and Rosenau (1990) discuss the advantages of using role theory; few have taken up the challenge until very recently (e.g., Harnisch et al. 2011; Thies and Breuning 2012). This may be the result of confusion about the appropriate level of analysis for the role concept (Kowert and Legro 1996: 477). Role theory might be mistakenly viewed as solely appropriate for the study of individuals, such as the leaders of states. Yet role theory developed in the interdisciplinary field of social psychology and can be appropriately applied to both individuals and corporate entities (Walker 1979: 173; Stryker and Statham 1985: 330; Barnett 1993: 274).

Role theory may seem incompatible with the dominant realist tradition in international relations, though the work that has been done with role theory has always been attuned to realism. Holsti's (1970) seminal study on national role conceptions noted the frequent use of roles such as "aggressor," "defender," and "balancer" in balance of power theory. Walker's contributions to foreign policy informed by role theory have also been sensitive to realism and even employed in conjunction with Waltz's neorealism (e.g., Walker 1987). Role theory is quite compatible with Waltzian neorealism for several reasons (Thies 2003, 2010a, 2010b).

First, role theory, like neorealism, presents a highly structured view of reality (Stryker and Statham 1985: 311). Second, role theory posits that established roles and the role location process reduce the variety of possible behaviors and outcomes in society in a manner compatible with Waltz's socialization proposition (Sarbin and Allen 1968: 501–503). Third, role theory has a great deal to say about socialization and can offer insight into this process for neorealism. Role theory's articulated views on the socialization process stand in stark contrast to the underdeveloped models of socialization associated with the current interest in norms. In particular, socialization can be conceived of as a *role bargaining process* (Stryker and Statham 1985: 351) occurring between actors in a *role system* (Sarbin and Allen 1968: 507).

Fourth, roles can bridge the different levels of analysis, from the individual to the state to the international system. Roles thus offer a way to bridge the theoretical gap between structure and agency in Waltzian neorealism. As such, roles offer a way to understand the interplay between foreign policy and world politics.[2] Even Waltz (1990: 37) has suggested that "systems populated by units of different sorts in some ways perform differently, even though they share the same organizing principle. More needs to be said about the status and role of units in Neorealist theory." This apparent opening to the functional differentiation of units in the system will receive confirmation in the model developed later in this chapter.

Finally, Waltz has explicitly used the language of roles and role theory in a discussion of the aftermath of the collapse of bipolarity. Waltz (1990: 222) argued that "the old and the new great powers will have to learn new roles and figure out how to enact them on a shifting stage. New roles are hard to learn, and actors easily trip when playing on unfamiliar sets." This language at least implies that roles are consistent with Waltz's general outlook on international politics, if not with his theory, as this book intends to demonstrate.

The term "role" is a metaphor borrowed from the theater. However, the metaphor has been applied in different ways to create different theoretical traditions (Biddle 1986: 68–76). Structural, functional, and organizational versions of role theory refer to roles as conduct that "adheres to certain 'parts' (or positions) rather than to the players who read or recite them (Sarbin and Allen 1968: 489)." Symbolic interactionist and cognitive approaches to role theory refer to roles as "repertoires of behavior, inferred from others' expectations and one's own conceptions, selected at least partly in response to cues and demands" (Walker 1992: 23).

Structural, functional, and organizational approaches focus on the individual as representative of a social position, while symbolic interactionist and cognitive approaches focus on the individual as a person. Roles tend to be tied to functions in structural, functional, and organizational approaches, while roles are directed toward another actor in the system in symbolic interactionist and cognitive approaches (Biddle 1986: 86–87). The result, as Le Prestre (1997a: 3–4) argues, is that the concept of a role can assume at least six different meanings: (1) a contribution or a function; (2) an influence or an impact; (3) expected behavior based on certain rules; (4) a part in a larger script or a course of action; (5) policy decisions; and (6) rank.

Biddle (1986: 86–87) views this theoretical divide among role theorists as the product of the failure of role theorists and researchers to integrate their work, and the fact that role theorists deal with a wide range of phenomena at different levels of analysis in different types of social systems. The result according to Walker (1979: 176) is that role theory tends to be "conceptually rich and methodologically poor." In order to alleviate this problem, Biddle (1986) and Stryker and Statham (1985) argue for an integrated version of role theory. Such a theory would incorporate propositions concerning the roles of individual actors and roles that are common to individuals in the same social position. The term "role" would refer to both "positions" in an organized group *and* to any socially recognized category of actors—for example, the kinds of people whom it is possible to be in a society (Stryker and Statham 1985: 323). I adopt the integrated version of role theory called for by these scholars in my own study.

ROLE THEORY

Role expectations, role demands, and audience effects are posited to affect the process of role location in this study.[3] These variables, working through the role location process, are also posited to affect role enactment. The selection of a role and its enactment also affect the construction of social identity within a society. A brief explanation of each of these concepts and their relationship to the study at hand is in order.

Role Enactment

Role enactment refers to how well a social actor performs a given role once it is selected. The focus of the researcher's attention is on overt conduct or behavior of the social actor. Sarbin and Allen (1968: 491–497) discuss the key dimensions of the social actor's role enactment: number of roles, effort expended upon a role, and time spent in one role in comparison to other possible roles. First, they argue that the more roles a social actor has in his repertoire, the better prepared he is to meet the demands of social life. In particular, a "skilled" role taker has a better chance than the "unskilled" in enduring the effects of novel and critical situations.

In my application to states, a "member" is more likely, due to previous experience, to be a "skilled" role taker with a variety of well-rehearsed roles than the "novice," which has not had the direct experience or anticipatory socialization to prepare it for multiple roles.[4] An examination of Holsti's (1970: 273–285) discussion of the number of roles held by states in his early study seems to support my contention. The states with the fewest number of role conceptions in the period from 1965–1967/1968 were largely the recently decolonized and independent states of Africa.

Despite Holsti's (1970: 277) admonishment to theorists to abandon the traditional view that states only play a single role in the international system, this tendency seems to persist even among recent applications of role theory. Bukovansky's (1997) account of the constitution of US identity through the War of 1812 focuses exclusively on the role adopted by the United States in promoting neutral maritime rights. Barnett (1993) extends the analysis to two roles available to Arab states prior to 1967: to act upon sovereignty, or to act upon the logic of pan-Arabism that would result in political unification. However, both authors may have chosen a particular role or two to study for the purpose of analytical clarity. Bukovansky demonstrates that the neutrality role could not be explained by neorealism or neoliberalism, but that it must be understood as grounded in conceptions of US identity. Barnett illustrates that conflict in the Middle Eastern subsystem prior to 1967 was often due to the incompatibility of the two dominant roles foisted upon those states.

Additionally, these two studies may shed light on the conduct of unskilled, novice states. Perhaps the leadership of the United States prior to 1812 was unwilling or unable to generate multiple roles and, thus, stuck to the neutral role, which nearly cost it its survival. New Arab states also had to deal with the first role ascribed to any state—that of a sovereign state—and deal with an ideology (or institution in Barnett's formulation) that intended to eliminate the first role. However, as Barnett (1993: 289) argues, over time, states like Egypt were able to reinterpret the meaning of the role derived from pan-Arabism from interstate cooperation (Faisal) to political unification (Nassar) to *raison d'etat* (Sadat).

The second dimension of role enactment refers to the amount of effort expended upon, or involvement, in a role. This can range from complete non-involvement in which the role does not implicate identity at all and no effort is expended to complete involvement, or engrossment, where the role *is* the identity and a great deal of effort is expended upon the role. My interest is in roles that fall somewhere between these two poles. In my discussion of roles in the international system, complete noninvolvement would probably correspond to Holsti's (1970: 270, 285–289) national role conception of the *isolate*, one of the most passive roles on his active-passive continuum (along with the *protectee* and *internal development* roles). The isolate focuses exclusively on the internal dimensions of the state and eschews interaction with other states, thus removing identity construction from social interaction. At the time of Holsti's study, states like Cambodia and Burma fell into this category.

At the other extreme, the picture painted by Bukovansky of the construction of early US identity is one of engrossment in the neutral role. Interaction with other states was unimportant to a US identity based on this role because no matter how other states would act, the United States maintained the attachment to the role. Since one of my aims in this study is to demonstrate how roles affect identity construction *through interaction in the international system*, my cases will likely be found between these two extremes.

The third dimension of role enactment is the amount of time that the individual spends in one role relative to other roles. The amount of time one spends in a role is a function of whether the role is ascribed or achieved (Sarbin and Allen 1968: 496–497). The amount of time spent in an ascribed role is not subject to a tradeoff. *Ascribed* roles are enacted all the time—the only variability in enactment is how salient the role is at any one point in time. Roles with an *achieved* aspect are subject to variability in the time spent in them compared to other roles. In my study, all states will have some ascribed roles, such as the role of the sovereign state.

Novice states will probably have more ascribed roles than achieved roles in their initial stages of development. Member states are likely to have multiple achieved roles in addition to their ascribed roles. This is because member states largely define the social reality. Member states choose roles for themselves and engage in *altercasting* to impose roles on novice states. Altercasting refers to situations in which the relevant others cast a social actor into a role and provide cues to elicit the corresponding appropriate behavior. Altercasting is a recognized method of socialization (Weinstein and Deutschberger 1963; Stryker and Statham 1985: 325; Biddle 1986: 80; Earle 1986).

Role Expectations

In an integrated version of role theory, role expectations consist of norms, beliefs, and preferences concerning the performance of any individual in a social position relative to individuals occupying other positions (Sarbin and Allen 1968: 497; Stryker and Statham 1985: 330–331; Biddle 1986: 69). Role expectations thus provide the conceptual bridge between the individual and social structure. For some positions, role expectations may be uniform across occupants, but for others, role expectations may vary across occupants.

An individual's role behavior must take into account the role behaviors of the occupants of other positions, thus the concept of a role is essentially interbehavioral (Sarbin and Allen 1968: 498). According to Stryker and Statham (1985: 323), it is nonsensical to talk about a role without reference to an implicit or explicit counterrole involved in ongoing interaction. Interdependency is inherent in the nature of role relationships. The occupant of a position is expected to perform certain acts (and not others) and is expected to perform those acts in specific ways at the proper time and place. Role enactment is thus constrained by the expectations of other individuals.

Role expectations vary on several dimensions: their degree of generality or specificity, their scope or extensiveness, their clarity or uncertainty, the degree of consensus among other individuals, and whether the positions are formal or informal (Sarbin and Allen 1968: 499–500). The latter dimension requires some elaboration in the context of the international system. Formal positions are denoted by widespread public knowledge of their existence and reasonable consensus on their role expectations. Few formal roles exist in the international system other than the role of the sovereign state, the role of an ally, and perhaps the great power role. Most roles in the international system are informal creations. Formal designations of these roles do not usually occur. Rather, role expectations in an informal social system may be referred to as *social types* (Klapp 1962). Social typing refers to the qualities of the individual, emphasizing the kind of individual who acts in a particular way, or a socially recognized category of actors in Stryker and Statham's (1985: 323) formulation. Social typing may be the origin of social roles that later develop into formal positions. So, in the international system we may see social types develop into the kinds of role conceptions described in Holsti (1970), such as "bastion of revolution-liberator," "defender of the faith," or "faithful ally."

Formal and informal roles may also support or conflict with each other. Barnett (1993) shows how the formal role of sovereign state conflicted with the informal role for the state derived from pan-Arabism. However, we can also conceive of the formal role of the sovereign state supporting an informal role of "balancer" in a balance-of-power system. The key to smooth social interaction is for the interested parties to know the role expectations attached to both formal and informal roles, and as Barnett (1993) suggests, which role is active at which time.

Role expectations may vary depending upon whether they are held by the role occupant (in which case they may be called *role conceptions*), by occupants of complementary positions, or by the audience. Role expectations define the range of tolerated behavior. Role expectations encourage conformity to group norms. In the extreme case, a failure to conform will result in removal from a formal or informal position. Conformity to role expectations may occur even if the performer has no strong commitment to the role because of his sensitivity to the reaction of others in complementary or audience roles.

Social interaction is made possible through the sharing of role expectations by individuals. If role expectations are unclear or ambiguous, then behavior is less predictable, and the possibility of conflict is introduced. The clarity of role expectations can be defined as the difference between operating under a condition of perfect knowledge about role expectations and imperfect knowledge, which is the amount of information usually available to a performer.

The performer may have imperfect knowledge for several reasons (Sarbin and Allen 1968: 503; Stryker and Statham 1985: 335–336). First, role expectations held by other individuals may be vague, indefinite, or ambiguous, which is also known as *role ambiguity* (Biddle 1986: 83). Other individuals may not have a clear positive conception of role expectations, but they are quite sure when those expectations have been violated. Second, clear expectations held by one individual may contradict equally clear expectations held by another. This occurs when occupants of complementary roles disagree on the expectations for the performer. The lack of congruence between role expectations is also known as *role dissensus*, or *intrarole conflict* (Sarbin and Allen 1968: 540). Third, the role expectations held by the performer may be clear, yet he may distort or misunderstand the expectations received from others. This kind of incongruity may be affected by past experience and interaction. Additionally, the degree of continuity or abruptness in the passage from one role to another will affect the clarity of the social actor's role expectations.

Role Demands

Role demands place constraints on the choice of role in a particular situation (Sarbin and Allen 1968: 510–514). Role demands call for a specific role enactment in a specific situation. Under ordinary conditions, role demands are implicit. However, some situations guided by certain norms demand certain roles. Such norms would include face-saving norms or reciprocity norms, which demand certain roles when they are in operation. In this case, it is the situation that dictates role expectations.

Audience Effects

The important actors in any role enactment consist of: (1) the role performer; (2) the individual in the complementary role; and (3) a third member who observes the process of interaction between the first two—the audience

(Sarbin and Allen 1968: 527–534). The audience may be passive or may actively respond to the performance. In order for the audience to react to the performer, the latter's role behavior must be public and open to observation. Public behavior makes the role behavior subject to positive and negative sanctions that will serve to shape future behavior.

Sarbin and Allen (1968: 534) mention several functions of the audience. First, they establish the consensual reality for the role. If the audience accepts the role enactment as appropriate, then it serves as confirmation of the reality of the role. Second, the audience provides *cues* to guide the performer's role enactment. Third, the audience engages in social reinforcement through the positive and negative sanctions associated with the role enactment. Fourth, the audience contributes to the maintenance of the role behavior over time. The enactment of a role without major deviation over time is likely due to the fact that the audience continually observes the enactment. Thus, the audience serves as a major source of continuous socialization pressure over time.

Role Location

Role location refers to the process whereby a social actor locates its proper role in a social structure. The actor must select a role that is appropriate to the situation. This is accomplished by locating the position of the self and other. If the actor is mistaken in assigning positions to itself and the other, then the role enactment will be inappropriate.

The role location process is the crux of my study of socialization. The role location process is where role expectations of the self and other, role demands of the situation, and cues from the audience all come together to produce a role for the actor and set the conditions for its appropriate enactment. Suitable roles are determined through the interaction of relevant actors in a role bargaining process. *Socialization itself is essentially a role bargaining process.* Socialization occurs throughout the life cycle of any social actor (Stryker and Statham 1985: 348–352). Thus, the socialization that occurs in the role location process is not just limited to emerging novice states, but it also affects already existing states in a new international system.

I have proposed a socialization "game" modeling the role location process (see further on). This game is a heuristic device used to model of the adoption of a single role by a novice state in the system. Most of the theoretical discussion so far has been concerned with the selection and performance of a single role; however, just as Holsti (1970) noted, most social actors will be confronted with the choice of a variety of possible roles for a situation. Social actors may also occupy many roles in a social system at any given time. This does not have to be a problem for the social actor, though, as multiple roles may be organized so that they are successfully enacted successively or simultaneously. Additionally, some roles may be active while others are latent.

The enactment of a large number of roles means that a social actor is linked with many other complementary roles in various areas of society and is therefore more closely integrated into society's norms. The connection of the social actor's roles to various other roles thereby ensures greater normative social control (Sarbin and Allen 1968: 540). Emerging states are unlikely to have multiple roles and, thus, are less likely to be constrained by the system. These states, in particular, will need to be socialized if the system is to be maintained. Small states that survive the transition from one system to another will retain many roles in the transition, thus maintaining their normative link to society. Therefore, the amount of socialization they require should be less than new states.

However, multiple roles are problematic when a social actor finds himself simultaneously in two or more positions requiring contradictory role enactments, also known as *interrole conflict* (Sarbin and Allen 1968: 540). Because the social actor occupies multiple roles, mechanisms must be found to reduce the incompatibility and conflict existing among several of the roles.

This situation of having multiple role demands that exceed available resources places a social actor in a cognitive state that Goode (1960) calls "role strain," or the felt difficulty of fulfilling role obligations. Three factors are important to determining the allocation of time and effort among one's roles and to determining which of several contradictory roles will be enacted in a situation: the social actor's norm commitment (some roles have much greater salience for the actor than others), the estimate of reward or punishment by role partners, and the estimate of reactions of a third party or an audience (Sarbin and Allen 1968: 539). These are the same types of factors that are present in the more general role location process. The socialization game that I propose can also be used to analyze the choice of which competing role to enact in a situation.

THE SOCIALIZATION GAME

The "game" or heuristic model illustrated in Figure 2.1 depicts the socialization process that occurs when a new state begins to adopt roles for itself in the international system (or subsystem).[5] This model is based on insights from both role theory and cognitive dissonance theory. In fact, the model is so general that it could be applied to the socialization of the constituent units of any type of social system.

This model consists of only three players: nature (N), an emerging state (Player 1), and a socializing state (Player 2). Nature in this game can be thought of in two ways. First, nature may be conceived of as the structure of the system acting as a "selector." According to Waltz (1979: 74), structures select by rewarding some behaviors and punishing others. Structures do not exercise direct effects, or act as agents do, but rather affect behavior indirectly through socialization and competition. Structure is the ultimate

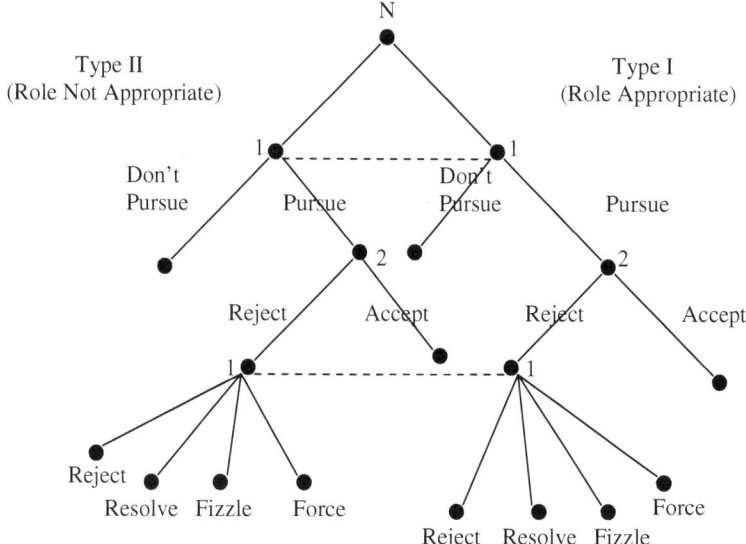

Figure 2.1   The Socialization Game

arbiter of whether the role chosen by any state is reflective of the underlying "reality." For example, a state with few capabilities could choose to enact the role of a great power but would be punished by other states acting on structural imperatives.

Second, in accordance with role theory, nature may be thought of as the audience of interested third parties in the interaction between ego and alter. Once again, the audience will have demands regarding the role(s) that the ego selects for itself. The audience in the international system will depend on the geographical and issue domains that the emerging state considers in exercising its role(s). The states of the audience are essentially "structural police." These states, having engaged in the practice of international relations for some time, know the expected norms and roles for interaction in the system.

The emerging state (Player 1), or ego, enters the system with little or no prior knowledge of how the system works. It must be socialized into the appropriate norms, roles, and behaviors for social interaction. The socializing state (Player 2), or alter, is the necessary complement to the emerging state in this situation. Role theory is premised on the notion that interdependence is inherent in the nature of role relationships. All roles exist in complementary pairs. So, if ego tries to adopt a role, it implicates an alter that must respond.

The socialization game involves the choice of a single role by the emerging state. Holsti (1970) has identified at least 17 types of national role conceptions, such as regional-subsystem collaborator, independent, faithful ally, mediator-integrator, regional protector, and protectee. We could imagine that the emerging state chooses any one of these roles. However, unlike Holsti, I explicitly posit that the adoption of a role by the emerging state (ego) implicates an existing state (alter) that must respond to the emerging state's announcement.

The game begins with Nature selecting whether Player 1 is a Type I or Type II player. A Type I player is a state for whom the role is appropriate, and a Type II player is a state for whom the role is not appropriate from the vantage point of the structure of the system. This selection would be based upon the emerging state's capabilities and status in the system. This selection occurs once the state has emerged and prior to the emerging state announcing a role.

Player 1 then makes a choice to pursue or not to pursue the role. The catch is that Player 1 is unclear whether it is a Type I or II player. Because it is a new state, it may not have the ability to correctly interpret cues from the audience of other states. Player 1 is therefore engaged in a game of imperfect information. It must make its choice about pursuing the role or not under some uncertainty. If Player 1 is a Type II state and doesn't pursue the role, then it has acted in accord with structural imperatives. Similarly, if Player 1 is a Type I state and it pursues the role, then it has also acted in accord with structural imperatives.

However, in the case where Player 1 is a Type I and does not pursue the role, it should feel increasing pressure to pursue it at some future point. In the case where Player 1 is Type II and does pursue the role, it will feel structural pressure to abandon that role. Punishment is likely in both of these cases from member states acting as socializers.

If Player 1 chooses not to pursue the role under either condition (Type I or II), then the game is over (for this iteration at least). If Player 1 chooses to pursue the role under either condition, then Player 2, the socializer, must respond. Player 2 must choose to accept or reject the role because it is a partner in enacting it. Player 2 is aware of the condition under which Player 1 is laboring. Player 2 steps out of the audience and represents the "family" of states in this situation.

If Player 2 accepts the role in either condition, then the game ends. If Player 1 is a Type I player and Player 2 accepts the role, then both have acted in compliance with structure. Player 2 rewards Player 1 by accepting its part in enacting the role. The socializer has thus confirmed that Player 1's behavior is in compliance with its place in the structure. However, if Player 2 accepts the role when Player 1 is Type II, then both players are acting contrary to the structure. They achieve some benefit from cooperating on role enactment, but at some future iteration they will likely be punished.

Player 2's other socializing action occurs when it rejects the role under the Type II condition. The socializer is providing a strong cue that the role adopted by Player 1 is inconsistent with its structural position. Player 2 could also conceivably act contrary to structure and reject the role even though Player 1 is a Type I player. Player 2 may try to bluff Player 1 from achieving a role that is due to it. For example, Player 2 may want to prevent a rise in the status of Player 1, so it suggests that the role is inappropriate.

If Player 2 rejects the role under either condition then Player 1 will experience dissonance. The dissonance is due to the fact that Player 1 desires the achievement of the role but now suspects that the role is not appropriate to its type. According to Elster (1998), there are five possible responses that Player 1 could choose to reduce the dissonance. First, Player 1 could try to modify the world so that it does achieve the role. This would occur through the exercise of its capabilities. Second, Player 1 could simply accept that the role would not be achieved. Third, Player 1 could update its own beliefs so that it is certain that it should achieve the role. Elster refers to this as "wishful thinking." Fourth, Player 1 could stop desiring that it adopt the role. And, finally, Player 1 could come to desire that it not adopt the role. Elster refers to this as "adaptive preference formation." These options are quite similar to those offered by Sarbin and Allen (1968: 541) to reduce "cognitive strain," by Hall (1972) to reduce "role conflict," and by Goode (1960) to reduce "role strain." All of these mechanisms attempt to reduce tension between the individual and others' expectations concerning the choice of a role.

In determining choices in a game, it is difficult to incorporate "desires" and "beliefs" into separate actions. My initial cut at the problem is to create four choices of dissonance reduction for Player 1: Force, Fizzle, Resolve, and Reject. Player 1 could choose Force and use its capabilities to modify the world so that it can adopt the role. This would entail forcing Player 2 to accept its part in the role enactment. If Player 1 is Type I, then it is likely to prevail against Player 2.

Player 1 could also choose Fizzle and update its beliefs to accept that the role could not be achieved *and* stop desiring it as well (Elster's second and fourth responses). The Fizzle choice under Type I conditions would be similar to simply not pursuing the role, but this would entail greater costs for Player 1. The Fizzle choice under Type II conditions would also be a suboptimal version of simply not pursuing the role.

Player 1 could choose Resolve, which involves updating beliefs so that the emerging state is certain that the role is right for it and the alter. Resolve is somewhat of a stalemate between the emerging state and its socializer. This type of "wishful thinking" would be dangerous for the new state in the Type II condition.

Player 1 could also choose Reject, in which it no longer desires the role for itself. This is what Elster called adaptive preference formation. This is a clear case of socialization at work: the socializer rejects the role, and, despite its beliefs and desires to the contrary, the emerging state also rejects the role. Player 1 has adapted its preferences to Player 2. This is an ideal ending for the game under Type II conditions because Player 1 has indeed "learned" something about itself and its place in the system through the socialization process. However, under Type I conditions, the emerging state has been misled by the socializer to reject a role that is appropriate.

The game that I have created would apply mainly to roles that an emerging state was trying to *achieve* in the system. Minor revisions could create a game in which the socializing state engaged in *altercasting*, in which the member state suggests a role for the novice. In this type of game, Player 2 (in our formulation) would make the first move with full knowledge of Player 1's Type. Player 1 would then accept or reject the role. Player 2 would then be subject to the dissonance reduction mechanisms if Player 1 rejects the role. This type of game would also be appropriate to roles *ascribed* to an emerging state in the system.

SOCIAL IDENTITY

Models of social identity based on role theory generally point to three crucial dimensions: the status, value, and involvement dimensions (Sarbin and Allen 1968: 550–557; Stryker and Statham 1985: 345–348; Vertzberger 1990: 282–295).[6] The status dimension refers to a position in a social structure and its associated duties, rights, and legitimated power or authority. That position, or status, implicates a number of normative expectations concerning the proper role, and enactment of that role, by the occupant. Some of these status roles are ascribed, and others are achieved.

The status ascribed to a state by others may not match the status the state believes it has achieved. This kind of status discrepancy may lead to internal conflict over a state's identity and, depending upon the resolution of the internal debate, externalized conflict to resolve the discrepancy. The ensuing interaction with other states should determine how realistic the state's role conceptions were in comparison to the relevant others' expectations for the state's role (Vertzberger 1990: 291–292; Cashman 1993: 228–232). Most versions of realism and neorealism at least implicitly, if not explicitly, recognize perceived status discrepancy to be a source of change in the system (e.g., Gilpin 1981; Schweller 1996).

The value dimension refers to how relevant others evaluate an actor's role enactment to be. The value dimension varies along the achieved versus ascribed continuum as well. In general, negative valuations are not placed on actors who fail to perform, or perform poorly, in achieved roles in specific instances. However, if nonperformance or poor performance persists, then the relevant others will no longer recognize the actor in the achieved role. The proper enactment of achieved roles usually does lead to positive valuation. On the other hand, the proper enactment of ascribed roles generally will not receive much positive valuation because it is expected. However, nonperformance or poor performance in ascribed roles will lead to strong negative valuations (Sarbin and Allen 1968: 552).

There are two aspects to the involvement dimension for states: the concept of belonging and the amount of effort or participation. According to Vertzberger (1990: 282), the conception of being part of a functional or regional group of states determines the expectations it has toward other states, and vice versa. This can lead to contradictory expectations of state behavior if a state is a member of several groups and thus is involved in enacting several roles, perhaps simultaneously, as was discussed earlier in the chapter. It is crucial at this point to determine which role is most salient to the situation (Stryker and Statham 1985: 345).

The second aspect of involvement refers to the amount of effort expended upon a role. As was stated previously, this can range from complete noninvolvement, in which the role does not implicate identity at all, to engrossment, where the role is the identity. Empirically, it is likely that the cases I will examine will all fall somewhere between these two extremes.

If social identity can be determined from the three dimensions of status, value, and involvement, then where should we look to analyze them? According to Sarbin and Allen (1968: 514), role location is the first, and role enactment is the last stage of the social act. Social identity is naturally implicated in this process. Social identity is partly created from interactions with other members of the role system enacting complementary roles. The shaping of identity is also dependent upon the positive and negative socializing sanctions placed on a social actor's public conduct (role location and enactment) by relevant others (audience). The starting point for the analysis of social identity is the role location variable—the placement of self and other, according to Sarbin and Allen (1968: 550).

Additionally, the role location process is the point where leadership has the greatest impact on negotiating a society's identity. At the stage prior to the start of the socialization game, the leader is engaged in negotiating a proper external role for the state with domestic constituents. As the leader attempts to negotiate the role agreed upon by domestic constituents with other states, he or she alone represents the domestic society's identity and interests. In effect, the role location process is a two-level game (Putnam 1988), with the leader acting as the fulcrum between domestic and international societies' conceptions of the appropriate role and implicated identity for a state. Level I is the negotiation within the domestic sphere, and Level II is the international negotiation of a role as portrayed in the socialization game.

The leader's own identity may become enmeshed in this process as well. Another concept from role theory, self-role congruence, examines how well an individual is suited for a role (Sarbin and Allen 1968: 522–527). Leaders may evaluate the appropriateness of a state's role and associated identity with reference to their conceptions of their own individual role(s) and identity (Walker 1992). In a state with a dominant, maximal leader, the negotiation for roles at the domestic level may be inappropriate. Instead, the leader may negotiate a personal role used to represent his or her state with other states. Whether the leader is negotiating a role on behalf of domestic constituents, or just him or herself, a thorough examination of the role location process and its impact on role enactment should lead us to a greater understanding of social identity formation in emerging states.

This argument suggests that Waltz may be mistaken in his assessment of leadership. According to Waltz, leadership should largely be irrelevant to the socialization process. "Chiliastic rulers occasionally come to power. In power, most of them quickly change their ways" (Waltz 1979: 128). Essentially, leaders should act as conduits for affecting structural imperatives on the states they represent. A leader should have no independent effect on the type of role adopted by the state in the system. Yet Waltz does have one disclaimer in his broad statement about leaders. Leaders can refuse to adapt to the system, and hope to survive, only if their state is relatively unaffected by the competition of states. Socialization, according to Waltz (1979: 128), proceeds at a pace set by the extent of a state's involvement in the international system. Thus, according to Waltz, leadership should only exert a noticeable impact when a state is not subject to extensive involvement with the international system and its socializing agents.

WALTZIAN EXPECTATIONS FOR ROLE-BASED SOCIALIZATION

The obvious question after an exposition of a role-based approach to socialization within a neorealist system is what would Waltz's (1979) structural theory expect from socialization? It is difficult to know exactly what Waltz would expect from socialization other than that it should reduce the range of observable behavior in the system. This is also what role theory would predict. However, there are several possibilities concerning the types of roles we should observe in the system based on Waltz's theory.

The first possibility is that the only role of any importance in the system is the role of the sovereign state. This is deduced from the Waltzian premise that states are the actors of consequence in the system; they seek security in order to ensure their survival; and they are functionally undifferentiated. Thus, rational, egoistic states all fulfill essentially the same role. If they do not fulfill the role of the sovereign state, they will be punished and possibly eliminated. However, by confining Waltzian expectations to a single role, I think I would be creating a straw man. Empirically, from Holsti (1970) we know that states do indeed profess a variety of roles for themselves. Indeed, Waltz himself introduces a role-based distinction in his version of neorealism.

This leads to the second possibility, that roles are based on capabilities (Wish 1987). In particular, Waltz specifically mentions a different role, or function, for the great powers. This leads to a bit of schizophrenia in his theory, since the theory's assumptions relate to all states as formal equals (functionally undifferentiated), yet the balance-of-power system he describes really only concerns the great powers. Waltz (1993: 49) has written about Britain and France continuing to enact the great power roles into the 1950s despite a structural shift to bipolarity. Their capabilities may have allowed them to try to maintain their positions in the system, yet by the Suez Crisis of 1956, the United States succeeds in socializing them out of that role.

Further, Waltz (1993: 55) states that Japan is ready for the mantle of great power status "if only it will reach for it." Waltz argues that as a state's capabilities increase to the level required of great powers, it should become increasingly difficult—due to structural imperatives operating through competition and socialization—for the state to shrug off the great power role. So, there is precedent in Waltz to consider differentiated roles in the international system based on capabilities.

This capability-based precedent leads to the third possibility: that a variety of roles, in addition to the great power role, are possible in the system. Virtually any role is open to a state that has the capabilities to enact that role. This allows us to extend Waltz's analysis to the regional subsystems where we should expect to find the kinds of roles identified by Holsti (1970), including regional leader, regional protector, active independent, and protectee. The variation in capabilities observed in the international system and regional subsystems allows for functional differentiation to creep back into the analysis. Obviously, great power or regional power status is based on relatively greater capabilities, but relative to whom? The role of regional protector (greater capabilities) implicates a role of protectee (lesser capabilities), and so on. In fact, the broad notion of functional undifferentiation is probably incompatible with the notion of socialization. However, we may find that certain types of states perform certain functions in the system—a limited form of functional differentiation.

Walker (1987: 77–79) essentially reached the same conclusion in his deduction of foreign policy roles from neorealism as informed by social exchange theory. Walker deduced five general roles from propositions culled from neorealism. The *consumer* role refers to a state attempting to gain or maintain assistance (economic, military, or diplomatic) from another state through its foreign policy. The *producer* role refers to the state that is providing the assistance. The *belligerent* role is adopted when the potential producer resists requests for assistance, or when the potential consumer presses demands for assistance in the face of resistance. The *facilitator* role attempts to establish or maintain the exchange process between states. The *provocateur* role attempts to disrupt existing exchange relationships or prevent them from being established.

It is this third possibility that will inform this study's expectations about socialization based on Waltz's theory. A state may offer any role it wishes in the role location process I model in the socialization game. As long as it has the capabilities to support the role, it will likely prevail. My characterization of Waltz's expectations for socialization appears to leave little room for social identity. This is in accordance with most characterizations that pit self-interested behavior based on calculations of capability against identity-based behavior (Katzenstein 1996: 23; Katzenstein et. al. 1998). However, Jepperson et al. (1996: 34) suggest that Waltz implicitly talks about identity when he argues that anarchy produces "like units." More explicitly, I expect that the interactive processes of role location and enactment will be shaped by state identity and will in turn shape state identity (Wendt 1994).

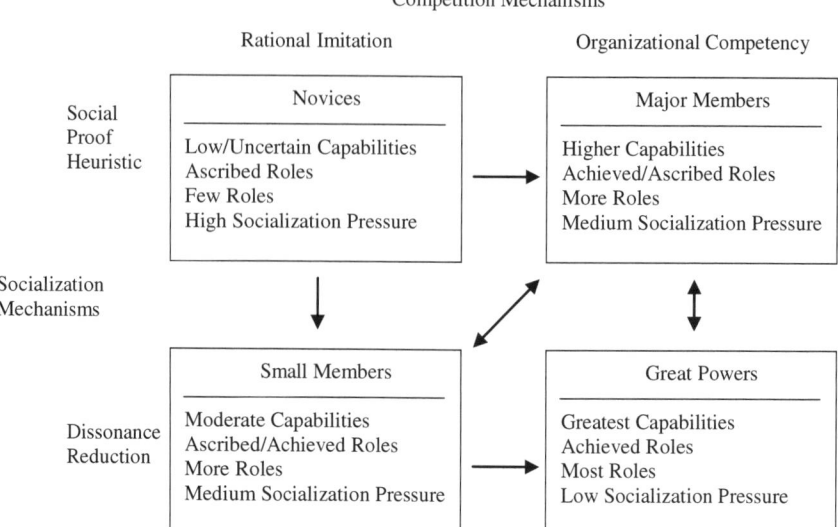

Figure 2.2 The Four Master Statuses. Reproduced with permission from Thies (2001).

Previously, I stated that this study would only consider competition as it interacted with socialization to produce the sameness effect. Figure 2.2 considers the impact of the interaction between the competition and socialization mechanisms on role location. The interaction of these structural forces produces four master roles in the international system—novice, small member, major member, and great power. Each of these master roles or master statuses describes a familiar ranking in the international system. As such, the master roles also implicate a state's social identity. Each master status also limits the kinds of auxiliary roles we should expect states to achieve.

Emerging states should be most circumscribed in their behavior. These novice states will probably engage in imitative behavior for their internal organization and their external policies. They will have few, well-defined roles in the system, and the roles they have are likely to be ascribed to them by member states. Emerging states will be subject to the most intense socialization pressure of any kind of state in the system and the least likely to resist such pressure because of their low or uncertain capabilities.

Small member states will have a larger number of roles, and more well-developed roles in the system than emerging states. Small states, having a greater sense of their capabilities and identity, will attempt to achieve roles in the system in addition to their ascribed roles. These states will most likely still be imitating others for their internal organization, but their role location efforts may subject them to the dissonance reduction process if other members disagree with their role conceptions. Small states may be both members of an established system and novices when the system changes.

Major member states, or regional powers, due to their greater capabilities, will have a greater array of well-developed roles that include more achieved than ascribed roles. The greater capabilities that regional powers have are partly a function of their natural endowments, but also a function of their ability to innovate their internal organization to make the best use of those capabilities. Major members are responsible for socializing emerging states and small states in their geographic subsystem. However, regional powers cannot act with impunity, as they are still subject to socializing activities by the great powers at the level of the international system and in the regional subsystem if it is a great power's traditional sphere of influence.

Great powers, due to their overwhelming capabilities in comparison to these other types of states, will have the largest number of well-developed roles. These roles are likely to largely reflect the achievements of great powers based on their capabilities. Great powers are still subject to socializing influence as members of a system, but due to their capabilities, they can force the adoption of a role for themselves in the dissonance reduction stage of the role location process. Great powers maintain their status in the system due to their innovations in internal organization that allow them to fully develop and exploit their capabilities.

States can be expected to move through these statuses over time. All states will begin their life in the emerging state category, as imitators and adaptors to the international system. As they successfully endure in the system, emerging states will at some point enter one of the other categories of states. Most states will move to the small state category and be resocialized as full members as the system changes over time. Other small states may become "members" of the system, not because of their own capabilities or intentions, but because other states tolerate them as members despite their imperfect imitation of the form and function of states. I am referring to those members of the system labeled quasi-states by Jackson (1990).

Emerging states that develop a higher level of organizational competency are able to make better use of their capabilities to achieve more roles in their subsystem, possibly including that of a major member. States can move between the major member and small member state roles as the system changes and as their organizational competency and capabilities change. Some emerging state may eventually attain the capability to exert influence beyond their subsystem into the international system. These states attain the role of great power if other great powers concur that their capabilities match the expectations of the role. If other great powers do not accept the state making a bid for great power status, then balancing will occur.

Figure 2.2 describes a dynamic, role location process in the international system. All states begin life in the system as an emerging state. However, the path they take from that point will largely be determined by the competitive and socialization mechanisms that drive their internal and external behavior. Some emerging states will simply become small member states, while others may become regional or great powers. Some emerging states may take an indirect path that leads them through the small state role, to the regional power role, and possibly to the great power role. These four roles by no means exhaust the types of roles that states may adopt. However, each of the four roles may be a "master status," or a role that is salient in every situation (Stryker and Statham 1985: 357)—hence an important aspect of social identity. States will pursue auxiliary roles that are consistent with their master roles or will be subject to socializing pressure to abandon those auxiliary roles or make the transition to a different master status.

This figure implies that Waltz's sameness effect should be strongest among emerging states. Emerging states are subject to adaptive and imitative behavior both internally and externally. Small states and regional powers will be subject to imitation—the strongest version of the sameness effect—only through competition or socialization, but probably not both. Great powers will be least subject to the sameness effect. Great powers are the innovators of internal organization and external policy and are the predominant socializers of the system. They determine what existing roles are appropriate to themselves and others and when new roles need to be created to meet new situations. However, great powers, and indeed all states, will engage in imitation at times, but in order to attain and retain their high status, great powers must innovate.

The cells of the figure also give us a broad picture of the social identity of actors in the various categories of states. As you will recall from our earlier discussion, social identity is thought to vary along status, value, and involvement dimensions. Status is incorporated into this figure through capabilities. The evaluation of role enactment varies according to the ascribed or achieved nature of the role. Finally, involvement concerns the number of roles a state adopts. Therefore, the greatest variance in social identity should be between the various categories of states, not within them.

How Structure Induces Foreign Policy Roles

The master statuses derived from the interaction of the mechanisms of socialization and competition also further our understanding of the impact of structure upon agents. The structure of the international system works through socialization and competition to produce four master roles for units within the system. These master roles further constrain the behavior of states once they assume that role. Thus, only certain types of auxiliary foreign policy roles should be expected in each master status. For example, we might expect a novice state to adopt a neutral role, but we should not expect a great power to adopt that type of foreign policy role. If states attempt to adopt foreign policy roles that are inconsistent with their master status, then socialization activity will occur on behalf of structure to prevent the enactment of these roles. All of this activity occurs within the role location process as modeled in the socialization game.

This conception of the international system helps to fill out Coleman's (1986) macro-micro-macro model, as elaborated upon by Hedstrom and

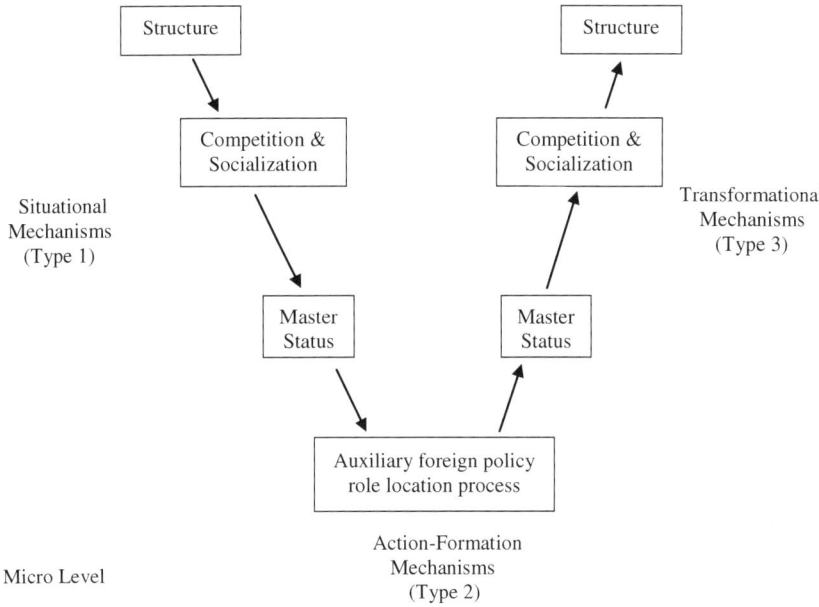

Macro Level

Situational
Mechanisms
(Type 1)

Transformational
Mechanisms
(Type 3)

Micro Level

Action-Formation
Mechanisms
(Type 2)

Figure 2.3 The Macro-Micro-Macro Model of Structural Change

Swedberg (1998: 21–23), and described in Chapter 1. I have expanded Waltzian neorealism to show how structure affects the units through socialization
and competition, thus explicating a Type 1 mechanism. The role location process, in which the units interact to select auxiliary foreign policy roles, offers a
Type 2 mechanism. Finally, the appropriateness of those auxiliary roles, or the
transitions to different master roles, explains the reproduction and possible
transformation of the system—a Type 3 mechanism (see Figure 2.3).

The next three chapters examine the United States and Israel in their
foreign policy role location processes. As seen in Figure 2.3, the role location process—or socialization process that occurs at the micro level of Coleman's (1986) model—is the key to the maintenance or transformation of the
system. The US cases, examined in Chapters 3 and 4, demonstrate how the
socialization process that occurs at the micro level can have implications for
the structure of the system. The Israeli cases, examined in Chapter 5, demonstrate the same for the structure of the regional subsystem.

3 Socializing the United States
Emergence to Major Member

In this chapter I begin to examine the socialization process in the international system. In each of our cases, I examine the history of interaction between the United States and its socializer and the relevant audience through the lens of the socialization game. The socialization game models the role location process. The analysis focuses on the major roles ascribed to, or achieved by, the United States during four periods of its early history: emergence (1776–1783), novice state (1783–1815), small member state (1815–1848), and major member state (1848–1898). Each of these periods of history is marked by a critical juncture that brings a change in the master status of the United States, and consequent changes in associated roles.

First, I examine the emergence of the United States from 1776 to 1783. The analysis finds the United States engrossed with pursuit of the role of the sovereign state, which it achieves despite the efforts of its primary socializer, Britain, to thwart it. Upon official recognition of the sovereign state role for the United States, I examine its tenure in the system as a novice state from 1783 to 1815. During this time period, the United States is still attempting to enact the sovereign state role, but it also becomes heavily invested in achieving a neutral role. In fact, it attempts to enact this role twice, with the second attempt resulting in the War of 1812 with Great Britain. Despite its failure to achieve the neutral role, the United States becomes firmly established as a sovereign state at the close of the war.

The United States becomes a small member state at the close of the war in 1815 and persists in that role until the conclusion of the Mexican-American War in 1848. The United States resists British attempts to ascribe the role of regional collaborator and instead enunciates a role of regional protector for itself in 1823. That role is largely uncontested, but not properly enacted until the Mexican-American War. At the close of this war, the US status changes to major member state, which it retains until the conclusion of the Spanish-American War in 1898. Despite a brief respite from role enactment during the Civil War, the United States achieves and enacts the regional protector and regional leader roles during this time period.

Since the data employed in this research is derived from secondary sources produced by historians, it is important to understand the impact of historiographical trends upon that data. In science there are no abstract "facts" that exist apart from the theories that are used to interpret them (Kuhn, 1970). That events occur in history is true, but what those events mean is always a matter of contention. As Lustick (1996) and Thies (2002) remind political scientists, unwarranted selectivity in the choice of historical source material can lead one to find false confirmation for a theory. In order to avoid this charge, I briefly describe the major trends in US historiography and how my sources fit into those trends. I then explain how I determined the aforementioned periods of US history and how they map onto US master statuses before analyzing the role location process associated with each.

THE HISTORIOGRAPHY OF US FOREIGN POLICY

The academic study of the history of US foreign policy began in earnest immediately following World War I.[1] The first generation of scholars, mostly trained as political historians, operated out of two different perspectives: nationalist and progressive. The nationalist historians, such as Samuel Flagg Bemis and Dexter Perkins, focused on the continuities and successes in the American diplomatic tradition. These scholars, along with Thomas Bailey and Julius Pratt, are often referred to as the early consensus historians (Dull 1981). These scholars tended to concentrate on interstate relations, particularly with respect to US-European relations. Progressives, such as Charles and Mary Beard, highlighted domestic, economic, and intellectual factors that guided US foreign policymaking. Progressives thus saw conflict and change, rather than consensus and continuity in US foreign policy.

The optimism that usually accompanied the writings of the nationalists was soon replaced after the horrors of World War II and the start of the nuclear age with the more pessimistic tone of realist historians, such as George F. Kennan and Hans J. Morgenthau. The realist historians were also primarily concerned with interstate relations and policymaking elites. The realists were less concerned about the internal sources of US foreign policy that was the hallmark of progressive research. In fact, the realists blamed the failings of US foreign policy on public opinion, partisan rivalry, and excessive legalism or moralism. As Hoffman (1977: 47–48) pointed out, this is exactly what US policymakers wanted to hear at the start of the Cold War.

The revisionists, writing in the 1960s and 1970s, expressed a renewed interest in the internal sources of US diplomacy. William Appleman Williams almost single-handedly launched the New Left revisionism in 1959, with the publication of *The Tragedy of American Diplomacy*. Revisionists like Williams emphasized the impact of the ideology of liberal capitalism on US foreign policy. Revisionists also shifted attention away from US–European relations to US relations with the Third World.

Critics of the revisionists, such as Bradford Perkins (1984), argued that the revisionist approach was monocausal in its reliance on economic motives to explain US foreign policy. These critics charged that revisionists failed to recognize legitimate national security concerns and the actions of other states on foreign policy. The postrevisionists, such as John Lewis Gaddis (1983), began to return to realist assumptions starting in the early 1980s. Postrevisionists have returned to a focus on interstate relations, policymaking elites, and traditional notions of the balance of power and national security. Postrevisionists generally find US diplomacy to be successful, and when they are skeptical, the blame is usually assigned to the culprits blamed by traditional realists. Incorporating some of the criticism of the revisionists, postrevisionists treat economic factors as important to grand strategy. However, economic factors are still subordinate to security and geopolitical concerns.

Diplomatic history has become somewhat marginalized with the rise of social history. US diplomatic history has been criticized for ethnocentrism, parochialism, a lack of theoretical rigor, and methodological stagnation.[2] Gaddis (1990) explained the lack of methodological innovation as the result of a tendency to seek synthesis through reductionism, the exaggeration of US influence on other states, and a parochial attitude that assumed the uniqueness of the US experience. The solution, according to Gaddis, is to borrow from international relations and political science to increase the methodological and theoretical sophistication of diplomatic history.[3]

McMahon's (1991) response to calls for international history, rather than simply US history, revolves around the types of questions that guide diplomatic historians. McMahon (1991: 15–16) suggests that the two principle questions guiding research in US diplomatic history are: why has the United States followed the international course that it has, and how have important policy decisions been reached? Both of these questions are US-centric and demand knowledge of US history, culture, and archival sources. McMahon suggests that work in foreign archives will illuminate these questions only at the margins. As LaFeber (1981: 326) states,

> The present world system, to a surprising extent, has been shaped not by some imagined balance-of-power concept but by the initiatives of Woodrow Wilson and his successors. The United Nations, multilateral trade institutions, ideas about self-determination and economic development, determining influences on international culture, and strategic military planning have sprung from the United States more than from other actors in the global theater.

While LaFeber justifies a focus on the United States, this quotation also demonstrates the unfortunate fact that most current research in diplomatic history tends to be on the contemporary post–World War II period. Further, the research tends to be driven by presentist concerns (McMahon 1991: 21).

Paterson (1991: 37–38) also suggests that calls for international history set nationalist history up as a straw man. Nationalist history may focus on the United States, but it does not have to involve removing the United States from the international context. Paterson argues that a focus on US diplomatic history does not necessarily entail assuming that the United States is responsible for everything that happens in the world, that its power is unlimited, that weaker states do not possess countervailing power, or that the United States is exceptional. Diplomatic history should proceed by examining US foreign relations from several levels of analysis, including the international, regional, national, and individual levels. No one of these levels should be seen as more appropriate or superior to the others.

The research presented in this book is an attempt to marry international relations theory, foreign policy analysis, and diplomatic history. This interdisciplinary approach, plus the solid foundation in neorealist theory, places me firmly in the postrevisionist camp of diplomatic historians. This research also seeks to avoid some of the criticisms leveled at diplomatic history. First, I am heeding Gaddis's advice and interpreting history through a theoretically and methodologically rich lens. Role theory might seem strangely applied to diplomatic history, but psychological and social psychological approaches to diplomatic history have been around since the 1980s.[4]

Second, although my research focuses on the United States, it is international history. I seek to answer McMahon's question: why has the United States followed the international course that it has? I answer this question by explaining how the United States achieves certain roles in the international system through time. Those roles must be negotiated with other states. Other states may attempt to socialize the United States into certain roles, or out of others. Additionally, when the United States achieves great power status, LaFeber's (1981) assertion is essentially correct. The United States becomes the primary socializer in the international system. Thus, although I focus my analysis on the United States, my theoretical approach demands that I take into account US interaction with other states.

Third, I do not treat the United States as an exceptional or unique case. The theoretical approach to socialization that I have developed should apply equally to all states in the international system. In my analysis of the early United States, I do not foreshadow it as a great power. In fact, early US role location processes brought it dangerously close to extinction as a sovereign state.

Fourth, my choice of the United States as a case was not based on parochial or ethnocentric concerns. Two factors were determinant: the United States makes the transition through all of the master statuses identified by my theoretical approach, including the great power role during which its history *is* international history; and finally, there is a large body of secondary literature on the diplomatic history of the United States.[5] If anything, my research could unflatteringly be accused of consigning diplomatic historians to the role of "hewers-of-wood and the drawers-of-water" for my theoretical use.[6]

Given that the nationalists, realists, and postrevisionists share an approach to history that focuses on interstate relations and policymaking elites, I draw my secondary source materials from scholars working within each of these approaches. From the early nationalists, I draw heavily on the work of Bailey, Bemis, DeConde, Perkins, and Pratt. These scholars provide the background historical narrative for much of my research on the United States, particularly in its early history. I also draw on the work of realists such as Kennan, Morgenthau, and Spanier, on and postrevisionists like Gaddis. As a careful analyst of previous research, I do not uncritically accept any of these scholars' interpretations of history. My interest in most of their work, particularly that of the nationalists, is to obtain a factual account of the manifest events that comprise US history. The nationalists are still the best source of the complete history of the United States, as modern realists and postrevisionists tend to focus only on US history since World War II.

The Periodization of US Diplomatic History

Dull (1981: 3) notes that the first problem in studying US foreign relations is the need to fix an appropriate beginning. Dull offers a concise review of the literature dealing with American colonial foreign relations prior to 1776. This literature often attempts to locate the origins of US diplomatic principles in the colonial past. Conversely, Hatzenbuehler (1981) suggests that we examine US foreign policy only after the adoption of the constitution with a centralized government in 1789. However, my interest in the United States begins when it declares its independence from Britain. This is the point at which the socialization of a state into the international system begins.

Once we have determined a starting point, we must also consider how periods of US history coincide with the master statuses developed in Chapter 2. Bailey (1969: 30) decries the pitfalls of periodization in the history of US foreign policy. For example, during the time he was writing, Bailey says that all schoolchildren were taught to accept uncritically that the United States was a great power after 1898. Bailey takes issue with this periodization but is quick to offer one of his own. Bailey (1969: 31) suggests that the United States was a "world power" at birth on July 2, 1776. A world power is "a nation with sufficient power in being, or capable of being mobilized, to effect world politics positively over a period of time." Bailey (1969: 43) also argues that the United States was a European power at birth. But Bailey (1969: 49) does not consider the United States a great power until the end of the Civil War.

Charles and Mary Beard (1921) also assert that the United States was a world power from the time of Edmund Burke's March, 1775, speech on conciliation. However, Bailey's and the Beards' views on the subject are not the standard interpretation. Almost every historian has a different way of classifying periods of diplomatic history according to the perceived status or capabilities of the United States. Bemis (1962a: 3) offers a categorization scheme that is not even mutually exclusive.[7] For example, he considers the period 1776–1823 the era of revolution and emancipation, and the period from 1815–1915 as the era of isolation and security. Varg (1990) offers six such periods of foreign policy transition in US history.

Klingberg (1983, 1996) identifies five periods in US foreign policy: 1775/76–1824 (the revolutionary period), 1824–1871 (rounding out the nation), 1871–1917/18 (becoming an industrial power), 1917/18–1966/67 (world crisis for freedom), and 1966/67–present (the search for world peace). These periods are further divided into eight international mood phases reflecting introversion or extroversion in US foreign policy. These periods are demarcated by a mixture of domestic-level events, such as the unrest over Vietnam during the Johnson Administration, and international-level events, such as World War I. The problem with this periodization, as well as those employed by many historians, is that the demarcations are caused by dissimilar events.

Since my analysis is located primarily at the level of the international system, I need demarcations that are international events. My attempt at periodization will employ the notion of critical junctures. The major wars in which the United States has participated serve as these critical junctures and mark shifts in pressures exerted by the competition and socialization mechanisms described in Chapter 1. These wars serve to reorient the master status of the United States as it endures in the system. The United States fights its war of independence from 1776 to 1783, during its period of emergence. After the treaty with Britain, the United States enters the system as a novice state until the War of 1812. After the truce with Britain, the United States endures as a small member state from 1815 until the Mexican-American War. The United States then makes the transition to a major member state from 1848 to 1898. The Spanish-American War marks the transition to great power status for the United States, which it has occupied for the last century.

Within each of these periods we find a number of lesser foreign policy crises which enable policymakers to achieve auxiliary roles in the regional or international system. For example, during the novice state period for the United States, policymakers attempt to achieve the role of a neutral twice. Further, during the century of great power status, US policymakers enact a number of roles in response to crises in Southeast Asia, Central America, and China.

EMERGENCE, 1776–1783: SEEKING THE ROLE OF THE SOVEREIGN STATE

The theoretical expectations for a state during its period of emergence are similar to those for novice states and can be derived from our discussion of role theory. First, novices are likely to be unskilled role takers with a limited number of roles. In fact, for an emerging state, seeking the role of the sovereign state will probably be the only role it has the ability to perform. This was the case during the emergence of the United States. Second, the role of the sovereign state may be either ascribed or achieved. However, when a state is emerging from colonial rule prior to the twentieth century, this is in all likelihood an achieved role, as it was for the United States.

Third, a state with relatively few roles is less likely to be integrated into the system and, thus, less likely to be subject to normative control than a state with a large number of roles. An emerging state attempting to enact one major role (i.e., the sovereign state) will be unconstrained by the normative bonds of the system. Therefore, socialization attempts upon the emerging state will usually reach the dissonance reduction stage of the socialization game to take the form of force, either to prevent the state's independence, to turn the independent state into a client, or conversely, to promote full independence. The United States, in its role location process, forced its role of the sovereign state upon its primary socializer, Great Britain. Finally, an emerging state will have low or uncertain capabilities. This was indeed the case for the United States, which caused it to ally with France in order to achieve its role as a sovereign state.

The United States declared its independence in 1776, but the role of the sovereign state is a socially granted phenomenon, not a unilateral decision. No state in Europe officially welcomed the "militia diplomats" sent out by the United States on behalf of its cause. This is because official reception of US envoys would be perceived as official recognition of a colony seeking independence. None of the European powers was willing to take that step and risk war with Britain, the most powerful of the great powers, and the colonial master of the fledgling United States.

At this point in time, the United States existed in a situation of fairly low interaction capacity due to its geographic isolation from Europe. It took at least two months or so to get diplomatic communication across the Atlantic to the militia diplomats, and many times these were lost as vessels were seized (Bailey 1980: 28; Bemis 1962a: 165–166). This situation of low inter-action capacity, or low impact of structure, allowed the United States some additional maneuvering space that might not have been available if it had emerged on the European mainland, where the impact of structure was at its highest. Role theory is also clear that social deviance may persist in a situation of structural failure, such as a low level of interaction. Thus, we should expect that an emerging United States would have some latitude in rejecting socialization attempts to maintain its colonial status by Britain.

The United States also had low and/or uncertain capabilities during its emergence. The fact that the emerging state was actually thirteen separate entities only exacerbated the difficulty of marshaling military capabilities or of knowing the true extent of military and economic potential. Without early help from the French, the US rebellion probably would not have survived. The French courtier Beaumarchais, with the French and Spanish governments as silent partners, created a company that shipped all sorts of weapons and supplies to the United States beginning in 1775. French authorities also allowed US privateers to outfit and operate out of French ports in order to prey on British commerce.

THE ROLE LOCATION PROCESS

Let us examine how the role location process for the sovereign state role proceeded from 1776 to 1783 through the lens of the socialization game.[8] According to Figure 3.1, Player N represents the structure of the international system. The structure ultimately determines whether the roles chosen by any state are reflective of underlying reality. In the international system, the great powers are the main interpreters of structural constraints and act as the audience for the performance of any role in the system. The great powers are the primary socializers and competitors in the system. Since socialization and competition are the two methods by which structure indirectly affects agents, the primary agents of socialization and competition will exert the direct effects on lesser agents in the system. In this time period, the system is multipolar, with Britain, France, Spain, the Netherlands, and Russia occupying roles as great powers. In a small international system, the great powers will always be the interested audience when a new state attempts to emerge.[9] Of these five states, Britain and France are the most powerful.

Britain is considered a hegemon during this time period by the Leadership Long Cycle research tradition (Modelski 1987), with France as the principle challenger to its leadership. It is clear that Britain emerged from the Seven

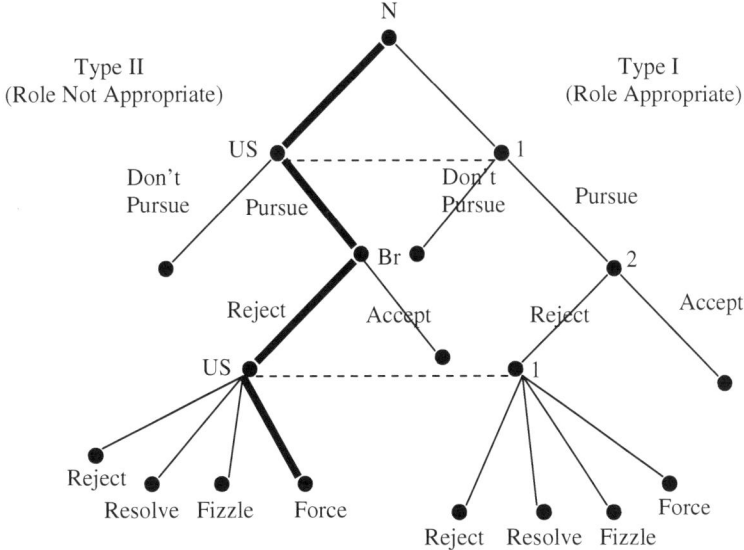

Figure 3.1 The Socialization Game for the Role of the Sovereign State

Years' War (1756–1763) as the most powerful state in the world. This war was fought on the North American continent between France and Britain as well, and was known as the French and Indian War (1754–1763). The result of the war was the loss of French colonial possessions in North America. Therefore, it is logical that these two great powers would be contenders for the socialization of the American colonies. However, since Britain was more powerful overall with a dominant position on the North American continent and a vested interest in preventing American independence, it is clear that the structure of the system in 1776 is disposed against the role of the sovereign state for the United States.

The American colonies (Player 1), acting through the Continental Congress, declared their independence anyway. The Congress must have known that the structural deck was stacked against them; however, the declaration of independence was also a plea for a partner in their choice of the sovereign state role. The Congress knew that the audience of European powers, still smarting from the Seven Years' War, would be enticed by the possibility of breaking up the British Empire through covert aid, rather than overt war with Britain.

Britain (Player 2) is the dominant socializer for the United States at this time. Britain, of course, rejects the role of sovereign state for the American colonies and sends troops to quell the rebellion. The Americans choose "Force" in the socialization game, which means that the Americans choose to use their capabilities to modify the world so that they can adopt the role of the sovereign state. This entails forcing Player 2 (Britain) to accept its part in the role enactment. After the surrender of the entire British invasion force from Canada at Saratoga, New York, on October 17, 1777, it appeared that the United States would prevail in its role location process.

Benjamin Franklin entered into negotiations with both the British and the French at this point. Franklin played on fears of an American reunion with Britain in talks with the French Foreign Minister Vergennes and insisted that France openly support the American rebellion. Vergennes was persuaded that France should declare war on Britain while its strength was dispersed in dealing with the rebellion. It is clear that Vergennes also expected commercial gains from winning the American trade and preventing further British encroachment against the French West Indies sugar trade.

Unfortunately for Franklin, France was not entirely free to pursue war with Britain. The other member of the interested audience of great powers was Spain, which also had considerable interests on the North American continent. France and Spain were bound together by the Family Compact of 1761, which required them to act together in decisions involving war. Spain was not prepared to go to war with Britain, despite a history of humiliating defeats at the hands of the British. The main reason for Spanish reticence was the fear of a powerful, independent American state that might challenge her colonial possessions in North America. Related to this concern was the fear that support of anticolonial rebellion in North America might spread to

Spanish colonial possessions in South America. Ultimately, France decided to support the sovereign state role for the United States despite the lack of Spanish support and its own fear of British military power.

On February 6, 1778, the United States and France signed the Treaty of Amity and Commerce. The signing of this treaty constituted official recognition of the United States by France. At this point, France stepped out of the audience of nations to support the United States in forcing Britain to recognize the United States in the role of sovereign state. The Franco-American Treaty of Alliance pledged both states to fight until US independence was "formally or tacitly assured" (Bailey 1980: 36). It also provided that neither side could make a separate peace with Britain, and that both states would guarantee the possessions of the other in America against all other powers. In recognition of the sovereign state role, Louis XVI appointed a full-fledged minister to the United States, Conrad Alexandre Gerard.

Britain had already started to consider conciliatory gestures toward the rebellious colonies. Prime Minister Lord North asked Parliament to grant the Americans home rule in December 1777. Parliament approved his conciliation bills on March 9, 1778. Unfortunately for the British, the French treaties had already been signed. The American colonists would accept nothing less than the sovereign state role at this point. France and Britain therefore went to war in June 1778.

The War of the American Revolution in Europe (1778–1783) that resulted from the United States' early role location process spiraled out of control for Britain. Spain joined France in the conflict on April 12, 1779, by convincing France to fight until Gibraltar was back in Spanish hands. Spain, however, refused to recognize the independence of the United States, to join an alliance with the United States, or even to officially provide any loans. The Netherlands also joined the war against Britain in 1780 when Britain seized the Dutch Caribbean island of St. Eustatius, which had quickly become the entrepôt for an enormous volume of European-American trade during the war. Things were already looking quite bleak for Britain at this point, as the most of the great powers of Europe aligned against her.

Although the War of the American Revolution is not generally considered a systemic war, it did provide the opportunity for smaller states to challenge some of the principles of the prevailing normative order.[10] While the structure of the system, in terms of the number of poles, is not challenged in this war, the audience of great powers is in disarray over the role sought by the United States. No longer is the question of sovereignty solely between the emerging state/rebellious colony and the dominant socializer/colonizer. The outcome of US role seeking is caught up in balance of power politics.

Russia, though not a combatant in this war, took the lead in organizing the Baltic countries into the Armed Neutrality of 1780.[11] This group of states eventually included Denmark-Norway, Sweden, the Holy Roman Empire (1781), Prussia (1782), Portugal (1782), and the Two Sicilies (1783). These small, neutral trading states took advantage of Britain's weakened position to advance certain principles of international law. They argued against "paper blockades"—meaning that for a blockade to be binding it must be enforced. They also argued for less confiscation of neutral goods regarded as war materials by belligerents. Finally, they proclaimed the principle of "free ships, free goods"—the immunity of noncontraband enemy goods carried on neutral vessels. Many of these principles were also contained in the Franco-American Treaty of Amity and Commerce.

Developments during the War of the American Revolution demonstrate that change in the international system is the direct result of agent action. Further, the direction that such change takes may be rather unpredictable. The United States during its emergence was a weak state militarily; alone, it did not pose a threat to Britain. However, when the United States sought the role of sovereign state, it unleashed a process that challenged some of the fundamental tenants of British predominance at sea. In negotiating with France for recognition of its sovereign role, the United States advanced rights for neutral ships within the confines of this bilateral relationship. Once the war with Britain widened, these principles were adopted by the Armed Neutrality. These neutral trading states were not considered military rivals to the great powers, yet the ideological challenge to British rule of the waves was unmistakable. The United States would later adopt the neutral rights role, based on its original innovation, and the agreement of an audience of interested small member states.

American diplomacy for recognition as a sovereign state continued during the war. In April 1782, John Adams secured official recognition from the Netherlands and a loan that prevented outright US bankruptcy. Later, in October, Adams also concluded a treaty of amity and commerce with the Netherlands. At this point, the United States had secured official recognition of its role as a sovereign state with two of the great powers. This decisive blow, plus faltering public support in Britain for the war, led to negotiations between the United States and Britain. Despite its treaty obligations with France, the United States opened separate negotiations with Britain, and signed the preliminary treaty of peace on November 30, 1782. The final Anglo-American treaty was signed on September 3, 1783, with the full permission of France. Britain acknowledged the United States in the role of a sovereign state and settled the boundaries of the US and British possessions. Britain also signed peace agreements with France, Spain, and the Netherlands on the same day.

The United States emerged from the war having forced the role of the sovereign state upon its primary socializer, Great Britain. It accomplished this unlikely task by turning to an alliance with France in order to add to its capabilities. Now that the United States had completed its first role location process, what types of role expectations and demands did the audience of nations have for it? Apparently, they had very few expectations. The new state did not command respect abroad. When states did take note of the United States, it was in the hope that the democratic experiment would fail.

In that event, monarchy would prevail, and US territory could once again be carved up by the European powers. The European states did not view the United States and its successful revolution as a real threat to their security; thus, they did not form an overwhelming coalition to defeat it, as they attempted after the French Revolution.[12]

The United States certainly took its role as a sovereign state seriously. John Adams was sent to Britain in 1785 as the first minister of the United States. While Adams was received cordially by George III, he was virtually ignored during the remainder of his time in Britain. Britain also refused to reciprocate by accrediting a minister to the United States. Given that Britain emerged from the War of the American Revolution with her position in world affairs largely unaltered, this snub was not a good sign for the United States as it embarked upon its tenure in the system as a novice state. The next several years in Anglo-American relations saw many violations of the peace treaty by Britain and significant infringements upon US commerce.

Relations with France at this time were actually not much better than those with Britain. Thomas Jefferson served as US minister to France and was constantly reminded of the enormous American debt of 35 million *livres* owed to the French government. Further, France preferred to keep the United States weak in order to promote its own interests in North America. Altogether, the performance of the United States in its role as a sovereign state was rather weak during its early history. This is largely because the partners in its role enactment were not fully committed to the role.

In terms of social identity, the early United States was understandably engrossed in the sovereign state role. This role was the only role to have been achieved by the United States as an emerging actor in the system. As described in Chapter 2, the status, value, and involvement dimensions can give us some insight into the social identity of the early United States. The status dimension refers to a position in a social structure, and the normative expectations concerning the enactment of its associated roles. As previously mentioned, the status that the United States thought it had achieved in obtaining the sovereign state role was not really respected by the great powers. This kind of status discrepancy can lead to internal conflict over social identity and also to externalized conflict to resolve the discrepancy.

The value dimension refers to how the relevant others evaluate an actor's role enactment. Generally, negative valuations are not placed on actors who fail to perform, or who perform poorly in achieved roles, especially as they are engaged in aligning behavior. However, the proper enactment of achieved roles usually leads to positive valuation—but not in this case. The United States was rebuffed by Britain in attempting to enact its role as a sovereign state by sending a minister to London. The United States also failed to receive positive valuation from the French.

The involvement dimension in this case refers to the amount of effort expended upon a role. As mentioned previously, the United States was fairly engrossed in the role. The sovereign state role was the status of the United

States at this point, especially since, under the Articles of the Confederation, no other form of unified identity existed for the separate states.

In general, the analysis of social identity created by the sovereign state role and its enactment suggests that the role was not socially accepted in the international system despite its *de jure* recognition. The expected result of such a discrepancy is both internal conflict over social identity and possible externalized conflict to resolve the issue. Because social identity is a *social* construction, the polity must adjust its internal role conceptions to match those of other states implicated in its identity construction. The adjustment can be accomplished by reconceptualizing roles within the polity or by forcing other states to change their conceptions. Both adjustment processes can entail conflict.

NOVICE STATE STATUS, 1783–1815: SEEKING THE NEUTRAL ROLE

Seeking the Neutral Role, Act I

What kind of theoretical expectations do we have for novice states? The discussion of the interaction between the socialization and competition mechanisms described in Chapter 2 predicts several things. First, novice states will have low or uncertain capabilities. This was certainly the case for the United States at the close of the Revolutionary War. In fact, Britain still had large, well-equipped armies stationed at strategic points in the United States at the close of the war. Without the distractions of the war in Europe, Britain could certainly have defeated the colonial armies. The British also refused to turn over to the United States a long chain of military posts from Lake Champlain to Lake Superior. Further, Spain disputed the territorial boundaries of the United States where they overlapped with Spanish claims near Florida, including the fort of Natchez that controlled commerce on the Mississippi River. Both Spain and Britain armed Native Americans and encouraged attacks against American settlers and property.

Through this policy of retaining forts and arming Native Americans, Spain and Britain exercised virtual control over nearly one-half of the territory of the newly independent United States from 1783 to 1794 (Bailey 1980: 57–60, 72). As DeConde (1956: 503) suggests, the United States was "relatively so insignificant . . . that in any struggle in which the major maritime powers took a real interest it could be little more than a pawn."

Theoretically, we should also expect that a novice state will have few roles in the international system. Further, these roles will largely be ascribed to it by its socializers. A novice state should be subject to the most intense socialization pressure of all states. This is due to the fact that a novice state will most likely be imitating other states in terms of its internal organization and external behavior. However, with relatively few roles, such a state may still be less subject to normative control than a state that has many roles and is thus better integrated into the system.[13]

The pace of socialization will vary with the novice's level of involvement in the international system, the number of other novices entering the system at the same time, and the extent of cultural differences between the novice and member states. Novices are likely to be unskilled role takers with a limited number of roles, and thus less equipped to deal with novel and critical situations. Role ambiguity, role dissensus, and other sources of imperfect information about role expectations will make the role location process conflictual for novices.

It is during the period of the novice state when domestic politics becomes important to the socialization process. Novice states may have some choice in determining which member state will serve as their socializer. It is at this point that domestic politics becomes important to international socializing activities. During the American Revolutionary War, the fledgling United States allied with France in order to force the sovereign state role upon its dominant socializer, Britain. This was certainly not an easy choice for the United States, given the large number of casualties and property damage caused by the French against American settlers in the French and Indian War (1754–1763). Further, France was a monarchy, just like Britain, which the United States was trying to replace with a new republican form of government. However, if the United States was to attain the sovereign state role, it had to augment its capabilities to attain it by force against Great Britain.

Domestic politics in postindependence United States began to revolve around those that favored closer relations with Britain and those that favored closer relations with France.[14] The political party system evolved out of this bifurcation of elite opinion during President Washington's first administration.[15] Alexander Hamilton formed the Federalist Party, which favored closer cultural and political ties to Britain.[16] Thomas Jefferson formed the Democratic-Republicans, which favored closer relations with France. The popularity of Jefferson's party received quite a boost from the French Revolution that started in 1789. Many Americans believed that their own example in throwing off the tyranny of monarchy inspired the French people to do the same. In 1793, after the execution of Louis XVI, France declared war on Britain. The US Federalists were appalled that the tyranny of monarchy was replaced by the tyranny of the masses. The rancor between the Federalists and the Democratic-Republicans was so strong that business, religious, and social life was divided along these lines. The Federalists began to call for intervention in the war on the side of Britain, while the Democratic-Republicans called for intervention on the side of France. President Washington instead sought a neutral role for the United States with his Proclamation of Neutrality on April 22, 1793.[17]

Two British decrees directly challenged the US neutral role.[18] The Order in Council of June 8, 1793, authorized the seizure of all neutral (American) cargoes of food bound for France, or ports under French control. The Order in Council of November 6, 1793, provided for the detention of ships carrying the produce of a French colony or supplies for a French colony. This meant that French property on neutral American ships would be confiscated. This directly contradicted the principle of "free ships, free goods" that the United States had set out in the Franco-American Treaty of Amity and Commerce.

The British immediately began seizing American vessels in the West Indies and jailing or impressing their crews into the British navy. The US Congress responded with a thirty-day embargo on all shipping in US harbors bound for foreign ports on March 26, 1794. This was an enormous financial drain on the United States, as much of its trade, including 90 percent of its imports, was with Britain. Further, three-fourths of the US Federal Government's revenues were from customs duties on imports. If the carrying trade between the United States and Britain were to stop, the United States would be bankrupt.

The United States and Britain were again on the verge of war. The United States sent John Jay to Britain in April 1794 to negotiate concerning the forts still under British control on the Great Lakes; compensation for seized cargoes on American ships; an opening of the British West Indian trade; and a commercial treaty with Britain. The only immediate concession that Jay won from the British was their evacuation of the forts they were pledged to surrender under the Treaty of 1783. The issues of compensation and some territorial questions were left to arbitration commissions. In fact, modern international arbitration is generally dated from Jay's Treaty. This is another instance of the inexperienced US state participating in the transformation of the normative order of international relations.

Jay's Treaty did yield greatly on the principle of "free ships, free goods." Jay agreed that, in some circumstances, French property and food bound for French ports could be seized if paid for by the British. Jay's Treaty was ratified by the US Senate in secret because, once the terms were made public, the outcry was enormous. President Washington could have vetoed the treaty, but the choice seemed to be between this treaty and war. Washington's choice in pushing for ratification was wise in the judgment of many historians because it postponed war with Britain for another 18 years, while allowing the United States to increase its capabilities and establish its footing in world affairs (Bailey 1980; Bemis 1962a, 1962b; Combs 1970; Varg 1963).

It is important to note that France did not respect the neutral role that Washington sought for the United States either. France retaliated against the British Orders in Council by seizing US ships bound for Britain. The supplies were confiscated and the crews were treated poorly. When President Washington agreed to accept a minister, Genet, from the French Republic, thereby officially recognizing the new regime, the minister orchestrated the seizure of British vessels off the American coasts upon his arrival in the United States (Ammon 1973).

In fact, there was not much difference in the numbers of American vessels seized by the French and British. In order to avoid war with the French, President Adams (a Federalist) sent three emissaries to the French Directory in October 1797. The French suggested that a bribe of 1.2 million *livres*, and a loan of 32 million *livres* (which would essentially be a gift), would be required to open negotiations. The US emissaries left in disgust and, when the news of their treatment was made public, opinion shifted in favor of war with France.[19]

In both May and July 1798, Congress authorized the capture of French armed ships, and in June 1798 it suspended trade with France. On July 7, 1798, Congress declared the two treaties of 1778 with France void. The subsequent undeclared Quasi-War with France lasted approximately two and a half years and was largely confined to the sea. A cessation to hostilities was finally secured by the Convention of 1800, which voided the treaties of 1778, substituted a commercial treaty that was less favorable to France, and gave responsibility to the United States for compensating its own citizens for losses due to French seizures on the high seas.

What does this round of the role location process tell us about the United States as a novice state? The audience of interested states, primarily Great Britain and France, were predisposed against the neutral role for the United States, as described in Figure 3.2. The United States attempted to pursue this role when Washington announced his Proclamation of Neutrality. The role was rejected by Britain, but held onto with resolve by the United States despite its acceptance of the terms of the Jay Treaty. The role was also

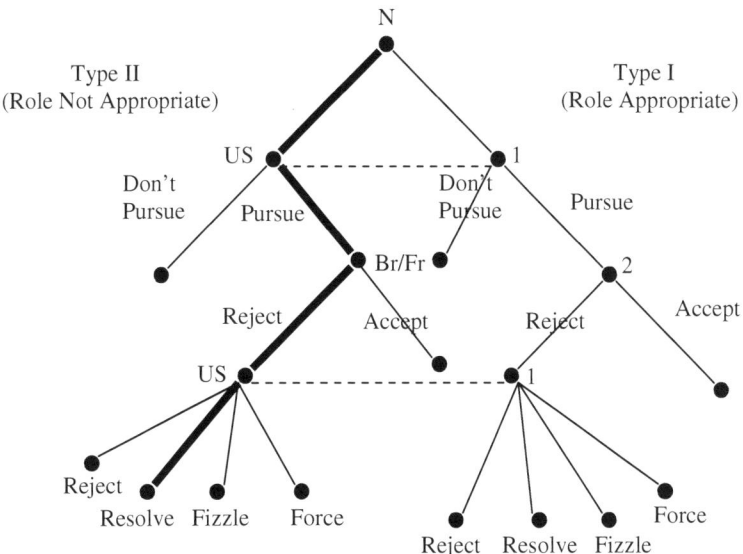

Figure 3.2   The Socialization Game for the Neutral Role I

rejected by France and held onto with resolve by the United States despite its nullification of the Treaty of Amity and Commerce of 1778, which guaranteed "free goods, free ships" between France and the United States.

Altogether, this suggests that a novice state will have a difficult time trying to achieve roles as it enters the international system. Neither Britain nor France accepted the neutral role, yet despite setbacks, the United States appeared to hold onto this role with resolve. The neutral role was only the second major role the United States attempted to enact. As discussed previously, states with few roles are less likely to be subject to normative control. Hence, socialization efforts by Britain and France to convince the United States to abandon the neutral role failed. However, it is impossible to enact such a role in isolation. Both France and Britain violated this role with impunity.

Seeking the Neutral Role, Act II

The United States became the most important neutral carrier from 1803, when Napoleon reopened hostilities with Britain, to 1812, with the outbreak of its own war with Britain.[20] Strangely enough, despite the rejection of the neutral role by France and Britain, neither state interfered with US commerce for the first two years of renewed hostilities. American shippers began to reap high profits and venture into previously restricted markets. France and Spain were forced to open their normally closed West Indian ports to US traders during the war because of the dominance of the British navy.

British shippers were unhappy with the growing wealth of the American merchant marine. Britain soon invoked the notorious Rule of 1756—that trade not open in times of peace could not be open in times of war. The British again began seizing cargo and sailors. The British navy also took up positions off of US ports to establish a virtual blockade. They exercised their right as a belligerent to search neutral ships. The British also continued their practice of impressment of sailors. Approximately 8,000–10,000 US citizens were impressed during this time (Bailey 1980: 116–120).

President Jefferson sent envoys to Britain in 1806 on a failed attempt to negotiate an end to impressment and to seek remuneration for seized cargo. Meanwhile, Britain and France had begun to declare a series of paper and actual naval blockades. By the middle of 1806, American ships were once again at risk of being seized by both the British and French if they attempted to carry trade to either belligerent or their colonies. Public outrage in the United States over impressment and seizure of cargoes was at an all-time high. After the attack upon the US frigate *Chesapeake* by a British frigate looking for escaped impressed sailors, public opinion was strongly in favor of war with Britain. President Jefferson chose instead to impose an embargo on all trade with Europe. The Embargo Act was passed by Congress in December 1807. Jefferson expected that both France and Britain would be forced to reconsider their heavy-handed practices with American vessels (Tucker and Hendricksen 1990: 204–209).

The embargo did cause distress to the parts of the British Empire dependent upon imports of American foodstuffs and cotton for textile manufacturing, though the impact on France was not as troubling. The state that suffered the most from the US embargo was the United States itself, as its economy went into a tailspin. Ironically, unemployed sailors were forced to join the British navy, from whom they had originally feared impressment. The embargo grew increasingly unpopular at home, and even President Jefferson declared that it was three times more costly than a war. Congress repealed the Embargo Act on March 1, 1809, and substituted the Nonintercourse Act that legalized US trade with all ports, except those under British and French control, until the neutral role was respected.

As a response, Britain sent several negotiators to the United States in 1809 in an attempt to end the embargo, the second of which was Francis James Jackson (also known as "Copenhagen" Jackson for his presentation of the ultimatum that preceded the confiscation of the Danish fleet at Copenhagen in 1807). Negotiations went nowhere, and Napoleon's response was to issue the Rambouillet Decree of March 23, 1810, which confiscated all American ships in French ports. With the Nonintercourse Act set to expire, Congress replaced it with Macon's Bill on May 1, 1810.

Macon's Bill permitted commerce with both England and France. However, it provided that if France repealed her offensive measures, then the United States would renew nonimportation against Britain. And, if Britain repealed the Orders in Council, the United States would renew nonimportation against France. In both cases, the United States could export to, but not import from the nonrepealing state. Napoleon sent communication to President Madison announcing the repeal of the offending decrees but with enough added conditions to make implementation nearly impossible. Nonetheless, Madison informed the British, and Congress passed legislation implementing nonimportation only against Britain on March 2, 1811.[21]

US public opinion continued to fester in anger over the treatment of the United States by Britain. On June 1, 1812, President Madison sent his war message to Congress. He gave first place on his list of grievances against Britain to the impressment of sailors. Second, he decried British naval ventures into US waters to conduct seizures. Third place went to the notorious Orders in Council, which injured US exports. Finally, he accused the British of encouraging the renewal of Indian warfare.

The United States was completely unprepared for war with Britain. The army and navy were inadequate, and there was not widespread support for the war. Federalist, pro-British New England, whose members in Congress had voted against the war, withheld militia from service and sold provisions to the British invaders. The Canadians, many of whom were descendants of the Loyalists expelled from the United States, threw back US invasion forces in 1812 and 1813. By 1814, the United States was desperately trying to defend its own territory. At the close of fighting, the British held a large portion of US territory in the Great Lakes area and along the northern frontier.

Battles at sea had reduced the US navy from sixteen men-of-war to three, while the British still had over 800 ships (Bailey 1980: 146–147).

Negotiations to end the war started one week after the declaration of war on June 26, 1812. The issue of impressment was the main obstacle in the negotiations. The British had already suspended the Orders in Council on June 16, 1812. Czar Alexander I of Russia offered to mediate, and this offer was quickly accepted by Madison but rejected by the British. Yet in order to mollify its ally, Russia, the British agreed to enter into direct negotiations for peace in November 1813. Negotiations did not actually commence until August 8, 1814, in Ghent. The US State Department had instructed its envoys to insist on the abandonment of impressment, the cessation of illegal blockades, and satisfaction of other neutral rights in dispute. British demands included a forfeiture of US rights to fortifications or ships on the Great Lakes by transfers of land in and around the Great Lakes to Canada and the creation of an enormous Indian buffer state south of the Great Lakes. This last condition was an indispensable condition of peace for the British.

These British demands were met with indignation in America and by the envoys, who rejected them outright. Considerable changes occurred in the demands of both sides as the war progressed, and one side appeared to gain the upper hand, only to be replaced by the other. In the end, both sides relinquished their indispensable conditions for peace. The United States gave up on impressment, and the British gave up on their territorial demands. The final treaty said absolutely nothing about neutral rights, which is what the United States presumably went to war for in the first place. Both sides simply agreed to stop fighting and return to the status quo. The defeat of British forces at New Orleans by General Andrew Jackson two weeks after the signing of the peace treaty lent to the American public's perception that it had won and exacted a victor's terms from Britain. President Madison, of course, knew this was not true but was happy to let this legend take root.

What does the socialization game tell us about the second round of the US neutral role location process? Once again, the structure of the system, as represented by Britain and France, is predisposed against the neutral role, as displayed in Figure 3.3. The US attempts to enact the neutral role by continuing trade with Britain and France. The neutral role is rejected by both France and Britain as each resumes seizing cargoes and sailors. The US attempts to force the neutral role by declaring an embargo on trade with Europe. The attempt at using trade to augment its capabilities in forcing the neutral role fails miserably, even to the extent of reducing US economic capabilities. Successive iterations of the embargo lead to war with Britain in the attempt to force the role. The war ends with a resumption of the status quo. Finally, the neutral role is not formally acknowledged in the Treaty of Ghent, reflecting the US choice to let the neutral role fizzle.

The War of 1812 is a crucial juncture in the history of American foreign policy. It is often called the second war for American independence. Despite

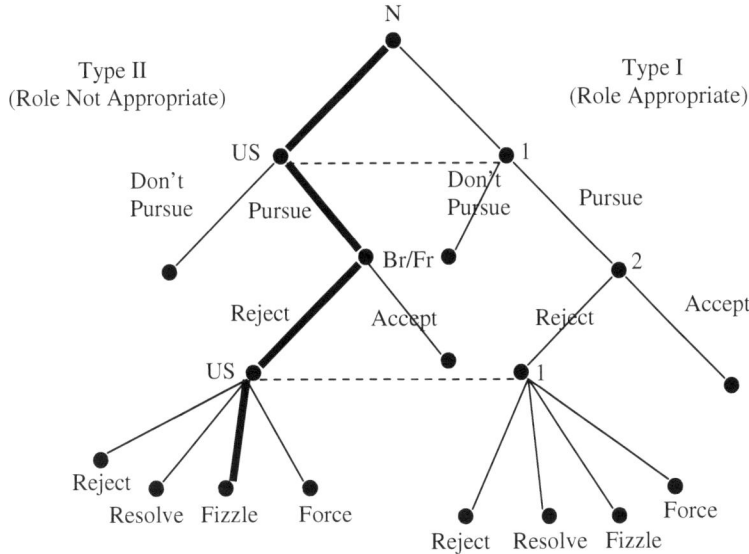

Figure 3.3   The Socialization Game for the Neutral Role II

the fact that France and Britain had previously formally acknowledged the United States as a sovereign state, from this point on, they will treat the United States as a formal equal. The United States moves from the novice state to the small state category at the close of this war. With Napoleon's defeat in 1815 at Waterloo, Americans finally felt as if they were free of European entanglements. As Bailey (1980: 163) aptly puts it, prior to 1815 "the United States had been a kind of tail to the European kite." The United States would not be involved in a European war again until World War I, 100 years later.

In terms of social identity, the United States is now fully accepted as a sovereign state. It has fought a war with its primary socializer as a sovereign state over its attempted enactment of an achieved role. The United States still lacks the capabilities to have its neutral rights role respected by the great powers, yet as expected, it externalized the conflict over this discrepancy in round two of the role location process. The neutral rights role became central to US identity during this period (Bukovansky 1997), and the United States refused to relinquish this role despite its lack of willing partners in its enactment.

It is also important to note that overall, British attempts at socializing the United States were rather mixed during this early period. This is despite the fact that the United States was the only state entering the system at the time, and the cultural differences between the United States and Britain were not great. Both of these factors would seem to predict rapid socialization and conformity for the United States. However, the United States sought and succeeded in gaining the role of the sovereign state. The United States also sought, and fought for, the neutral rights role, which it ultimately allowed to fizzle. Another determinant in the pace of socialization is the level of involvement in the international system. The fact that the United States sought a neutral role, free of entanglements, may have slowed the pace of its socialization. The United States, after Washington's proclamation, attempted to keep the level of involvement in the security sector of the system to a minimum.

In fact, the United States at this stage could be considered a rogue state. The impact of structure, as acted upon by Britain and France, is becoming stronger during this period, yet the level of US conformity to structure's dictates is still low. The United States failed to balance against Britain in 1794, preferring to sign Jay's Treaty instead. Further, the United States failed to balance against Napoleonic France, when it engaged in the War of 1812 with Britain. Thus, a strict Waltzian neorealist explanation of early US behavior fails because of its strict focus on capabilities and lack of regard for the social nature of the international system.

SMALL MEMBER STATE STATUS, 1815–1848: SEEKING A REGIONAL ROLE AT A YOUNG AGE

At this point, the United States begins its tenure as a small state in a new international system.[22] Thompson's (1988) survey of the literature finds that the series of wars of the French Revolution and Napoleonic Wars (1792–1815) is unanimously considered as a systemic war. What happens to the makeup of the great powers? Certainly, Britain remains the dominant power in the world. However, Russia and France remain great powers. Spain and the Netherlands fall from great power status. These changes in the pool of possible socializers prove important to the United States initially as a small, and later major, member state. Theoretically, we should expect small states to have moderate capabilities. They will begin to have a greater number of roles in the international system. These roles will include a mixture of ascribed and achieved roles. Small states will also be subject to continued socialization pressure, but not of the magnitude felt by novice states.

The United States made the Louisiana Purchase in 1803, thereby more than doubling its territory. It also made moves into Spanish Florida, which eventually culminated in Spanish cessation of Florida to the United States in the Adams-Onis treaty of 1819. President Monroe had put off recognizing the newly emerging Latin American Republics while negotiations with Spain for Florida were underway. However, in 1822 the United States exercised its rights as a member state by officially recognizing the new republics and, due to the diminished capabilities and status of Spain, was able to ignore Spain's protests. Fear of European monarchical aspirations was growing in the United States, especially in response to the Quadruple Alliance of Russia, Austria, Prussia, and Britain (expanded to include France in 1818 at the Quintuple Alliance, or Holy Alliance, as it is often called). The Holy Alliance's successes in Spain and Italy, and their perceived designs on Latin America, in addition to Russian maneuverings in the Pacific Northwest, prompted President Monroe to include the Monroe Doctrine in his annual message to Congress on December 2, 1823 (Crabb 1982: 12; Bailey 1980: 177–180).

The US Role: Regional Collaborator or Regional Protector?

In issuing his statements, President Monroe was attempting to achieve the role of regional protector. According to Holsti (1970: 262), this role conception may imply special leadership responsibilities in a regional or issue area, but its first and foremost concern is the function of providing protection for adjacent regions. This may seem an odd choice for a small state, yet it makes sense considering the United States' recent history in that time period. The Monroe Doctrine was also a reaction against British efforts to altercast the role of regional-subsystem collaborator to the United States.[23] In August 1823, British Foreign Secretary Canning proposed to US Minister Rush that the United States join Britain in a manifesto to prevent intervention by the European powers in the New World. Such a proposal essentially amounted to an informal alliance with Britain.

President Monroe's initial reaction to the proposal was favorable. Monroe consulted past Presidents Madison and Jefferson, who were both strongly in favor of cooperation with the British.[24] However, upon closer scrutiny, Secretary of State Adams discerned that the proposal meant British military and commercial leadership in the region (Varg 1963: 249–250; Bemis 1969: 400–401). The proposal also hinted that neither the United States nor Britain would seize any part of Spanish America. Adams did not wish to prevent US acquisition of Texas, California, Cuba, or other areas (Perkins 1955: 67). If Britain could limit increases in US territory, it was quite possible that it could eventually emerge as the dominant power in the Americas. Adams further reasoned that the possibility of the Holy Alliance actually engaging in military action to return the Latin American republics to Spain was extremely low. Adams argued that the United States could safely reject the British proposal and issue a manifesto of its own (Bailey 1980: 181–182; Crabb 1982: 14–15). The rejection of the regional collaborator role is portrayed in Figure 3.4.

The Monroe Doctrine is derived from several passages in Monroe's annual message to Congress. Monroe states that the American continents are not open to future colonization by any European powers. Monroe also says that any attempt to introduce the monarchical political system in the Americas will be considered as dangerous to US peace and safety. Monroe further states that the United States will not interfere with existing European colonies, but that any attempt by European powers to reassert control over those states that have declared their independence will be viewed as the "manifestation of an unfriendly disposition toward the United States." Finally, Monroe pledged not to interfere in the internal concerns of any of the European powers (Bailey 1980: 183–184; Crabb 1982: 13–14).

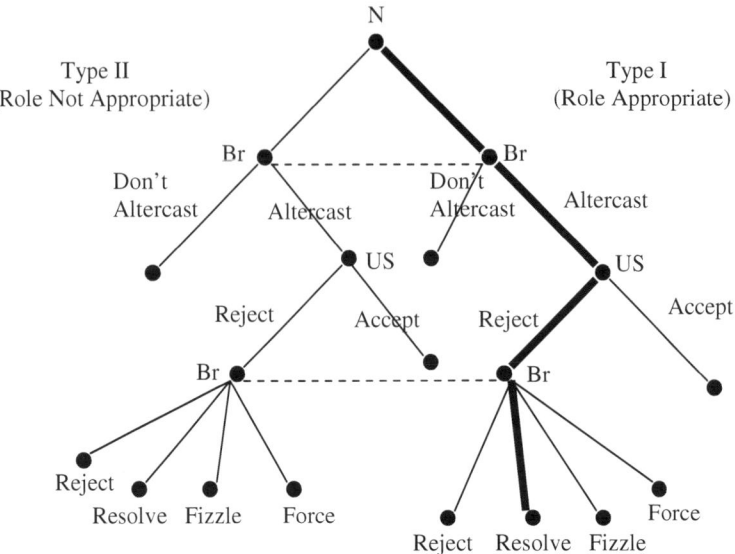

N

Type II
(Role Not Appropriate)

Type I
(Role Appropriate)

Br
Don't
Altercast

Altercast

Br
Don't
Altercast

Altercast

US

US

Reject

Accept

Reject

Accept

Br

Br

Reject

Resolve   Fizzle   Force

Reject   Resolve   Fizzle

Force

Figure 3.4   The Socialization Game for the Altercast Role of Regional Collaborator

President Monroe proposed a number of roles for the United States in his message to Congress. The roles of liberation supporter and anti-imperialist agent can be discerned in Monroe's statements.[25] However, it seems that the role of regional protector encompasses these roles at the time. The United States' concern was to secure the independent, republican states of Latin America. The security of the United States was perceived as wrapped up in the entire region's security. If the European powers were allowed to become entrenched again in the Americas, then the United States could be drawn into further wars within the region, or in Europe (Crabb, 1982: 17–18). This underlying security motivation is often used to interpret the Monroe Doctrine as a call for isolationism. However, it should be clear from Monroe's statements that he was not adopting the role of an isolate.[26] Monroe would fight for the independence of a foreign state within the Western Hemisphere. Monroe essentially carved out a sphere of influence for the United States and warned the European states to stay out (Bemis 1969: 397–398; Lieuwen 1965: 127).

How did the United States' dominant socializer and the audience of states react to the Monroe Doctrine? British Foreign Secretary Canning was understandably livid that Monroe stole his thunder. However, Britain tacitly supported the American policy. Britain did not favor a restoration of Spanish power in the Americas. Further, Britain was prepared to use its naval preponderance to prevent the Holy Alliance from attempting to reassert Spanish control with or without the Monroe Doctrine. Canning had actually already received a memorandum from the French Ambassador that formally denied

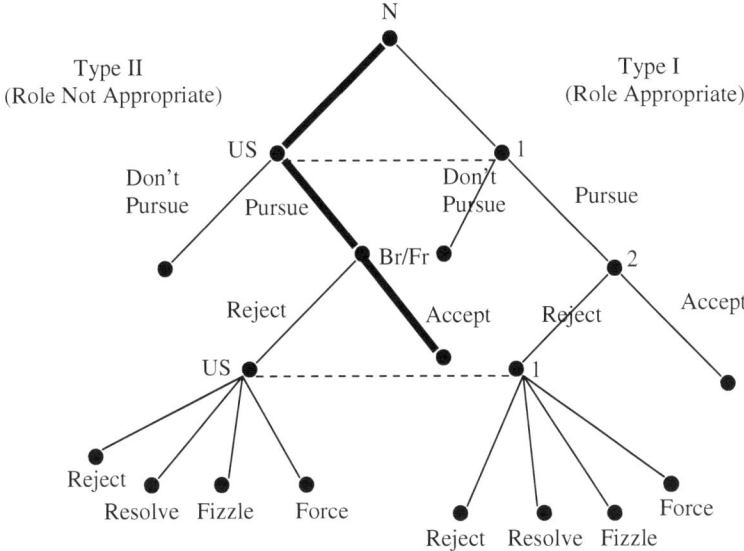

Figure 3.5   The Socialization Game for the Role of Regional Protector

any intention by France to invade Spanish America—two months before the Monroe Doctrine. Thus, the outcome of the issuance of the Monroe Doctrine was favorable to British interests, with the exception that the injunction against colonization in the Western Hemisphere could be applied to Britain as well (Bailey 1980: 186–187). Thus, the role of regional collaborator that Britain originally tried to altercast to the United States was rejected by that country in favor of its own role conception as regional protector (see Figure 3.5).

Did the United States have the capabilities as a small state to back up the role of regional protector? The reaction of L'Etoile (Paris) was representative of the general feeling in Europe.

> Mr. Monroe, who is not a sovereign, has assumed in his message the tone of a powerful monarch, whose armies and fleets are ready to march at the first signal . . . Mr. Monroe is the temporary President of a Republic situated on the east coast of North America. This republic is bounded on the south by the possessions of the King of Spain, and on the north by those of the King of England. Its independence was only recognized forty years ago; by what right then would the two Americas today be under its immediate sway from Hudson's Bay to Cape Horn. (Perkins 1927: 30)

The United States was militarily weak at the time of Monroe's speech to Congress. Further, after the speech, neither the President nor Congress showed any inclination to expand the navy to the level required for the doctrine's effective implementation (Whitaker 1941: 508–511). Crabb (1982: 16) suggests that the United States relied mainly on British naval power to deter the Holy Alliance from intervening in Latin America.

The fact that British naval power guaranteed independence for the Latin American republics was not lost on the republics themselves. The Monroe Doctrine appears to have been greeted with indifference in most of Latin America. According to Bailey (1980: 188), three of the republics applied to the United States for assistance, while Colombia and Brazil interpreted Monroe's comments as an invitation to form an alliance against European aggression. Monroe turned down all of these requests and offers, in order to make it clear that the United States would not act unless a general European intervention went unmet by the British navy.

No serious challenges to the US role of regional protector were mounted in the aftermath of its proclamation. In fact, Bailey (1980: 191) labels the period from 1825–1840, the "awkward age of diplomacy" for the United States, simply because not much worth noting happened in US foreign policy during that time. Bailey credits this lull in activity to the US focus on internal expansion and a general quietness in European affairs. The United States settled disputes with Britain over the Oregon Territory and the Maine boundary during this time period. But in general, the United States seemed to implicitly adopt the internal development role.[27] This remained the case until the annexation of Texas and the war with Mexico.

Transition to the Major Member Status

Texas achieved independence from Mexico in 1836, with assistance and the support of public opinion in the United States. Texas offered itself for annexation to the United States, yet the issue became so embroiled in the slavery question that it withdrew its offer in 1838. The emerging state of Texas sought to secure its position by seeking recognition and assistance from the European powers. Both Britain and France recognized the Republic of Texas and signed treaties of amity and commerce with it. However, Texas again courted annexation by playing the British and Americans against each other. Finally, on March 1, 1845, Texas was officially annexed by the United States.

Mexico had threatened war with the United States if it annexed Texas. However, the US declaration of war on May 13, 1846, was largely the result of President Polk's expansionist policies. The peace treaty signed on February 2, 1848, gave New Mexico and California to the United States and secured its title to Texas down to the Rio Grande. With the Oregon dispute settled, and the Mexican cessation of territory, the "manifest destiny" of the United States to stretch from the Atlantic to the Pacific was achieved. The Mexican-American war vastly augmented US potential capabilities. It demonstrated to the world that the United States would enforce the Monroe Doctrine and would not allow the European powers to exercise control of independent states in the Americas.

President Polk reinforced this notion in his message to Congress on April 29, 1848, regarding the Yucatan. Polk's message was in response to a rumor that the local Mexican rulers of the Yucatan were about to transfer their land to Britain. The "Polk Corollary" to the Monroe Doctrine stated that the United States would not consent to the transfer of "dominion and sovereignty" over the Yucatan to any foreign power, even at the invitation of the inhabitants. European states were warned not only against armed intervention, but also against diplomatic maneuverings and intrigue (Crabb 1982: 35). This was essentially Polk's motive for annexing Texas as well—to prevent Britain or France from setting up a puppet government in an independent state bordering the United States (McCoy 1960: 110–111; Perkins 1955: 75–77).

The Mexican-American War marked the transition from small member state status to major member state status (or regional power) for the United States. The regional protector role that President Monroe adopted in 1823 could now be enacted properly. The increase in US territory certainly augmented its capabilities. It also increased the American sense of security. The United States underwent two interesting role location processes during this period. First, it was able to reject the regional collaborator role that Britain attempted to altercast to it (see Figure 3.4). It was able to accomplish this goal by offering its own achieved role of regional protector. The British had no reason to challenge this role because the outcome of the policy was the same for them (see Figure 3.5). The British would use their navy to prevent Spain and the Holy Alliance from reasserting control in the Americas either way.

No serious challenge was mounted to the self-proclaimed regional protector role by any great power. Many states rightly doubted US ability to enact this role without the surrogate capabilities it found in British naval power. The audience of states in Latin America discovered that this role did not include any proactive measures from the United States when their expectations for aid and treaty commitments fell on deaf ears in the United States. These expectations from states weaker than the United States did not detract from the regional protector role for the United States. In fact, this role conception probably did not become an integral part of US social identity until after the Mexican-American War, given the mismatch between the status of the role and the actual capabilities available to defend the role when announced in 1823; the lack of positive valuation given the role by the relevant others; and the little time and effort expended by the United States in this role.

MAJOR MEMBER STATE STATUS, 1848–1898: THE UNITED STATES ATTAINS THE REGIONAL LEADER ROLE

Theoretically, we should expect major member states to have a greater array of well-developed roles that, on the balance, include more achieved than ascribed roles. The greater capabilities major members have are partly a function of their natural endowments, but also a function of their ability to innovate their internal organization to make the best use of those capabilities. Major members are responsible for socializing emerging states and small states in their geographic subsystem. However, major members cannot act with impunity as they are still subject to socializing activities by the great powers at the level of the international system and in the regional subsystem if it is a great power's traditional sphere of influence.

Polk's Corollary to the Monroe Doctrine was a declaration of the role of regional leader for the United States concerning all of the Western Hemisphere.[28] Once again, Britain would occupy the role of the primary socializer for the United States in its attempts to enact this role.[29] Britain was alarmed at the outcome of the Mexican-American War, with the consequent increase in American territory. Britain was also worried that US expansionism would now continue to push southward toward its own territorial enclaves in the Caribbean, including Jamaica and British Honduras. After the Treaty of Guadalupe Hidalgo, and the discovery of gold in California at approximately the same time, it became crucial to the United States to have a fast and convenient water route to the Pacific coast. The search for a canal route through the Central American Isthmus was bound to lead the United States and Britain into conflict.

A canal across Nicaragua was regarded as the most feasible waterway at this time. In order to prevent US action in the area, the British seized San Juan at the mouth of the San Juan River in 1848. This action was supposedly to protect the Mosquito Indians. It also had the effect of controlling the proposed terminus of the canal. The United States and Britain entered into negotiations concerning the proposed canal route through Nicaragua. The United States actually held the upper hand in these negotiations, as several Central American states had come to the United States seeking protection from Britain, including Nicaragua—thus providing positive valuation for the enactment of the regional protector role. US Secretary of State Clayton informed the British minister that several of the Central American states had even offered to be annexed to the United States Further, the United States had already concluded several treaties conveying exclusive canal route rights with Central American states.

Despite having the upper hand in terms of regional support of its leadership and protector roles, the United States largely capitulated to Britain with the Clayton-Bulwer Treaty of April 19, 1850. Both the United States and Britain agreed to cooperate in any ventures leading to the construction of a canal. Both agreed never to fortify such a canal, or exercise exclusive control over it. Finally, and most detrimental to US expansionist interests, neither the United States nor Britain was to occupy, colonize, or exert dominion over any part of Central America. It was unclear whether this included territories already occupied by Britain in British Honduras and the Mosquito Coast, or whether it only prevented future colonization.

The Clayton-Bulwer Treaty was approved by the Senate but quickly became very unpopular in the United States for several reasons. First, it bound the United States not to acquire any of Central America. And second, it appeared to violate the Monroe Doctrine by allowing the British to keep their current holdings in Central America. However, this Treaty may be interpreted as actually having strengthened the Monroe Doctrine, since Britain accepted the principles underlying the noncolonization clause of the Doctrine (Bailey 1980: 276).

Both the regional protector and regional leader roles are in question in this interaction between the United States and Britain in Nicaragua. The United States offers up both roles for British approval. Britain initially rejects both roles. The United States chooses to pursue the roles and ends up at resolve in the dissonance reduction phase of the game (see Figure 3.6). The Clayton-Bulwer Treaty was a stalemate of sorts between the United States and Britain. In order for the United States to fully enact its regional roles, Britain would have to withdraw from the Mosquito Coast to allow US control of a proposed canal, but that did not happen. The regional protector and leader roles were certainly accepted by the local audience of states, many of which sought protection and annexation from the United States in fear of British designs in the region.

Due to the stalemate over the US role conception in the region and the consequent Clayton-Bulwer Treaty, the next decade in US–British relations in the region was rather rocky. An attack on a US diplomat in San Juan/Greytown in July 1854 led the US naval commander in the area to blow the town off the map. In 1855, a group of Americans led by William Walker seized control of Nicaragua. US President Pierce extended diplomatic recognition to Walker's

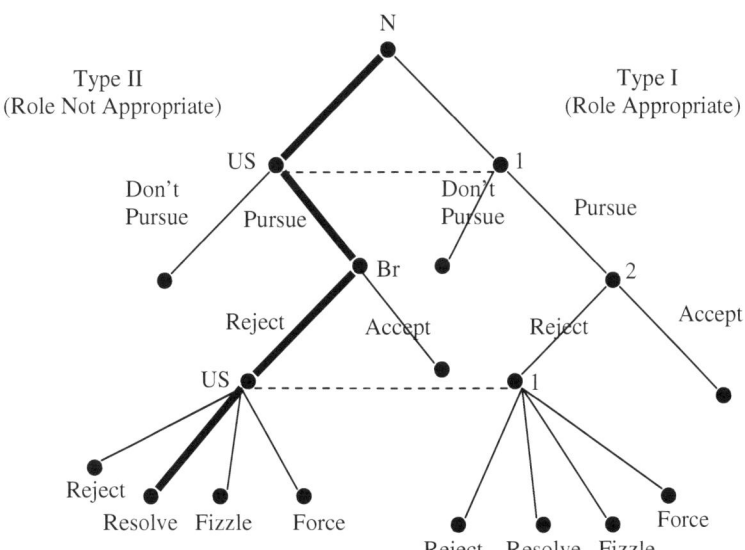

Figure 3.6 The Socialization Game for the Roles of Regional Leader and Protector

dictatorship of Nicaragua in 1856. Britain viewed these actions as flagrant violations of the Clayton-Bulwer Treaty and an attempt to further extend US territorial control in the region. It appeared that the United States and Britain were headed for war.

Matters were made worse when the British minister in the United States, John Crampton, started to enlist American volunteers for the Crimean War in 1856. This act was in violation of the US neutrality law of 1818. The British also began systematic searches of US merchant ships suspected of being slavers in early 1858 in the Caribbean. After US protests, the British stopped the searches. Largely due to the draining of resources for the Crimean War, the British were in the mood to settle their disputes with the United States. However, the route they took was indirect. Britain signed agreements with Honduras in 1859 and Nicaragua in 1860, giving up the disputed territory in the region. It is important to remember that although the United States got its way in Central America, it did not get validation for its role conceptions from the British.

The United States was also seeking to expand into Cuba during this time period, for the same reasons they were seeking a canal. Cuba was a natural port of call for ships headed from the US East Coast to the West Coast. Cuba also offered control of the shipping lanes in the Caribbean. The United States offered to buy Cuba from Spain in 1848, and again in 1854. Its offers were refused both times. Britain and France attempted to get the United States to agree not to let Cuba fall out of Spanish hands starting in 1852, but the United States would not acquiesce to such a proposal. Undoubtedly, the United States was pushing for increased territory, which meant increased security. It was also acting upon the regional protector and regional leader roles set out in the Monroe Doctrine and Polk's Corollary. However, neither of those roles was ratified by Britain, France, or Spain in these early machinations over Cuba. The socialization game ends in resolve over enactment of these roles in Cuba, just as it had in Central America.

In 1858, US Secretary of State Cass declared that the United States would not allow the establishment of European protectorates in the Western Hemisphere, or any other efforts to subjugate independent American states. This minor doctrine of US foreign policy was directed at the problem of failing Spanish authority in the Americas (Crabb 1982: 35–36). The Civil War made this doctrine, and indeed the Monroe Doctrine and the Polk Corollary and their associated roles, rather hollow from 1861 to 1865.

Temporary Retreat from the Regional Leader Role, 1861–1865

The US Civil War began on April 12, 1861, with the attack on Fort Sumter. With its powerful navy, Britain became a focal point for the foreign policy of the North and the South during this conflict. The North feared intervention by Britain on the side of the South, due to its dependence on US cotton exports. The North thus worked toward keeping Britain out of the war.

Anglo-American relations were at a high point following the settlement of the controversy in Central America. In fact, British opinion was initially favorable to the cause of the North because it was assumed that the struggle was over freeing the slaves—an issue the British had long been pushing.

However, until the Emancipation Proclamation, Lincoln had declared that the war was about preserving the Union, not freeing the slaves. Many British thus felt that they should support the South on the principle of self-determination. The ideal of union, of purposefully supporting the enormous country the United States had become, was not especially appealing to all Britons. British aristocrats also felt greater affinity for the "Southern gentleman" than they did for the brash and vulgar Yankee. There was also some fear that if the North did prevail, then the masses in Britain would be encouraged to pursue democracy at home (Bailey 1980: 319–321).

Further, the United States was seen as a growing rival, a powerful commercial competitor, and a threat to Canada and other British possessions in the Western Hemisphere. If the United States were split in two, Britain would no longer need to fear a unified, aggressive democracy. The balance of power principle could be extended to the two states that might form out of the old United States.

On April 19, 1861, President Lincoln proclaimed a maritime blockade of the seceded states. The implementation of this blockade was never fully effective. However, the great powers recognized it as binding. The British navy did not insist on high blockading standards, and maintained a neutral stance while in American waters. US naval vessels intercepted British merchant ships suspected of attempting to circumvent the blockade without official British protest. Thus, during the Civil War, the British played the role of neutral carrier, while the Union played the role of dominant sea power (Bailey 1980: 324–325).

Britain issued a proclamation of neutrality on May 6, 1861, recognizing the belligerent status of the Confederacy. This caused some consternation in both Britain, which desired to remain neutral, and the Union, because it was one step short of recognizing the independence of the Confederacy. The British declaration allowed the South to send out privateers and commerce destroyers and to issue bonds. The Confederacy believed that it would soon be recognized by Britain. Britain attempted to sooth the Union's anger over the issue by forbidding privateers of either belligerent from bringing their prize to British ports. This was a deathblow to Confederate privateers cut off by the Union blockade.

The United States as a novice state championed the rights of neutral ships carrying trade to belligerents. The Declaration of Paris of 1856 attempted to abolish privateering and paper blockades (blockades not properly enforced). It also proclaimed the principles of "free goods, free ships" and "free goods, always free." The United States failed to ratify the Declaration because it did not want to give up privateering, which essentially functioned as the seagoing militia of small-navy states during this time period. The fact that the

British overlooked the Union-imposed paper blockade and prevented Confederate privateers from anchoring in British ports worked to the Union's favor. The Union almost undid this good fortune by seizing two reviled Confederate emissaries from the British mail steamer *Trent* off of the coast of Cuba, thus reenacting the old British practice of boarding US merchant ships and removing men, which had led to the War of 1812. Lincoln eventually released the prisoners, with Secretary of State Seward noting that Britain had finally accepted the principles for which the United States had fought in 1812 (Bailey 1980: 326–329).

Britain and France both toyed with intervention and mediation as the fortunes of the belligerents in the US Civil War rose and fell. Napoleon III favored a separation of the United States into two separate states to establish a balance of power in the region. This balance of power could ensure the success of the puppet regime he installed in Mexico. Relations between the United States and Mexico, and between the great powers and Mexico, were strained when the Mexican Congress passed a law in July 1861 that suspended payments on the government's foreign obligations for two years. In October 1861, representative of Britain, France, and Spain signed the Convention of London, which provided for a joint military expedition to Mexico to collect the debts in default. The Spanish captured Vera Cruz in December 1861, yet both Spain and Britain withdrew from the expedition soon thereafter. The French remained and finally occupied Mexico City in June 1863. In October 1863, a delegation of Mexican monarchists offered the throne to Maximilian of Austria—the handpicked choice of Napoleon III. Maximilian accepted and signed the Convention of Miramar that guaranteed French military support until 1867.

The Union was unable to enact its roles as regional protector or regional leader until the tide of the Civil War turned in its favor. Secretary of State Seward was loath to push the Mexican issue with the French too hard, fearing the formation of a French alliance with the Confederacy. However, public opinion and Congress were both calling for the expulsion of the French and their imposed monarchy by early 1864. At the close of the Civil War, the Union had almost one million men in its armies. Seward sent a diplomatic mission to France urging Napoleon to withdraw from Mexico. Napoleon agreed that France would withdraw its troops from Mexico over a period of nineteen months. On June 19, 1867, Maximilian was executed by firing squad.

The United States' roles as regional protector and leader were also challenged by Spain. The Dominican Republic asked for reannexation to Spain, which occurred in May 1861. Seward had protested this move, while not referring to the Monroe Doctrine or the Polk Corollary. Spain failed to acknowledge the United States' protests, but the situation seemed to take care of itself. Soon enough, the oppressive methods of the Spanish turned the islanders to revolt. Just as the Union succeeded in defeating the Confederacy in the Civil War, Spain voluntarily pulled out of the Dominican Republic in 1865.

Both of these incursions into the Americas by France and Spain were serious threats to the Monroe Doctrine and the Polk Corollary, and to the role conceptions that went along with them. The United States had little capability to try and enforce the regional protector or regional leader roles when it was involved in a conflict to preserve its own state. However, once the Civil War was finished, France and Spain could no longer reject the enactment of these roles by the United States. The experience of the United States during the Civil War makes it clear that regional roles require the capabilities to back them up. Foreign policy doctrines and their associated roles are simply words when a lack of available capabilities prevents their enforcement through deeds.

Interest in foreign affairs declined for a number of years after the close of the Civil War. Secretary of State Seward was attempting to purchase as much new territory as he could, eventually succeeding only in the Virgin Islands (1867) and Alaska (1868). The Treaty of Washington (1871) dealt with a number of outstanding disputes with Britain, including the Northwest Water Boundary (San Juan Islands), fisheries, and the *Alabama* claims, resulting from Confederate commissioned destroyers built in British ports. Most of the United States' energies after the Civil War were wrapped up in the internal development role.

Reasserting the Regional Protector Role

The United States attempted to enact the regional protector role established by the Monroe Doctrine in a boundary dispute between Venezuela and the British colony of Guiana. The Venezuelan government actually induced the United States to enact this role when it employed a propagandist to produce a pamphlet entitled "British Aggressions in Venezuela, or the Monroe Doctrine on Trial" in 1894. The boundary dispute between Britain and Venezuela immediately captured public attention as the pamphlet circulated through Congress. Secretary of State Olney sent a communication to Britain in July 1895 that interpreted the Monroe Doctrine as prohibiting any European interference in the affairs of the New World. Olney even went so far as to declare that the United States is "practically sovereign on this continent, and its fiat is law upon the subjects to which it confines its interposition" (Crabb 1982: 37).

Lord Salisbury's response was essentially that the principles espoused by President Monroe had absolutely nothing to do with this boundary dispute between British possessions that had been in existence long before the Republic of Venezuela. President Cleveland decided that the disputed territory must belong to Venezuela and that the United States should do whatever was required to keep it in Venezuelan hands. War again seemed eminent between the United States and Britain. Cooler heads prevailed, and Britain agreed to submit to arbitration, signing a treaty with Venezuela in 1897. The resulting settlement in 1899 was not much different than what Britain had offered to Venezuela previously.

The prestige of the United States was boosted greatly by British capitulation. Bailey (1948: 447) suggests that this incident, rather than the Spanish-American War, may better date the emergence of the United States as a great power. This seems odd given that the British fleet still was vastly superior to that of the United States. In fact, the United States had done little to improve its naval position in the years following the Civil War, despite its increased interest in the Caribbean and the Pacific. One of the outcomes of this near-war with Britain was the negotiation of a general arbitration treaty with Britain in 1897. The Senate failed to ratify the treaty despite strong favorable public sentiment. Perhaps the rejection by the Senate of the idea that Anglo-British conflicts should be settled by arbitration, rather than force, should mark the transition to great power status for the United States.

Transition to the Great Power Master Status

Most observers mark the transition to great power status for the United States at the Spanish-American War. The United States had long had an interest in Cuba, as mentioned previously. Insurrection against the Spanish had been an ongoing occurrence on the island since the 1850s. Early in 1895, a new revolt against the Spanish began. The revolutionaries adopted a scorched earth policy that made US investors nervous. In fact, they attacked US property, hoping to encourage US intervention. The Spanish redoubled their efforts by sending General Weyler to Cuba in 1896; Weyler proceeded to place the population in barbed-wire "reconcentration" camps. US public opinion was outraged and Congress passed a resolution favoring recognition of Cuban belligerent status. President Cleveland refused to grant that status during the ongoing presidential election campaign between Bryan and McKinley.

The so-called yellow press pioneered by William Randolph Hearst flooded the public with horror stories of Spanish atrocities and damage to US investments. Some of the stories were true, and many were exaggerated, but conditions in Cuba were horrible. In January 1898, the *Maine* was ordered to Cuba on a friendly visit. An explosion sunk the *Maine* in Havana harbor with the loss of over 250 lives on February 15, 1898. The sensationalist press urged intervention and retribution for the *Maine*, even though the cause of its destruction was unknown. Congress voted $50 million for war preparations on March 9, 1898. On March 28, the American Court of Inquiry declared that the vessel had been destroyed by a mine. The report did not assign responsibility for the mine, yet the public perceived Spain to be behind the plot.

President McKinley tried to settle the issue diplomatically despite public protests. The Spanish were willing to revoke the reconcentration orders in Cuba and grant an armistice. However, this was not enough to satisfy public opinion or Congress. On April 11, 1898, two days after the diplomatic capitulation by Spain, McKinley sent a war message to Congress. The joint resolution that was passed on April 19, 1898, declared Cuba free, demanded the withdrawal of Spain, directed the President to use the military to these ends, and disavowed any intention to annex Cuba.

Britain was the only European power to welcome US intervention in Cuba. This was probably due to growing concern about another rising great power—Germany. Britain maintained official neutrality, yet public and governmental sentiment lay with the United States. The rest of the great powers were wholeheartedly on the side of Spain. Germany, France, and Austria-Hungary all favored mediation or intervention to prevent hostilities, though none was willing to take the lead. The United States was now a formidable power in its own right, with the British navy in a position to prevent European action.

The US navy sailed into Manila harbor and destroyed the antiquated Spanish fleet to take the Philippines. The small American army took Cuba as the Spanish fleet fled. At the close of the war, the US army also took Puerto Rico. On April 12, 1898, hostilities ceased. The final peace treaty signed on December 10, 1898, had Spain relinquish sovereignty over Cuba. Further, the Philippines, Puerto Rico, and Guam were ceded to the United States.

The debate over the peace treaty revolved around the issue of the United States as an imperial power. The anti-imperialists argued that the United States had acquired territory that could not be Americanized and turned into states. They further decried the annexation of peoples against their will as being contrary to the spirit of the Declaration of Independence. The expansionists/imperialists argued the economic and strategic advantages of the new territories and the humanitarian and civilizing impact the United States would have on our "brown brothers" (Bailey 1980: 475–476). The Senate ultimately voted with the imperialists, and the United States became a great power with interests and territory that spanned the globe.

A number of subsidiary roles were enunciated during the Spanish-American War. The United States took the role of liberator, by freeing Cuba from Spain (Holsti 1970: 263). It also fashioned itself in the developer role by offering assistance to the underdeveloped peoples of the newly acquired territories (Holsti 1970: 266). One might also argue that the United States created an imperial role for itself, but, since all of the great powers at the time were also imperial powers, these two roles were coincidental.

The United States underwent huge changes in its status and social identity during its tenure as a major member of the international system. It enacted a number of achieved roles, including regional leader and regional protector, along with liberation supporter and developer. It underwent some early rejections of these roles, most notably by Britain with the Clayton-Bulwer Treaty and by Britain, France, and Spain in Cuba during the early 1850s. Further, while the United States was engaged in its own civil war, it was unable to enact these roles, which were rejected by France in Mexico and Spain in the Dominican Republic. However, by the late nineteenth century, the United States was instructing its former socializer, Britain, on how it would act with its protectee, Venezuela, and defeating another major member of the system, Spain, in a war that marked the US ascension to great power status.

4 Socializing the United States
Structural Imperatives and Great Power Status

Theoretically, great powers, due to their overwhelming capabilities in comparison to the other types of states, will have the largest number of well-developed roles in the international system. These roles are likely to reflect the achievements of great powers based on their capabilities. Further, great powers maintain their status in the system due to their innovations in internal organization that allow them to fully develop and exploit their capabilities.

Great powers are the primary socializers of novice states in the international system and regional subsystems that are their traditional spheres of influence. Great powers are also responsible for resocializing all states when the system changes. Great powers are still subject to socialization attempts as members of a system, but due to their capabilities they can force the adoption of a role. However, if that role challenges the status of other great powers, the state runs the risk of leading the others to balance against it to prevent enactment of the role.

The number of great powers in the system at any one time affects the probability that a particular great power will be subject to socialization attempts. The probability increases directly with increases in the number of great powers, assuming the distribution of capabilities is relatively equal among them. Thus, in a multipolar system with six members, any one of the great powers will still be subject to the role location process modeled in the socialization game.

However, when the number of great powers is reduced to two, the probability of one state successfully socializing the other is very low. Rather, the two poles will socialize states with lesser capabilities both within and outside their spheres of influence. In a bipolar system, the socialization game still models the role location process for all states other than the two great powers. Since these two great powers have the capabilities to adopt a role by force in the system, our analysis will focus on how well that role is enacted in concert with those members of the audience that the role implicates. The focus becomes how well the United States in its role as great power socializes lesser states into the order that it is attempting to create. However, should the distribution of capabilities between the two great powers become imbalanced, then we may see socialization efforts exerted by the stronger power upon the lesser one.

Since great powers express many roles in the international system, and since the United States has been a great power for a century, this analysis will focus on the roles expressed by the United States in its major foreign policy doctrines and during systemic crises. The following analysis will deal with the Open Door Policy and Stimson Doctrine, the Roosevelt Corollary to the Monroe Doctrine, World War I and the Versailles Treaty, World War II, and the "roles of bipolarity" enunciated during the Cold War. All of these policies and doctrines were issued in response to crises that developed while the United States occupied the status of great power. Leadership is crucial in the development and negotiation of roles for the state during these crises. This should be obvious from that fact that these doctrines bear the names of US presidents.

THE OPEN DOOR POLICY: A REGIONAL ROLE TO PLAY IN ASIA

The set of diplomatic guidelines that regulated US foreign policy in Asia after 1899 is known as the Open Door policy.[1] This policy was announced in two stages in the attempt to limit colonial rivalry in China. On September 6, 1899, Secretary of State Hay sent a diplomatic note to Great Britain, Germany, Russia, France, Italy, and Japan. In the note, Hay sought agreement on the principle of perfect equality of treatment in the great powers' commercial relations with China. The Open Door concept prevented any one state from gaining a dominant position to the detriment of other states' commercial interests in China. This initial version of the Open Door policy was actually quite limited. It maintained the treaty system of foreign concessions in China and the spheres of interest that the great powers had carved out for themselves.[2]

As Crabb (1982: 58) argues, this was a unilateral policy pronouncement of the United States masquerading as a multilateral agreement.[3] The United States was the concept's main supporter and interpreter—it failed to even consult with the Chinese (Cohen 1971: 50).[4] The initial version of the Open Door policy expressed the role of balancer for the United States in China.[5] It was clear from Hay's communication that the United States would prevent any single European power from gaining a predominant position in China. This role was accepted by the other great powers largely because it maintained the status quo and prevented the costly conflict it would take to expand their individual interests. If this policy had taken a multilateral approach to solving disputes over spheres of influence in China, the United States might have adopted the mediator-integrator role.[6] However, the unilateral policy pronouncement clearly indicates the role of balancer. In this situation, the role of mediator-integrator would most likely have been rejected by the other great powers. Only the balancer role, with its explicit reliance on capabilities, could maintain the status quo in China.

The Boxer Rebellion occurred soon thereafter, requiring foreign military force to quell it, thus undermining the already weak Chinese government.

Fearing a new colonial scramble, Secretary Hay issued another set of diplomatic notes to the great powers on July 3, 1900. In this note, Hay called for the preservation of the "Chinese territorial and administrative entity" (Bailey 1980: 482). Basically, Hay informed the great powers that the United States sought Chinese political independence. The great powers eventually acquiesced to Chinese independence because none of them were strong enough to challenge the others to prevent it from happening.

The enunciation of the Open Door policy was a firm announcement by the United States that it was playing the role of a great power. As a great power, it authorized Chinese political independence from the other great powers. The other great powers acquiesced to US demands, although many argue that they were just humoring the United States (Schulzinger 1984: 22–23; Bailey 1948: 287). In any event, the US presence in Asia had been growing steadily as it picked up possessions across the Pacific, from Hawaii to Samoa, to Wake Island and the Philippines. These territories placed the United States on equal footing with the other great powers in the region. Although US commercial trade with China was only approximately two percent of all US foreign trade, Hay and others saw the potential for expanded US interests in the region (Bailey 1980: 482). Further, a China carved up into great power colonies could pose a security threat to the Philippines.[7]

The second version of the Open Door policy articulated the role of regional protector for the United States in Asia. Not only would the United States balance against regional attempts at hegemony, but the United States now also assumed the responsibility of determining the sovereignty status of states in the region and of protecting those states from interference on the part of the European powers. Once again, the great powers accepted this role and its enactment in China. The Chinese, on the other hand, viewed the Open Door policy as simply an extension of the treaty system that imposed on Chinese sovereignty (Borg 1947: 2–7). The role of regional protector that the United States enacted with China was correctly viewed as placing China in the role of protectee. President Chiang Kai-shek viewed the policy as contributing to a sense of dependency and laziness on the part of the Chinese (Crabb 1982: 72).

In terms of the socialization game, both the role location effort for the balancer role and the regional protector role were initially favored by structure (see Figure 4.1). At the time, a rough balance of power already existed, and the dominant sea power, Britain, favored its maintenance. When the United States offered these roles for itself, no other great power had incentive to challenge the roles.

The United States did not have occasion to enact the balancer role, and the announcement of the regional protector role was an exercise in deterrence. Despite the fact that the United States did not have the naval strength to force such a role upon the other great powers, it accepted the protected status of China. Since these roles were very hollow in terms of role location and enactment, they did not implicate US social identity to any great extent.[8]

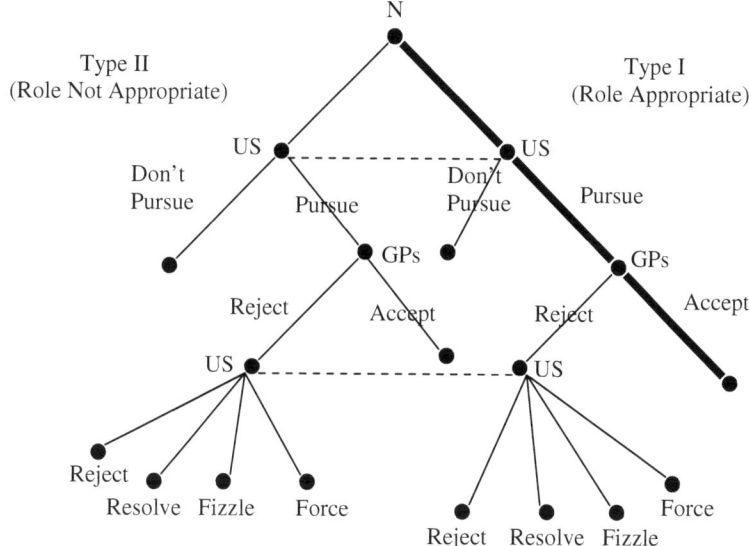

Figure 4.1 The Socialization Game for the Balancer and Regional Protector Roles in Asia

It is important to note that US policy regarding Chinese territorial integrity and political independence remained steadfast through successive administrations. When Sun Yat-sen assumed power after the Chinese Revolution of 1911, the United States under Wilson was the first to officially recognize his government, thus enacting its role as great power in determining system membership. In 1915, after Japan made its notorious "Twenty-one Demands" which would have essentially reduced China to a Japanese protectorate, Wilson informed Japan that the United States would not recognize any territorial changes made in China as the result of the demands.

As a newly emerged great power, Japan was attempting to achieve the role of regional protector for China. This was the first major challenge to the United States in its role as regional protector for China. Wilson's policy of nonrecognition, in combination with British opposition and naval power, compelled Japan to withdraw it demands in China (Crabb 1982: 75–76; Neu 1975: 85–88). Thus, although the regional protector role was initially challenged by Japan, it was supported by Britain, and ultimately Japan was forced to withdraw its claim to the role. This is a situation in which Japan as a great power attempted to achieve a role against other great powers' wishes, thus prompting Britain and the United States to balance against it to deny the role.

After Japan invaded Manchuria in 1931 to set up the puppet state of Manchukuo, and after the failure of the League of Nations to respond to the invasion, Secretary of State Stimson proclaimed a policy of nonrecognition of

Japan's territorial aggrandizement in China. The Stimson Doctrine accorded no legal recognition to the Japanese-created Manchukuo and affirmed the US commitment to the Open Door policy (Crabb 1982: 78–80).

In China, such verbal pronouncements were interpreted as the failure of the United States to properly enact its role as regional protector in the face of Japanese ongoing aggression (Hse 1975: 609). Japan's actions were a direct challenge to the US role of regional protector, which were met with words from the United States but not deeds. This was probably the result of conviction in the State Department that Japanese hegemony was inevitable in the region, and also of apprehension in the military about a contest between the Japanese and American navies (Crabb 1982: 84). In fact, Japan was launching its bid for the role of regional leader during this time period, having recently emerged as a great power itself.

Japan was able to force its role as regional protector and regional leader upon the states in the region, and upon the United States, which lacked the capabilities and will to enforce its claim to the regional protector role for Asia. It was not until the declaration of war with Japan in 1941 that the United States would attempt to reclaim and force its role of regional protector on the Japanese. The United States' social identity is affected by the regional protector role for Asia after World War II because of the heavy involvement in the role and the positive valuation it received from the audience of states in achieving the role. The fact that US social identity was involved with Asia is one of the factors that contributed to US involvement in Indochina. The First Johnson Doctrine is essentially a reassertion of the US role as regional protector in Asia.

THE ROOSEVELT COROLLARY:
THE REGIONAL LEADER ROLE, ACT II

During the early 1900s, the United States was faced with the problem of many of its Caribbean neighbors becoming heavily indebted to European creditors. Britain, Germany, and Italy had blockaded Venezuela in 1902 in the attempt to overthrow its dictator, Cipriano Castro, whose corrupt regime was proving ruinous to European investors. Germany eventually bombarded the Fort of San Carlos in Venezuela in 1903. By 1904 the Dominican Republic was bankrupt in the wake of a bloody civil war, and there was fear in the United States that the four major creditor states might attempt a forcible collection of the debts as they had in Venezuela. In order to deal with these financial crises without European intervention, Roosevelt issued his famous corollary to the Monroe Doctrine in his annual message to Congress in December 1904.[9] Roosevelt said that any Latin American state

> whose people conduct themselves well can count upon our hearty friendship. If a nation shows that it knows how to act with reasonable

efficiency and decency in social and political matters, if it keeps order and pays its obligations, it need fear no interference from the United States. Chronic wrongdoing, or an impotence which results in a general loosening of the ties of civilized society, may in America, as elsewhere, ultimately require intervention by some civilized nations, and in the Western Hemisphere the adherence of the United States to the Monroe Doctrine may force the United States, however reluctantly, in flagrant cases of such wrongdoing or impotence, to the exercise of an international police power. (Gantenbein 1950: 362–362)

The United States used this policy as justification to intervene in the Dominican Republic in 1905, and eventually to intervene in sixty other instances in Latin America (Gerassi 1965: 231). Bailey (1948: 261) argues that the Roosevelt Corollary marks the end of the Monroe Doctrine as a "defensive" doctrine and the beginning of a more active, or imperialistic, version of the doctrine. Crabb (1982: 39) suggests that British officials had urged the United States to adopt the principles expressed by Roosevelt as early as the 1860s, thus accepting the US role of regional leadership in the Western Hemisphere.

Roosevelt's language is the language of socialization.[10] Roosevelt would play the parent to the unruly children of the Caribbean who failed to learn the adult responsibility of paying their bills on time. At one point prior to the Dominican intervention, Roosevelt suggested that the Caribbean states deserved a "spanking" from Europe. But, rather than rely on others (European powers) to discipline his children, Roosevelt would take on that role. The United States would thus serve as an example or model for these states to emulate, but it would also engage in direct instruction, through force if necessary, to instill appropriate behaviors for membership in "civilized society." As Crabb (1982: 39) points out, Roosevelt intended his corollary to apply to the smaller, weaker American republics that were subject to chronic revolution and misrule, rather than the prosperous, civilized states such as Argentina, Brazil, and Chile. As one might expect, the Roosevelt Corollary was very unpopular among Latin Americans (Gerassi 1965; Crabb 1982: 40).

In terms of the socialization game, the structure of the system seemed favorable to the roles of regional leader and regional protector that Roosevelt's Corollary reasserted (see Figure 4.2). The dominant sea power, Britain, seemed to have favored these roles for the United States since the issuance of the Monroe Doctrine, or at least since the mid-1860s. Britain had accepted the US role in the Venezuelan crisis of 1895 as well. No great power challenged the United States as it reasserted these roles. The Latin American states, or the interested regional audience, had little choice but to accept the roles issued by the Colossus of the North.

By the 1920s, the United States began to realize that adherence to the Roosevelt Corollary made relations with its Latin American neighbors uneasy. President Wilson, the champion of self-determination, actually relied on the Roosevelt Corollary to actively intervene in the region more than Roosevelt

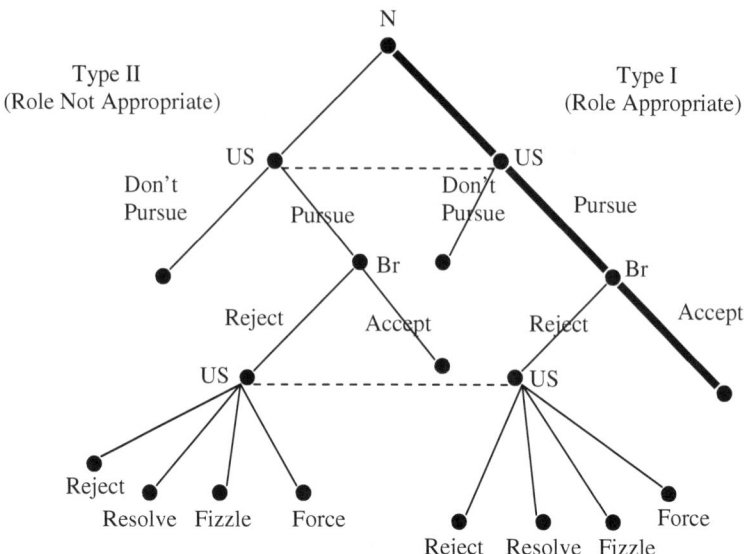

Figure 4.2   The Socialization Game for the Regional Leader and Protector Roles

did with his "Big Stick" diplomacy. In 1923, Secretary of State Hughes reinterpreted the Monroe Doctrine so as to exclude the Roosevelt Corollary. Hughes's reinterpretation would find support in Under Secretary of State Clark's memorandum of 1928. The key point of both men's work was that the Monroe Doctrine outlines the case of the United States versus Europe, not the United States versus Latin America.

Thus, intervention in Latin America would have to be based on other principles in the future, such as self-defense, treaty obligations, or the protection of humanity. Such intervention was not intervention at all, according to Hughes, but rather "nonbelligerent interposition" in our "sister republics" (Vinson, 1961: 146). After the publication of the Clark Memorandum, the United States began to liquidate its military forces in Latin America, with the last marines leaving Nicaragua in 1932. This paved the way for Presidents Hoover's and Franklin D. Roosevelt's Good Neighbor Policy for the region (Crabb 1982: 41–42). It also remarked a return to a more defensive posture for the Monroe Doctrine and attempts by Roosevelt to "multilateralize" the Doctrine through hemispheric defense pacts, such as the Act of Chapultepec (1945) and the Rio Treaty (1947).[11]

Historians have disputed whether the Roosevelt Corollary was the result of genuine security interests (e.g., Spyckman 1941; Osgood 1952), or purely economic interests (e.g., Williams 1962; LaFeber 1963). As in many instances of foreign policy creation, the Roosevelt Corollary probably had both security and economic motivations. The important point for this analysis is that Roosevelt reasserted for the United States the regional leadership and regional protector roles, which were generally accepted by the European powers, and grudgingly endured by the "sister republics" of Latin America. After numerous interventions in the region, Hughes and Clark rescinded the offensive version of the Monroe Doctrine espoused by Roosevelt, with a return to a more traditional defensive version that was more palatable to Latin Americans. Eventually, through defense pacts like the Rio Treaty, the United States began to use the regional leader role to encourage states to assist in their own defense, thus removing some of the stigma associated with their previous roles as protectees.

The evolution of the Monroe Doctrine through the Roosevelt Corollary, and the Hughes and Clark reinterpretations, is an example of a state changing the techniques and expectations for role enactment. The roles of regional leader and regional protector were achieved by the United States in 1823; yet as situations change over time, the methods of enacting a role are bound to change. We will see more evidence of the changing methods of enacting roles when we examine the major foreign policy doctrines issued in the post–World War II era.

WORLD WAR I AND THE TREATY OF VERSAILLES: ROLE TRANSITION FROM NEUTRALITY TO BELLIGERENCY

Seeking the Neutral Role, Act III

The start of World War I in Europe brought a declaration of neutrality for the United States by President Wilson.[12] Wilson was faced with public opinion that was largely in favor of the Allied Powers, despite an equally strong disinterest in becoming involved in the war. The United States was the wealthiest neutral state and the most important neutral carrier at the outbreak of the war. This led to difficulties with Britain over the rights of neutrals, just as it had during the Napoleonic Wars. Britain was still the dominant sea power in the world.

The British Order in Council of August 20, 1914, arbitrarily redefined contraband to include almost every article that could be of direct or indirect aid to its enemies. British naval practices at this time included the traditional search of neutral vessels on the high seas, but also increasingly involved bringing the vessel to port for inspection. This practice caused considerable loss to American shippers, often to the advantage of their British competitors. The British invoked an undeclared paper blockade of Germany. Further, Britain now stopped vessels destined for neutral ports, such as Holland and Sweden. Finally, on November 3, 1914, Britain declared the North Sea a military area and mined it so heavily that neutrals could not make the passage without prior approval at a British port.

Although the British blockade and searches reduced US trade with Germany by 93 percent from 1914 to 1915, and then virtually extinguished it altogether the following year, the United States did not fight for its neutral role with Britain by word or deed. The British generally compensated the US merchants, and the increased trade with the Allied powers more than made up for the losses with Germany. Further, Wilson was sympathetic to the Allied cause and though diplomatic protests were lodged by the State Department with the British government, no real action was expected or required (Bailey 1980: 570).

In late 1914, Wilson allowed bankers to extend credit to the Allied Powers, and in 1915 he allowed them to lend money outright. United States munitions manufacturers were also engaged in a vigorous trade with the Allies. The Germans responded by declaring a war zone around Britain in February 1915. Germany announced it would destroy all merchant ships found in the zone. This was the most flagrant violation of neutral rights yet. The traditional practice for belligerents was to stop a vessel, examine it, and then make provisions for the safety of its crew. However, the Germans intended to use submarines to simply destroy the vessels outright. Allied ships were sunk with regularity thereafter in the war zone, the most alarming for the US public being the *Lusitania*. Wilson sent several strong notes protesting attacks on neutral and civilian shipping to the German government, which gave orders not to sink liners without provisions for noncombatants.

Despite the obvious necessity of controlling the seas during the war, little effort or money was spent on expanding the US navy until 1916. The Naval Act of 1916 was passed in response to the British blacklisting of American companies with German connections. Wilson's response was "Let us build a navy bigger than hers [Britain's] and do what we please" (Bailey, 1980: 587). However, President Wilson won reelection in 1916 based on a pledge to keep the United States out of the war.

The years leading up to US involvement in World War I marked its third attempt to enact the neutral role—and its third failure. Once again, the other interested great powers fail to sanction the role. This time, as when the United States was a novice, Britain is the dominant sea power and prohibits the enactment of the neutral role. Germany also violates the rights of neutral US ships. The United States undergoes a great deal of interrole conflict, as discussed in Chapter 3, since the great powers are opposed to the neutral role for the United States and prefer it enact the role of a belligerent.

In terms of the socialization game that models the role location process, the structure of the system is disposed once again against the neutral role for the United States (see Figure 4.3). This is because World War I is a systemic war—a war being fought to change the fundamental nature of the international system. All great powers are compelled to engage in such a war—belligerency is thus an ascribed role for a great power during a systemic war. The United States attempts to pursue the neutral role, which is rejected in no uncertain terms by both Britain and Germany. How does the US deal with the dissonance created by this situation? It chooses "Fizzle" in the socialization game. This option for dissonance reduction means that the

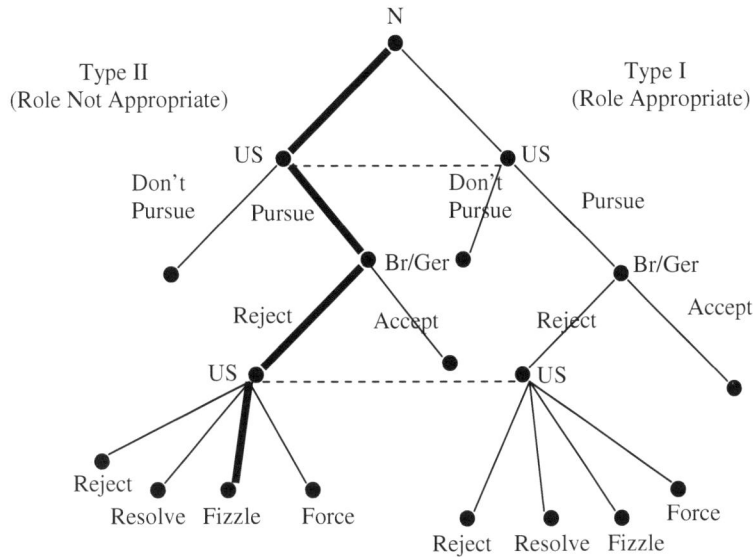

Figure 4.3   The Socialization Game for the Neutral Role III

United States updates its beliefs to accept that the neutral role could not be achieved, and it stops desiring the role as well. This is definitely the case by the time Germany engages in unrestricted submarine warfare.

Enacting the Great Power Role as a Belligerent

After Wilson's reelection to the Presidency, he went on a quest to negotiate peace among the belligerents. It was during this time that Wilson sought the role of mediator for the United States (Chotard 1997: 43).[13] His initial attempt to get the Allies and the Axis Powers to publish their war aims was met with hostility on both sides. On January 22, 1917, Wilson suggested the creation of a league of nations for establishing world accord. Unfortunately for Wilson, the Germans' reply on January 31, 1917, was unrestricted submarine warfare against all ships in the war zone—a clear rejection of the mediator role for the United States, which the United States allowed to fizzle. Wilson severed diplomatic relations with Germany on February 3, 1917. The Zimmermann note, turned over to US authorities by the British on March 1, 1917, outlined plans for a German-Mexican alliance should war come with the United States. This communication dramatically turned the tide of public opinion against Germany.

In mid-March, the Germans began sinking unarmed US merchant vessels as they had promised. Wilson delivered his war message to the Congress on April 2, 1917, declaring that the status of belligerency had been "thrust" upon the United States. According to role theory, role demands are found in certain situations that constrain the choice of roles available to the actor. The unrestricted submarine warfare demanded the belligerent role—the situation determined the role, not the actor. Wilson felt as though he had little choice but to declare war.[14] However, moving from neutrality to belligerency was not an easy task for the United States. In fact, there was substantial anti-British feeling due to the blacklist and perceived abuse of US merchantmen. The United States moved to enact the roles of belligerent and ally.

In terms of the socialization game, after the other great powers reject the neutral role, and the United States allows it to fizzle, the great powers attempt to altercast the belligerent role to the United States. We can still use a reinterpreted version of the socialization game to understand the structure of this situation (see Figure 4.4). The structure of the system (N) favors the enactment of the ascribed, belligerent role for the United States. The great powers (Player 1) altercast the role of belligerent to the United States The United States (Player 2) still rejects the belligerent role, preferring to seek a peaceful resolution to the war. Player 1 creates a situation that demands the United States adopt the belligerent role—German unrestricted submarine warfare, which was not directed specifically at the United States, but would entail US casualties. This is a novel way to "Force" the United States to enact the belligerent role, and to accept an allied role with Britain.

Wilson delivered his Fourteen Points address to the Congress on January 8, 1918. The Fourteen Points were designed to present Allied war aims and serve as propaganda. The capstone point for Wilson was the Fourteenth Point—the League of Nations, which cast the United States in the roles

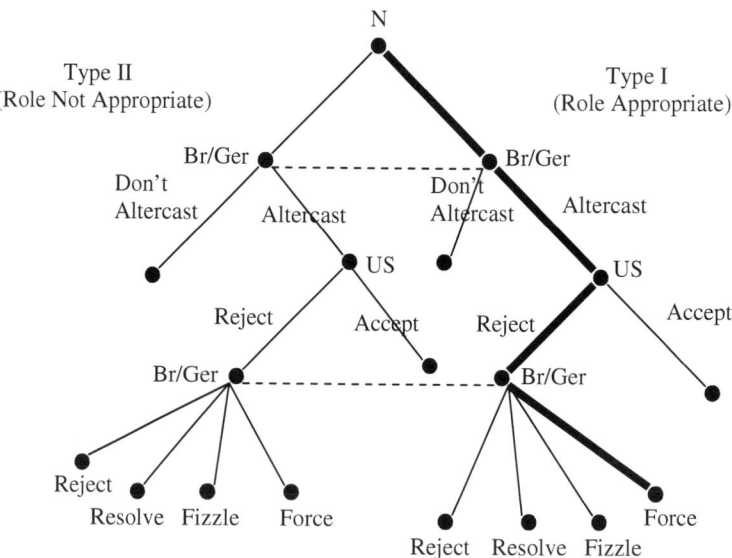

Figure 4.4   The Socialization Game for Altercasting the Belligerent Role

of peace builder and catalyst, which were ultimately accepted by all sides (Chotard 1997: 46).[15] Germany made it clear by October 1918 that it were willing to make peace based on the Fourteen Points. The Allies were somewhat less enthusiastic about this approach, since they had created a number of secret treaties amongst themselves to carve up the spoils of war. Britain objected to the Second Point, which would ensure freedom of the seas. France objected to the absence of a demand for war reparations from Germany. The Allies finally agreed to the Fourteen Points but included a demand for reparations. The Armistice was signed on November 11, 1918. After much deliberation, the Treaty of Versailles was signed on June 28, 1919.

Reaction to the Treaty was generally favorable among the US public. The major stumbling block appeared to be the provision for the League of Nations, which cast the United States in the role of peace organizer through collective security (Chotard 1997: 54).[16] However, thirty-two state legislatures had endorsed the League, with two others offering conditional approval. Thirty-three governors were on record as favoring the League (Bailey 1980: 617). The most vocal opponents were Republican Senators led by Henry Cabot Lodge.[17] After a barnstorming tour of the country supporting the League, President Wilson suffered a stroke and was out of the public eye for seven and a half months. Lodge attached a series of amendments to the treaty, which, when presented along with the treaty to the Senate, led to its defeat on November 19, 1919. Wilson probably could have persuaded some of the Democrats with mild reservations to vote for the treaty prior to his incapacitation, but he instead declared that the Lodge reservations emasculated the entire treaty. A second attempt at passage failed on March 19, 1920.

The debate and ultimate rejection of the Versailles Treaty demonstrates the role strain that active intervention as a great power caused the United States. World War I was the first occasion that the United States acted with force as a great power outside the Western Hemisphere. As such, the United States had little anticipatory socialization, other than its mixed success in the Asia-Pacific region, to ease the transition into the role. The lack of anticipatory socialization, in addition to the great amount of normative change required by the new role, as well as the perceived role strain of the new role, all led to a difficult transition into the active role of a belligerent.[18] The US public and government were loath to give up their adherence to the neutral role, despite the lack of willing partners to enact the role, until the German implementation of unrestricted submarine warfare demanded the belligerent role.

The isolationist impulse behind the neutral role is a strong force in US foreign policy (Spanier 1992; Klingberg 1983; Whitcomb 1998). The neutral role, and isolationism, is the comfortable position for the United States, but certain situations have demanded the United States take a belligerent role in wars, such as the War of 1812, World War I, and World War II. After the conclusion of the first of these two wars, the role strain caused a retreat from the active belligerent role into a more passive role. As Walker (1992: 31) suggests, the greater the role strain that results from performing a role, the easier it is to make the transition out of the role. The US Congress was not comfortable in performing an active role in global affairs after the conclusion of World War I. Thus, the Versailles Treaty was not ratified because of its provision for the League of Nations and the active role of peace organizer that it entailed for the United States.

The United States after World War I was in the curious position of being accorded the status of a great power but failing to live up to the expectations attached to that role, namely, the ascribed role of belligerent during a systemic war. Great powers are expected to be actively involved in international affairs, not passive observers. As we have seen, the United States has taken on a number of active roles within its region, such as regional leader, regional protector, and liberation supporter.[19] The United States even attempted to enact the balancer, and later, the regional protector role in Asia. These roles were met with skepticism but not completely rejected by the great powers, until Japan's invasion of Manchuria. Of course, outright rejection of the regional protector role by Japan occurred during the League years when the United States was not playing an active role in world affairs. The United States did remain committed to the regional leader role in the Western Hemisphere, as discussed previously. The United States would not fully accept its obligations as a great power until World War II. After World War II, the United States remains actively involved in global affairs, without a return to isolationism.

WORLD WAR II: ROLE TRANSITION FROM NEUTRALITY TO BELLIGERENCY II

Seeking the Neutral Role, Act IV

After the Japanese invasion of Manchuria in 1931, the Italian invasion of Ethiopia in 1935, and Germany's occupation of the Rhineland in 1936, the US public was once again clamoring for neutrality. In 1934–1935, Congressional hearings and articles in the popular press blamed US entry into World War I upon munitions manufacturers (Bailey 1980: 700–701; Schulzinger 1984: 158–159). Books like Engelbrecht and Hanighen's (1934) *Merchants of Death* described the interlocking international ties of the munitions business, and their attempts at starting wars so as to increase their profits.

In 1935, Congress passed the first in a series of Neutrality Acts.[20] The 1935 Neutrality Act provided that the president could forbid the sale or transportation of munitions to belligerents. With the *Lusitania* incident still fresh in lawmakers' memories, the president was authorized to warn US citizens that they traveled on belligerent ships at their own risk. The 1936 Neutrality Act forbade loans to belligerents, except for ordinary commercial transactions. However, an exception was made for Latin American republics fighting non-American states. This exception is an example of the United States' commitment to its roles as regional leader and regional protector in Latin America. These roles were obviously engrained in American social identity by this point, as they were made exceptions to general neutrality. After the outbreak of the Spanish Civil War, the Neutrality Act was extended to internal conflicts as well.

The 1937 Neutrality Act reaffirmed all the provisions of the 1936 Act but added the condition that any travel by US citizens on belligerent ships was illegal. However, certain raw materials could be purchased by a belligerent on a "cash-and-carry" basis. This series of neutrality acts were attempts at preventing the types of incidents that were perceived to have dragged the United States into World War I.

In March 1938, Germany annexed Austria. Late in 1938, Germany also demanded the Sudetenland. President Roosevelt convinced Hitler and Mussolini to meet with French and British leaders at Munich in September 1938. The Sudetenland was given to Germany in the hopes that its territorial aspiration would be appeased. However, in March 1939, Germany absorbed the remainder of Czechoslovakia. On August 23, 1939, Germany and Russia signed the infamous nonaggression pact. And, on September 1, 1939, Germany invaded Poland. Britain and France declared war on Germany on September 3, 1939.

President Roosevelt issued the standard proclamation of neutrality under the Neutrality Act of 1937. The "cash-and-carry" clauses of the 1937 Act had expired in May 1939. Roosevelt sought to reenact the "cash-and-carry" clause and prohibit US ships from sailing into danger zones. The debate between the repealists and noninterventionists was fierce, but both sides were committed to keeping the United States out of the war. The Neutrality Act of 1939 lifted the arms embargo and established prohibited danger zones for US ships. Allied purchasers of war materiel would now be allowed to proceed on a cash-and-carry basis.

As the war got underway, the Allies announced a blockade of Germany. Germany responded with a counterblockade of Allied coasts. In November 1939, Germany launched a floating magnetic mine attack upon Allied shipping. The Allies responded by extending their blockade to enemy exports and imports. The Allies included noncontraband goods that were exported through adjacent neutrals in neutral vessels. This practice was directly contrary to the principle of "free goods, free ships." The United States protested Allied actions, particularly the revival of the practice of forcing neutral ships to British ports for prolonged searches. However, just as in World War I, US protests were routine and not expected to be acted upon by the British. US public and government sympathy lay with the Allies.

Enacting the Great Power Role

The fall of France in 1940 forced the United States to abandon its technical neutrality toward Britain. In April 1940, the United States froze Danish and Norwegian assets in the United States so that they would be unavailable to

Germany. In June 1940, the United States began transferring old military equipment to the British through private channels. In September 1940, the United States turned over fifty old destroyers to the British who responded with a "gift" of sites for bases in Newfoundland and Bermuda, and rent-free leases on six additional sites. With the destroyer-for-bases deal completed, the United States really had shed any pretense at enacting the neutral role.

The lend-lease program was passed in January 1941, and marked the unofficial declaration of war on the Axis powers. Greenland was occupied by the United States in April 1941, as part of the enactment of the regional protector role for the Western Hemisphere. Since Denmark was under German control, this also contributed toward tension with Germany. In May 1941, the United States seized Axis-owned ships in US ports, many of which were transferred to Britain. On May 21, 1941, the US merchant ship *Robin Moor* was the first US ship to be sunk by the Germans. In August 1941, Roosevelt and Churchill met off the Newfoundland Coast and agreed upon the terms for a postwar peace in the Atlantic Charter. The Atlantic Charter marked a tacit alliance with Britain and acceptance that the United States was already at war with Germany.

After establishing convoy routes to Britain, with the consequent clashes with German submarines, the United States repealed the Neutrality Act of 1939 in November 1941. The day after the attack on Pearl Harbor, December 8, 1941, the United States was officially at war with Japan. The Axis partners of Japan, Germany, and Italy, declared war on the United States on December 11. On the same day, the US Congress voted for war with Germany and Italy.

Once again, the socialization game finds the United States attempting to achieve the neutral role when the structure is disposed against that role (see Figure 4.5). However, the pursuit of that role was rather weak. Japan rejects the neutral role in the Pacific by bombing Pearl Harbor, and Germany and Italy reject the neutral role in Europe by declaring war on the United States. The United States then rejects the neutral role. This is a case of adaptive preference formation (Elster 1998). It is also a clear case of socialization at work: the other great powers acting as socializers rejected the neutral role, and, despite the United States' beliefs and desires to the contrary, it also rejected the role. This is actually an ideal ending for the United States because it has learned something about itself and its place in the system through the socialization process.

What the United States has learned, and what is now a part of its social identity, is that the neutral role is inappropriate given its status as a great power. The neutral role did not receive positive valuation in World War I, and it does not receive positive valuation at the start of World War II either. By the start of World War II, the United States is not particularly heavily involved in the neutral role. Each of the Neutrality Acts passed before the outbreak of war subsequently authorized the United States to enact its neutral role in less and less neutral ways. The heart of neutrality was absent

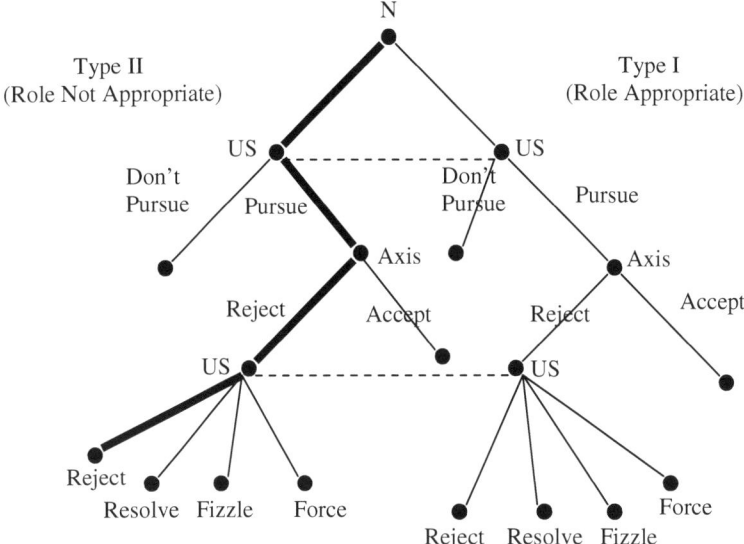

Figure 4.5 The Socialization Game for the Neutral Role IV

from the United States' role enactment by the time it was socialized out of that role by the Axis powers. What the United States needed was a push to realize that it could not pretend to be neutral, even if it had convinced itself that it was, in a systemic war. The United States then adopted the roles of belligerent and ally that were accepted by the audience of states.

With the lessons of World War I in the recent background, the United States had plenty of anticipatory socialization to assist in making the transition to the belligerent and allied roles. Although the United States passed four major neutrality acts leading up to World War II, those acts successively softened the neutral stance, until the technicality of the neutral role was replaced by the unofficial enactment of the belligerent and allied roles. The United States was much more prepared for an active role as a great power in this iteration of its role location process. As a systemic war, the United States as a great power could not remain neutral. Changes in the composition of the great powers affect the normative order of the system. The United States relinquished its right to affect the normative order after World War I, but after World War II, the United States became the primary creator of that order.

The end of the war marked the transition from a multipolar to a bipolar international system. Britain and France were exhausted from the war; Germany and Italy were defeated. The United States and the Soviet Union emerged as the two most powerful states in the system. At Yalta, Roosevelt and Stalin carved up Europe into their appropriate spheres of influence. Japan would soon be eliminated as a great power by the dropping of the atomic bomb on Hiroshima. The United States, in conjunction with Britain, also began to shape the postwar order agreed to in the Atlantic Charter, once again casting the United States in the roles of peace organizer, catalyst, and integrator (Chotard 1997: 55–59). This postwar order included the United Nations, the Bretton-Woods financial and monetary system, and NATO. The United States would now embark upon an active role as a great power, indeed one of two "superpowers," in the post–World War II international system. The United States would not revert to isolationism as it had after World War I.

The United States would no longer be subject to socializing attempts as it emerged as one of the primary socializers in the bipolar international system. The Truman Doctrine effectively notified the world that the United States was prepared to adopt the global leadership role that its capabilities demanded (Crabb 1982: 112). The United States was finally prepared to meet the expectations of the audience of states and to enact its role as a great power. The United States had learned in its experiences from World War I and World War II that the neutral role, and the isolationism that it implied, were inappropriate to its status in the system. Moreover, in the bipolar world that developed out of the conclusion of World War II, the United States would play the role of bloc leader for the free world.[21] The United States now viewed the regime type of states as fundamental to world order, and would therefore lead the bloc of free states opposed to the bloc of totalitarian states (Nathan and Oliver 1985: 64). The cornerstone of this bloc would be NATO, established in 1947, in addition to other multilateral security arrangements, such as ANZUS (1951), and bilateral pacts with Japan (1951) and the Philippines (1951).[22]

The language of the Truman Doctrine also implicates the role of defender of the faith.[23] The United States would seek to defend the values of democracy and capitalism—the American way of life (Nathan and Oliver 1985: 64). Scholars have noted that the "crusade" is a recurrent phenomenon in US foreign policy (Klingberg 1983; Spanier 1992). The Truman Doctrine launched one such crusade against tyranny and totalitarianism (Crabb 1982: 133). Further, when assistance was required by a state to defeat intervention by totalitarian forces, the United States would adopt the role of liberation supporter and supply economic and military aid. It is clear that aid would be extended to endangered states that were making some effort to preserve their own security and independence. Thus, the United States would act as a supporter of liberation, rather than as a liberator for the state.[24]

President Truman was the first US leader to negotiate a bipolar international system. The foreign policy doctrine he advanced did not involve efforts to socialize the Soviet Union into roles that were conducive to US interests. Instead, Truman suggested that the United States and the Soviet Union would occupy the roles of bloc leaders. The United States would focus its socialization efforts on states of lesser capabilities to maintain their position within its bloc. It was assumed that the Soviets would attempt to socialize states within its sphere of influence in the same manner. In states that were not aligned with either bloc, both states would compete for favor in the roles of liberation supporter and defender of the faith.

Competition to maintain the balance of power in a bipolar system requires that both poles adopt the same roles in the system. Bipolarity induced similar role conceptions adopted by successive US presidents. The roles of bloc leader, defender of the faith, and liberation supporter or liberator become the standard "roles of bipolarity" according to Thies (forthcoming). Further, these roles are enunciated in statements of "universal" foreign policy principles (Crabb 1982: 130). Therefore, they are not targeted at specific cases, such as Greece or Turkey, but stated as a universalistic, open-ended policy for US intervention. The roles offered in these universalistic policy statements are peculiar to great powers. Only a great power has the capabilities to assert a role, and not to fear punishment for failure to enact the role. Such universal roles may not have specific referents in actual situations, yet can still be considered achieved roles for the great power.

THE UNITED STATES AS A GREAT POWER

In dealing with major foreign policy crises, the United States has issued relatively few roles for itself as a great power. The neutral role was enacted, although somewhat feebly, before both world wars. This makes sense because structure induces great power participation in wars that alter the composition of the great powers and the normative order of the system. Essentially, the United States' capabilities were too great for other states to accept the neutral role after its transition to the great power master status. The other two occasions that elicited a neutral role from the United States were just prior to the Quasi-War with France (1798) and the War of 1812 with Britain. On those occasions, the United States had too few capabilities to enact the neutral role in opposition to the great powers.

As a great power, the United States found itself actively involved in a number of regions throughout the world. The United States made a short-lived attempt to serve as balancer in the Asian region under the first of Secretary Hay's Open Door notes. This attempt was made despite historic US concerns to stay out of balance of power politics. However, it was soon replaced by the role of regional protector in Asia. That role was accepted by the great powers, rejected by the rising Japanese great power, and then ultimately vindicated at Japan's defeat in World War II. A similar role for the Southeast Asian region was expressed by Johnson in his first doctrine. The United States also made clear its special relationship to the Americas by expressing the activist regional leader role of the Roosevelt Corollary and Johnson's Second Doctrine. Further, President Eisenhower, and later President Carter, outlined the role of regional protector for the Middle East.

The conception of the great power role has also changed at times from passive to active and back. The United States switched from a passive conception of great power to an active conception in World War I, then back to a passive conception that would only be replaced by an active conception at the start of World War II. The active conception of the great power role would persist from World War II until the Nixon Doctrine, when the president announced a retrenchment of US activities abroad. The passivity of the Nixon Doctrine would be replaced by an active conception of great power status during the Carter Administration.

The role location process modeled in the socialization game still applies to the United States during the early years in its great power master status. For example, the United States underwent a role location process during the Open Door Policy and during Roosevelt's reassertion of the regional leader and protector roles in Latin America. The socialization game also models the way in which the great powers rejected the United States in a neutral role before both world wars. Further, the game also models the only role successfully ascribed to the United States in our analysis—the belligerent role in World War I. Finally, the socialization game can also be used to model the only case in which the United States is socialized out of a role while a great power—during the application of the roles of bipolarity to Lebanon during the Eisenhower Administration (Thies forthcoming).

The transition from a multipolar to a bipolar world also constrained the choice of roles available to US presidents. As Thies (forthcoming) argues, the Truman Doctrine committed the United States to the "roles of bipolarity"—bloc leader, liberation supporter, and defender of the faith. The Reagan Doctrine revisited these roles as applied to the international system. The roles of bipolarity are also applied to specific subsystems by the Eisenhower Doctrine and both Johnson Doctrines. It should be noted that under the Truman Doctrine, the United States expresses general roles of bipolarity for the entire system. Successive presidents apply these roles to important regional subsystems as the United States extends its influence. Eisenhower applies the role of bipolarity to the Middle East, Johnson to Asia and then Latin America. Reagan rounds out the era of bipolarity by restating the roles of bipolarity for the entire system.

The collapse of the Soviet Union also led to the transition to a unipolar system. President Bush's New World Order was the first definition of the great power role in a unipolar system. This role envisioned the United States intervening with its international partners to uphold the rule of international law. Clinton's doctrine appeared to refine the great power role expectations enunciated by Bush by placing constraints on the conditions for intervention. George W. Bush's doctrine of preemption attempted to exert unilateral force throughout the world as one might expect of an unrestrained great power, yet the pushback by the audience of states was strong. Obama's doctrine again reflects the US interests as a great power, though it also commits to multilateralism. Thus, the initial exuberance the United States felt as the only remaining great power has been somewhat constrained by the pragmatics of implementing force as needed throughout the world.

The transition to unipolarity has obviously left the United States and its leaders in a quandary. The United States has the capability and influence to adopt any role in the system that it wishes, but which role(s) should it adopt? Le Prestre's (1997b: 68–71) brief survey of the academic and foreign policy elite search for appropriate role conception in the post–Cold War era finds arguments for all types of roles. The arguments often offer incompatible roles, such as the isolate and regional leader, or balancer and hegemon.[25] The fact that incompatible roles, and such a wide variety of roles, are offered in the national debate suggests that structure is not constraining US foreign policy at all like it did during the Cold War.

According to Layne (1993), the US is trying to maintain intact the international order it constructed after World War II as a benign hegemon. Layne argues that the strategy of preponderance will fail.[26] A strategy of benign hegemony does not prevent the emergence of new great powers. In fact, it allows others to free ride militarily and economically, eroding the hegemon's preeminence over time. Preponderance also articulates a vision of a US-led international order. Other states will fear that the United States will use its military power to compel them to give in on issue areas where the United States has less power. These states will react to the threat of hegemony, not to the hegemon's identity, because other states cannot afford to view the United States as a benevolent hegemon. Thus, new great powers will emerge, and we should expect a shift from unipolarity to multipolarity at the turn of the century (Mearsheimer 1990).

According to Layne (1993), Mearsheimer (1990; 1994/1995), and Waltz (1993), it is inevitable that states will seek to balance the power of the United States. The competitive nature of international politics manifests itself in balancing and the "sameness effect." Japan and Germany will seek to emulate the United States to acquire the full spectrum of great power capabilities, including nuclear weapons. Both will seek recognition of great power status. Already we have seen that both want a UN Security Council seat. Japan took the lead in implementing peace in Cambodia, and Germany took the lead in aid to the former Soviet Union and Eastern Europe.

Mastanduno (1997) similarly examines neorealist theory and unipolarity by testing Walt's (1987) balance of threat against Waltzian balance of power propositions. Mastanduno finds little evidence that states are balancing against the United States in the security realm. The United States is not behaving in a completely unconstrained way in its intervention, nor is it edging away from its alliance commitments, and other states are not seeking a revision in the status quo. However, he does find that balance of threat accounts for US security policy. The United States is seeking to preserve unipolarity, reassure the status quo states, engage and integrate undecided states, and it is emphasizing multilateralism.

Mastanduno's propositions for balance of threat theory are exactly what we would expect if socialization, in addition to competition, is taken into account. Layne (1993), Mearsheimer (1990; 1994/1995), and Waltz (1993) rely strictly on the impact of competition to make their predictions regarding unipolarity. If we include socialization, we expect a different version of events. Since the United States is the only remaining great power, the system has changed. The United States must resocialize all members of the system. This is what it appears to be doing according to balance of threat theory. The United States is attempting to reassure the status quo states like Germany and Japan. It is attempting to engage and integrate undecided states, such as China and Russia. The United States emphasized multilateralism in the first Gulf War, and even more overtly in the intervention in Kosovo. The George W. Bush Administration's much more aggressive foreign policy appears to be a temporary aberration, though coalition partners were emphasized in both the interventions in Afghanistan and Iraq. Obama's Administration returned to familiar policies of reassuring status quo states, engaging and integrating undecided states, and emphasizing multilateralism, including the "reset" in relations with Russia and the multilateral sanctions put in place on Iran's for its nuclear program.

5 Socializing Israel
Emergence to Major Member

This chapter examines the role location process for Israel in the international system and the regional subsystem of which it is also a member.[1] In each of the following cases of master status transition, I examine the history of interaction between Israel, its socializers, and the relevant audience through the lens of the socialization game. The analysis focuses on the major roles ascribed to, or achieved by, Israel during four periods of its international system history: emergence (1948–1949), novice state (1949–1956), small member state (1956–1967), and major member state (1967–present).

Each of these periods of history is marked by a critical juncture that brings a change in Israel's master status and consequent changes in associated roles. These critical junctures take the form of interstate wars, just as they did in the US case. In fact, the application of a general theory to the Israeli role location process should help alleviate the notion that it is a unique case (Barnett 1996: 3–25).

My use of the term master status is similar to Brecher and Wilkenfeld's (1997: 29) "power status." In their usage, power status denotes the scope of a state's potential impact—superpower, great power, middle power, or small power. They also acknowledge that a state may be a small power in the global power hierarchy, but a middle power, or even a great power, within its subsystem. They specifically refer to the cases of Egypt and Israel, which they suggest were small powers in global terms after 1956 but great powers in the Middle Eastern subsystem. This may be true in terms of application of capabilities to a specific geographic area, but my use of master status also denotes the social status of the state in the system. Social status and power status usually coincide, but it is not necessary for them to do so. I agree that the social status occupied by Israel and Egypt after 1956 in the international system is that of the small member state. However, in terms of pure capabilities, they may indeed have the impact of a great power within their geographic region.

I do not analyze the international system and regional subsystems as separate entities; rather I view them as intersecting, much as the circles overlap in a Venn diagram. However, certain roles will be primarily regional in nature, while others are international. I concur with Brecher's (1972: 47) conditions for the existence of a subordinate state system. First, a subsystem has delimited scope, with primary emphasis on a geographic region. Second, it contains at least three actors. Third, it must be recognized by most other actors as constituting a distinctive community, region, or segment of the international system. Fourth, it must contain the element of self-identification. Fifth, the units of the subsystem are relatively inferior in power to the units of the dominant system, using a sliding scale of power in both. Finally, more intensive and influential penetration of the subordinate system by the dominant system occurs than the reverse. The Middle East qualifies on all of these counts as a subsystem.

Which states qualify as members of the Middle Eastern subsystem and participate in the Israeli role location process? Gause (1999) reviews the approaches of several international relations scholars, including Barnett (1998) and Walt (1987), and finds that their definitions of system membership are too restrictive, or ad hoc in nature. Gause (1999: 24–25) argues that geography, self-identification, and a common social-historical background are important determinants of system membership to the extent that they lead to "sustained, durable interest and involvement, expressed in tangible commitment of resources, to a common agenda of issues among the states concerned." This definition leads him to include the eastern Arab states from Egypt to Iraq, Israel, Iran, Turkey, the United States, the Soviet Union/Russia, Great Britain, and France as current or past system members during the post–World War II era. Both Gause's and my own understanding of system membership include the notion of the density of interactions between the states.[2]

The two dominant structural features of the international system during most of Israel's history are anarchy and a bipolar distribution of capabilities. According to Safran (1969) and Barnett (1998), the distinctive feature of the Middle Eastern subsystem is pan-Arabism. Both Arabism and Islam contain elements committed to transforming the subsystem from an anarchic organization to a hierarchic one (Barnett 1998; Gause 1999: 26). The fortunes of pan-Arabism and transnational Islamic politics have waxed and waned during the post–World War II era, but neither has overturned the essential anarchic nature of international politics based on the sovereign state.[3] In fact, as the modern sovereign state becomes increasingly institutionalized throughout the Middle East, the salience of transnational ideologies and their potential to overturn anarchy decline (Gause 1999: 28–29).

The two great powers or superpowers during this time were the United States and the Soviet Union. As Gause (1999: 28) has remarked, there has been little sustained effort to examine how the global distribution of power affects outcomes in the Middle Eastern subsystem. This chapter will begin to contribute to that effort by examining the dominant socializers' impact upon Israeli role location in the international system during the post–World War II era. Further, we can assess any change in regional role location efforts that occurred when the international system changed to unipolarity in 1989 with the collapse of the Soviet Union.

In addition to anarchy, the dominant structural feature of the Middle Eastern subsystem during the post–World War II era was multipolarity. The constitution of the great Middle Eastern powers changed through this time period, yet a multipolar balance held (Walt 1987). Multipolarity may also help explain why pan-Arabism and transnational Islamic politics have never achieved the goal of unity. It may also explain why the artificial states created in the wake of colonial withdrawal have persisted intact (Gause 1999: 28).

What does a perspective that emphasizes socialization add to our understanding of the Middle East? As described in Chapter 2, balancing is itself a dissonance reduction mechanism. Balancing occurs when a state attempts to achieve a role that the socializer and audience believe to be inappropriate. The role location process offers the socializer the chance to direct the socializee to abandon an inappropriate role before such action is required. Further, a focus on socialization through the application of role theory may help us to understand why Israel has had such a conflictual history.

Israel's emergence as a state in the Middle Eastern subsystem was predestined to produce conflict from a socialization perspective. First, the pace of socialization into any system will vary with the extent of cultural, identity-based differences between the novice and member states. Obviously, a Jewish state in the midst of a predominantly Arab and Islamic region will make the socialization process difficult, if not impossible. In fact, the surrounding Arab states attempted to prevent Israel's emergence, and then to eliminate Israel after it declared independence. Subsequent socialization efforts were normally met with conflict, rather than cooperation.

Second, the pace of socialization of a novice state will vary with the number of other novices entering the system at the same time. Jordan, Lebanon, and Syria all emerged as independent states in 1946 prior to Israel's emergence in 1948. Under normal circumstances, the emergence of this many states in a small system would slow the pace of socialization, as regional powers attempted to acquaint these states with the appropriate norms and roles. However, the emergence of a cultural outlier like Israel probably speeded the socialization of Jordan, Lebanon, and Syria. But for Israel, the pace of socialization into the system was retarded by this fact.

Third, the pace of socialization will vary with the novice state's level of involvement in the system. Israel was involved in the subsystem because of the Palestinian Arabs that inhabited, or were expelled from, the territory under its control. The fate of the Palestinian Arabs would continue to determine Israel's interaction with the subsystem's members during its entire existence. The Palestinian problem, in addition to the lack of positive involvement in the system through economic or cultural integration, all contributed to a slow pace of socialization.

Fourth, novice states should look to peer groups for imitative guidance for role enactment as predicted by the social proof heuristic. Since most of the roles Israel has tried to achieve have been rejected by its peers in the region, the lesson for Israel has been that conflict is necessary to adopt and enact roles. Since conflict is used by the peers to reject Israel's roles, and Israel uses conflict to attempt to adopt and enact the roles, a vicious cycle of conflict ensues. This has led to a situation of "protracted conflict" (Brecher and Wilkenfeld 1997) or "enduring rivalry" (Goertz and Diehl 1993) between Israel and many of its peer states.

Finally, socialization into the developing regional subsystem may conflict with socialization into the international system. Roles that are appropriate in one system may be unacceptable in the other. Fundamentally, Israel in the role of the sovereign state was acceptable to both the United States and the Soviet Union at the level of the international system, but this role prompted subsystem members to launch a war to reject the role.[4]

THE HISTORIOGRAPHY OF ISRAELI FOREIGN POLICY

As we have seen, US historiography went through multiple phases since diplomatic historians began to focus on US foreign relations in the early twentieth century. The historiography of Israeli foreign relations seems to be marked by two periods—pre–Lebanon War and post–Lebanon War. The War in Lebanon caused many Israelis to seriously question government policy, since it was the first war that did not threaten the survival of the state. Further, it caused a movement among historians that challenged previous scholarship on the Arab-Israeli conflict. This movement is known as the "new history," "revisionist history," or perhaps most pejoratively, "history"—as opposed to the "prehistory" of an earlier generation of scholarship.[5]

The new historians work from a variety of methodological and philosophical approaches. Morris (1988a, 1990) is a conventional historian who employs a positivistic approach. Pappe (1988, 1992) draws on the work of Croce and Carr and admits to the presentist standpoint in his work. Despite differences in philosophical orientations, there are two main features that unite these scholars under the banner of the new history (Bar-On 1998: 23). First, the new historians seek to reinterpret the narrative of Zionist history, the history of the 1948 war, and the early period of statehood because they believe that earlier historians were committed to promoting Zionist propaganda. Second, the new historians believe that the myths created to justify Zionism need to be eliminated in order to prepare Israeli civil society to reconcile with the Palestinians and the Arabs in general.

The new history questions many of the assumptions of standard interpretations of Arab-Israeli interaction. Bar-On (1998) suggests that the new historians deal with themes such as the David and Goliath analogy, the "people who dwells alone" mentality, and Israel's commitment to peace throughout its history. In the specific case of the 1948 war, Finkelstein (1995: 51) suggests that the new history questions the standard interpretation by arguing five major points: (1) the Zionist movement did not support the partition of Palestine; (2) the neighboring Arab states did not unite to destroy the emerging Israeli state; (3) the war did not pit a weak and defenseless Jewish David against a strong Arab Goliath; (4) the Palestinian Arabs did not flee because of Arab orders to do so; and (5) Israel was not earnestly seeking peace at the end of the war.[6]

Finkelstein's (1995) main critique of the new historians is not that they are incorrect about some of their assertions, but that they often substitute new and ill-founded myths for the old ones. For example, Morris (1988b, 1990) destroys the myth that the invading Arab states ordered the Palestinian Arabs to leave. However, he goes further by asserting that the Zionists had no part in forcing them to leave either. The end result is that the refugees are "born of war, not by design"—700,000 Arab refugees "just happened" to leave the emerging state of Israel. This view has been challenged by Teveth (1990), as have many of the theses and methods of the new historians. Karsh (1997: 7) claims that the new historians may be engaging in the "New Israeli Distortiography."

My approach to secondary sources on Israeli foreign policy is to rely on the standard interpretations of events, except in cases where documentary evidence appears to be overwhelmingly in favor of a new interpretation. For example, I rely on Schiff and Yaari's (1984) reinterpretation of the war aims in Lebanon. However, the analysis of the rest of the international and foreign policy crises rely on standard interpretations.

Despite my concerns with the methodological and philosophical positions that some new historians have adopted, they have launched some important criticisms about Israeli historiography that should be addressed. The criticisms are similar to those recently leveled against US diplomatic history. First, new historians have called for an interdisciplinary approach to Arab-Israeli relations. Second, they have pointed out that Israeli historiography fails to incorporate the Arab version of events—a call for international history. Third, they deplore historical treatments of Israel that are infused with an ethnocentric bias. Fourth, some have also argued against treating Israel as a unique case. I have avoided these problems in the Israeli case, just as I did for the United States.

Once we have chosen the appropriate secondary sources of diplomatic history, we need to take into account the appropriate periodization of that history for analytical purposes. The periodization of diplomatic history for the United States and Israel is discussed in the next two sections.

The Periodization of Israeli Diplomatic History

The traditional approach to classifying periods of Israeli foreign policy, particularly in the context of the Arab-Israeli conflict, relies on wars for dating. The secondary sources used in this research are no exception. Generally, the historian analyzes each war, and then may search for similarities and differences between the foreign policies that led to, and were produced by, each. To my knowledge there is no "Klingberg" of Israeli foreign policy that seeks cycles of introversion and extroversion—perhaps because Israel has not had the luxury of being introverted as of yet.

Sandler (1993) offers a periodization based on a distinction between a statist (1949–1967), and an ethnonational foreign policy (1967–present). Undoubtedly, the priorities of state survival demanded that some aspects of the Zionist program be temporarily delayed during the early years of Israeli statehood, such as pressing the Soviets to allow Jewish emigration. Further, both US cycles of introversion and extroversion, and the Israeli "switch" from statism to ethnonationalism, are thought to be partly the result of domestic public opinion or mood. However, both the US cycles and the Israeli switch may be a function of social and power status. Most importantly in terms of dating periods of history, both the US and Israeli cases correspond with the dates of major wars, or in my terms, critical junctures.[7]

I argue that Israel passes through three of the master status categories described in Chapter 2. Israel undergoes its period of emergence from 1948 to 1949, when it forces the role of the sovereign state on its Arab neighbors. It occupies the novice state status from 1949 to 1956, when it becomes involved in the Suez Canal Crisis at the behest of France and Great Britain. The years 1956–1967 mark its duration as a small member state in the system. The Six-Day War marks its transition to major member status in the system, where it persists to this day. The Yom Kippur War of 1973 did not alter Israel's master status, despite the attempts of Egypt and Syria to rectify their 1967 defeat.

EMERGENCE, 1948–1949: SEEKING THE ROLE OF THE SOVEREIGN STATE IN THE INTERNATIONAL AND REGIONAL SYSTEMS

The theoretical expectations for an emerging state are similar to those of novice states and can be derived from our discussion of role theory in Chapter 2.[8] First, emerging states are usually unskilled role takers with a limited number of roles. The role of the sovereign state is probably the only role that most emerging states will have the ability to perform. This was the case with the United States, and it is the case with Israel as well. Second, the role of the sovereign state may be either altercast or achieved. However, Israel attempted to achieve this role on its own following the end of the British Mandate (1922–1948) and before debate on implementing the UN partition resolution was resolved. The partition resolution of November 1947 liquidated the mandate and defined the legal framework for a Jewish state in Palestine. If the leaders of the Jewish Agency had waited, the United Nations and its members would have probably ascribed the role of sovereign state to Israel, but perhaps with less territory than the leadership desired.

Third, a state with few roles will be poorly integrated into the system and less subject to normative control than a state with a larger number of roles. Since an emerging state will be focused on attaining the singular role of sovereign state, it will be fairly unconstrained by the normative expectations of system members. Thus, socialization attempts on the emerging state will probably reach the dissonance reduction stage of the socialization game. Force, either to prevent the state's independence, or to promote its independence, is the likely outcome of dissonance reduction in an emerging state's role location process. Israel, like the United States, had to force its adoption of the role of the sovereign state. As I will discuss shortly, Israel's situation was complicated by its emergence into both a strong regional subsystem and international system, whereas the United States did not have to contend with subsystem socializers.

Finally, an emerging state will have low or uncertain capabilities. The *Yishuv* had been stockpiling arms in its settlements long before the war, but these arms did not include tanks or planes needed to fight the militaries possessed by its neighbors.[9] The *Haganah* was able to hold its own against local Palestinian Arabs and the Arab Liberation Army that began pouring into Palestine in January 1948.[10] By May 2, 1948, the *Haganah* had secured territory roughly equivalent to that approved by the United Nations in November 1947. However, it was not clear at independence how the *Haganah* would fare as an army against the regular armies of its Arab neighbors.

Israel also emerged in a subsystem marked by high interaction capacity. Not only did it have a number of neighbors actively involved in the internal conflict in Palestine, but also a number of outside powers, including Great Britain, France, the United States, and the Soviets, were involved in subsystem affairs. Thus, Israel did not have the luxury of low interaction capacity that engenders the greater freedom of action that the United States enjoyed upon its emergence.

Israel declared its independence on May 14, 1948, just before the official termination of the British mandate in Palestine. The next day, Egypt, Syria, Transjordan, Lebanon, and Iraq sent their armies to assist the Arab Liberation Army and the Palestinian Arabs in destroying the emerging state. Let us examine the role location process for Israel in its attempt to achieve the sovereign state role.

First, the structure of the international system was bipolar, with the United States and the Soviet Union occupying the roles of the great powers. Both the United States and the Soviets had supported the partition resolution in November 1947. President Truman supported partition for both domestic political considerations and international concerns. Domestically, there is evidence that Truman supported partition to gain the Jewish vote at home. Internationally, Truman was concerned with containing Soviet influence, as expressed in the Truman Doctrine issued in March 1947. There was some concern that supporting partition might push Arab states into the Soviet sphere of influence, which would also endanger access to oil in the region. Further complicating the calculation was the fact that US oil companies owned about 42 percent of Middle Eastern oil supplies by 1947.

The ultimate downside for the United States in supporting partition would be a Jewish state emerging under Communist rule, with the Arab states seeking Soviet support and nationalizing US-held oil reserves. These fears were expressed by the State Department, but largely dismissed by Truman, who believed that Israel would become a bastion of democracy in the Middle East. However, the concerns about the Arab states siding with the Soviets, in addition to the 160,000 troops the Truman Administration estimated would be needed to implement partition, caused Truman to reconsider immediate partition in favor of some form of trusteeship in April 1948.[11] Truman thought a trusteeship might allow the Jews and Arabs to work out their differences before a final territorial settlement. The trusteeship proposal was abandoned by the United States and the United Nations on the day Israel declared independence. Overall, it appears that President Truman did favor Israeli independence. Truman granted *de facto* recognition to Israel as soon as news of the Israeli proclamation of independence reached Washington. In fact, Truman recognized Israel over the objections of Secretary Marshall, and without informing the US delegation at the United Nations.

The Soviet Union went even further by granting *de jure* recognition on May 18, 1947. The Soviets also favored the partition of Palestine from the moment the problem was brought to the United Nations by Britain in April 1947. Soviet interests in an independent Jewish state included the desire to eject Britain from the Middle East; the political presence in the region that support for Israel would bring; and, finally, the possibility of a socialist regime forming in the new Israeli state (Bialer 1990: 133–134). The Soviet Union had indirectly contributed to Jewish immigration by encouraging displaced Jews to emigrate to Eastern and Central Europe. The Soviets then pressured its satellite governments, particularly Poland, to allow the refugees to participate in the *aliyah* to Palestine (Bialer 1990: 68–69; Ro'i 1980: 20–33).[12] Thus, both the United States and the Soviet Union supported Israel's bid for the role of the sovereign state.

In terms of the international socialization game, Player N favors the role of the sovereign state for Israel. Israel pursues the role, and it is accepted by its socializers in the international system, the United States and the Soviet Union. As we know from the debate on partition in the United Nations, most of the member states of the General Assembly favored Israeli independence, with the exception of the Arab countries.[13] However, we know that Israel had to fight a war to secure its independence in the Middle Eastern subsystem. Israel was formally admitted as an equal member of the United Nations in May 1949.

The quest for the role of sovereign state was not as easy in the Middle Eastern subsystem. The structure of the regional subsystem was multipolar, with Egypt and Iraq being the major members of the subsystem that opposed Israeli sovereignty. Egypt and Iraq stepped out of the regional audience to serve as Israel's socializers. The socialization game proceeds as follows in Figure 5.1.

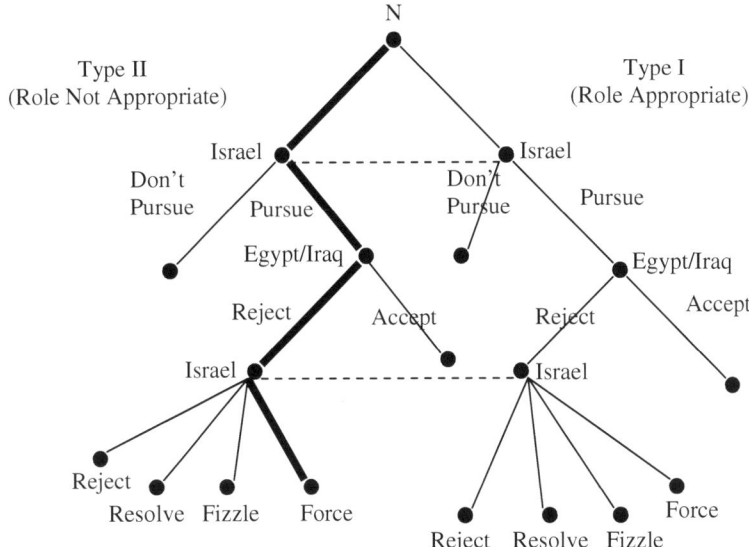

Figure 5.1 The Socialization Game for the Role of the Sovereign State

Player N is disposed against the role of the sovereign state for Israel because the major members of the Middle Eastern subsystem opposed it. Israel (Player 1) pursues the role. Egypt/Iraq (Player 2) reject the role by leading the Transjordan, Lebanon, and Syria in an invasion of Palestine to prevent enactment of the role. Israel (Player 1) chooses to "force" the role upon its regional socializers. Fighting with Iraq basically ceased after July 18, 1948. Fighting in the north with Lebanon and Syria ended on October 30, 1948. By January 1949, Egyptian forces were in disarray in Gaza and Negev. Egypt signed an armistice agreement with Israel on February 24, 1949, and Lebanon signed an armistice with Israel on March 23, 1949. Israel signed additional armistice agreements with Transjordan (April 3) and Syria (July 20) under UN auspices. Iraq refused to participate in negotiations for an armistice.

How did Israel manage to force the sovereign state role upon its regional socializers? First, the Arab armies performed poorly. In general, they were not well trained, with the exception of the British-trained Arab Legion of Transjordan. The Arab armies did not coordinate their actions well, nor did they make use of their armor effectively, apparently because they were unaware of the extent of Israeli weakness in this regard.

Second, the Arab states often had conflicting secondary interests in Palestine. Transjordan wanted to secure as much of Arab Palestine as possible, including Jerusalem. Syria also wanted this territory, but, failing that goal, both Syria and Egypt preferred that it not fall into the hands of King Abdullah of Transjordan. During the long battle for the Negev, no other

Arab army came to the defense of the Egyptians.[14] Thus, traditional Arab rivalries undermined the effort against a unified Jewish people (and Israeli Defense Force) fighting for their state's independence.

Third, the Israeli's used the first month-long truce, established by UN mediator Count Bernadotte, to build up their weapons supply. The Israeli's secured arms from Czechoslovakia with Soviet approval despite the weapons embargo placed on the belligerents by the truce. The increase in capabilities brought in from outside the regional system, in addition to the poor use of Arab capabilities, helped Israel to force the role on its socializers.

The armistice agreements signed between Israel and the Arab states gave Israel all of the territory allocated to the Jewish state in the original UN partition resolution, as well as the 2,000 square miles of the Arab portion that Israel had captured in the war. Egypt received the Gaza Strip; Transjordan (renamed the Hashemite Kingdom of Jordan) received what is now known as the West Bank and part of Jerusalem; four demilitarized zones (DMZs) were created along the armistice frontiers; and Israel was awarded the remaining majority of the territory in Palestine. On August 12, 1949, the UN Security Council formally recognized the end of the war by terminating the mediator position, occupied by Ralph Bunche since the assassination of Count Bernadotte.

How did the achievement of the sovereign state role affect Israeli social identity? The achievement of statehood for Israel was the fulfillment of a very old idea. One of the first Zionist movements was the *Hoveve Zion* (Lovers of Zion), which was formed in Russia in the 1880s. Its members advocated the resettlement of Jews in Palestine as a practical measure to solve the problem of persecution they experienced. Theodor Herzl published a pamphlet in 1896 called *Der Judenstaat* (*The Jewish State*), in which he argued that the Jew would always be a hated outsider in Europe. As a "nation without a land," the great powers should grant them a territory to fulfill their needs as a nation. Herzl convened the First Zionist Congress in 1897, which founded the World Zionist Movement. The goal of the Movement was to create a home for the Jewish People in Palestine with the backing of the international community and international law.

The Zionists had little success in obtaining recognition of their aspirations in Palestine from 1897 to 1917. However, in 1917 the British foreign secretary, in a letter to Lord Rothschild (a prominent British Zionist leader), issued the Balfour Declaration. This declaration of support for a Jewish homeland in Palestine set the stage for Jewish immigration to the area after the British occupied it in 1917. The *Yishuv* grew in size from approximately 65,000 in 1919 to 650,000 in 1948. The *Yishuv* transformed the idea of Jewish statehood into a reality through political parties that were created during the British Mandate. The dominant party of the *Yishuv* and early statehood was the *Mapai*, a social democratic party, headed by David Ben-Gurion. Ben-Gurion served as Prime Minister and Defense Minister from 1948 to 1963.

Ben-Gurion, reflecting the Zionism that brought him to lead an independent state, expressed his political philosophy in terms of the doctrine of *mamlachtiyut*. *Mamlachtiyut* expressed the centrality of the state and its superiority to any other value. It can be loosely translated as "statism." The state was so central to Ben-Gurion because it was the means to the end of saving the Jewish people. The achievement of the sovereign state role and the continued enactment of that role were wrapped up in the centrality of the state for Ben-Gurion (Sandler 1993: 91–100; Liebman and Don-Yehiya 1983: 84).

The involvement dimension of social identity refers to the amount of effort expended upon a role. As the brief review of Zionism suggests, the effort expended upon achieving the sovereign state role was enormous. Ben-Gurion, through the doctrine of *mamlachtiyut*, would attempt to further engross the Jewish people in the sovereign state role. The Israeli War of Independence was only the first in a series of wars that would threaten that role and the developing social identity of Israel.

In terms of the value dimension of social identity, the great powers and the United Nations positively valued the enactment of the sovereign state role by Israel. Israel's Arab neighbors did not value the achieved role at all. In terms of the status dimension, Israel had achieved the position of a new state in a still relatively small international system. Overall, the sovereign state role is crucial to Israeli identity.

NOVICE STATE STATUS, 1949–1956

The theoretical expectations developed for novice states in Chapter 2 include low or uncertain capabilities. This is certainly the case for Israel, which has a difficult time obtaining arms during this period. Second, novice states are expected to have few roles in the international system. Israel, like many novice states, seeks a form of neutrality after it secures its independence. However, it does seek several other roles with possible international and regional repercussions. Third, novice states are subject to intense socialization pressure; yet, with few roles in the system, they are also the least subject to normative control.[15] This allows Israel to navigate a course between the United States and the Soviet Union. Fourth, on balance a novice state should have more ascribed than achieved roles. Israel is able to achieve roles primarily because of its success in forging a "nonidentified" foreign policy.

Seeking the Nonaligned or Nonidentification Role in the International System

Ben-Gurion's dedication to the security of the state formed the basis of his grand strategy for international politics. One principle of that doctrine was insuring the support of at least one great power during the struggle for the state and then for state survival. However, Israel succeeded in securing the support of both great powers during its emergence. In order to maintain the support of both powers, Israel adopted the nonalignment or "nonidentification" role.[16] According to Sandler (1993: 110), the reason for the nonaligned orientation is not a lack of desire to identify with any side in the global struggle between East and West, but a wish not to exclude any potential ally that could increase Israel's security. According to Bialer (1990: 14), Foreign Minister Sharett referred to this role as a policy of "knocking on any door." Sharett viewed nonalignment as a practical necessity (Bialer 1990: 24). The fundamental tendency of Israel, which would remain hidden until the opportune time, was an orientation clearly leaning toward the West. In order to implement the nonaligned role, Ben-Gurion rejected domestic calls for exclusive alignment with Britain, the United States, or the Soviet Union.

Bialer (1990: 206–207) argues that there were five reasons for the policy of nonidentification, in addition to security considerations. First, Israel felt a sense of responsibility for the Jewish people scattered throughout both major blocs. Second, Israel acknowledged that both the United States and the Soviet Union had supported them in the sovereign state role. Third, Israel sincerely wished to refrain from encouraging rivalry between the great powers by identifying with one or the other. Fourth, Israel's leadership was motivated to keep peace within the ranks of its own labor movement. Finally, Israelis held an image of their role as "a people that shall dwell alone," unencumbered by entanglements that might prevent them from finding their own developmental path.

Let us examine the role location process for the nonaligned role (see Figure 5.2). First, what is the predisposition of structure (Player N) with

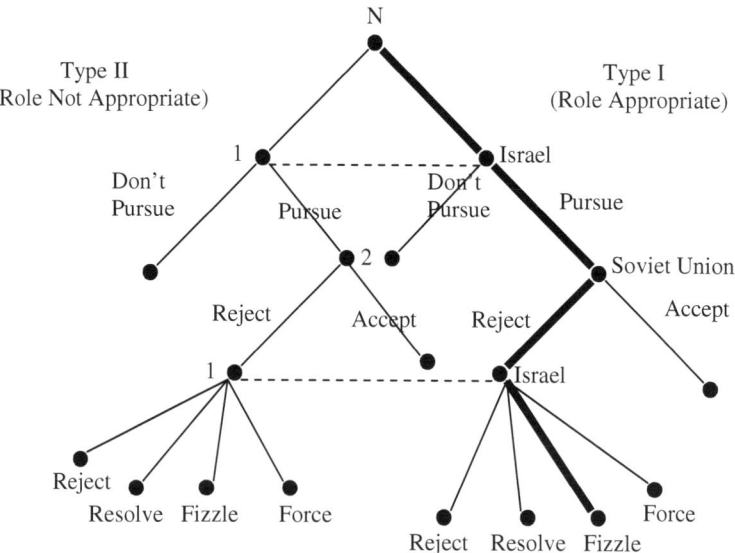

Figure 5.2　The Socialization Game for the Nonidentification Role

regard to the nonaligned role? The structure of the international system, represented by the United States and the Soviet Union, seemed initially predisposed to accept the nonaligned role. In February 1949, the Soviet ambassador to the United States explained to the Israeli ambassador to the United States that the Soviets had no intention of forcing Israel into its bloc. Further, the Soviets expected Israel to remain completely independent and that such independence ensured friendly relations between the two states. Israel was expected to follow a foreign policy of neutrality in the East-West conflict (Bialer 1990: 153).

The United States was certainly not making overt attempts to bring Israel into the Western bloc either. The United States imposed a strict embargo on the export of American arms to Israel until August 1949. The Truman Administration refused to lift the embargo during the war of independence for several reasons. First, Truman feared that a humiliating defeat of the Arabs might drive them into the Soviet's orbit. Second, the Arab states might retaliate with an oil embargo. And third, Britain might be prompted to renew delivery of weapons to Arab states. After this date, licenses were granted for the export of items with low military potential. The Truman Administration did not want to start an arms race in the region by delivering large quantities of weapons to Israel.[17]

Israel (Player 1) chose to pursue the nonaligned role. However, the Soviets (Player 2) rejected the nonaligned role by refusing to enact the role through economic, political, and cultural contacts. Between 1948 and late 1949, Russia had supplied Israel with fuel and wheat, which were both particularly hard to come by during the war. Israel attempted to expand economic relations with the Soviet Union thereafter, but to no avail. In February 1949, Israel received a loan from the United States for $100 million. Israel then approached the Soviets for similar financial credit. Again, the Israelis were rebuffed. Israeli trade with the Soviets dwindled and did not revive until 1954, when an agreement was struck to trade Soviet oil for Israeli citrus and cash (Bialer 1990: 124–131).[18]

Israel (Player 1) allows the nonaligned role to "fizzle." According to Brecher (1972: 5–6), from 1948 to 1950, Israel followed the path of nonidentification. After the decision to publicly support the United States on Korea in 1950, Israel moved toward *de facto* alignment with the West, and abandonment of nonidentification. Israel generally received the "cold shoulder" treatment from the Soviets after 1950. The pursuit of *aliyah* was at a dead end, economic cooperation was at a minimum, and the last attempt to arrange a meeting with senior Soviet leaders at the end of 1951 was flatly rejected by the Soviets. This was followed by the Prague trials at the end of 1952 and the "Doctors' Trials" of January 1953, which were both viewed by Israel as the reemergence of traditional anti-Semitism in Russia and Eastern Europe. The Soviets broke off diplomatic relations in February 1953 after a bomb exploded near their embassy in Israel. Soviet actions in the UN Security Council took a decided turn against Israel. The

Czech-Egyptian arms deal disclosed in 1955 sealed the rift between Israel and the Soviet Union.

Sandler (1993: 108–109) also argues that Israel's international orientation was largely a reflection of the personal orientation of Ben-Gurion, and he had long been a vocal critic of the Soviet Union. According to Sandler, Ben-Gurion despised the Soviet regime's treatment of its people, and Stalin in particular. Ben-Gurion perceived international communism as an instrument of the Soviet Union's global hegemony aspirations, with the Israeli Communist Party serving as an agent for pursuing that goal. Finally, Ben-Gurion decried the anti-Semitic practices of the Soviet Union. However, it is probable that Ben-Gurion would have continued to deal with the Soviets, despite his personal feelings, if he felt that they would be forthcoming with economic, political, or cultural assistance. When the Soviets failed to respond to Israeli overtures in these areas, Ben-Gurion felt he must turn to the United States and the West for aid.

Sandler (1993: 108) asks, "[I]f nonalignment was perceived as serving Israel's foreign policy interests, why did the Jewish state abandon this orientation in the midst of the Cold War when many of the new nations were adopting nonaligned orientations?" His answer is that nonalignment was a function of the global balance of power. Accordingly when Soviet and US interests were aligned in favor of Israel, it could adopt a nonaligned policy. Yet when Soviet and US interest diverged, it had to abandon the nonaligned policy. This truism masks an underlying feature of the international social system.

New states often seek a neutral or nonaligned role upon entry into the international system. This is essentially a policy of survival—the rejection of entanglements that may drag the state into war. The United States attempted to adopt the neutral role twice during its years as a novice state—recall President Washington's Farewell Address admonishing against "entangling alliances." Holsti's (1970: 290–291) analysis finds more states offering his "independent" role than the "faithful ally" role in the period of the mid-to-late 1960s. Most of these states are the newly independent African states. Indeed, the nonaligned movement took shape as many new states entered the system professing variants of the neutral role. As states mature in the system, they generally drop the neutral role in favor of a more active stance in world politics. The Switzerlands of the world are the exception, not the rule. The neutral role is probably coincident with the novice master status in the international system, but is not likely to be accepted or enacted upon transition to the other master roles (as the United States discovered before both world wars).

In terms of social identity, the nonidentification role did not have much time to make an impact on Israel, as it was only pursued in earnest from 1948 to 1950. Thus, this role was low on the involvement dimension of social identity. Further, this role was not valued highly by the Soviets, nor by many actors in Israeli domestic society. Finally, the status of the nonidentification role probably led to confusion on the part of other international actors in terms of the expectations attached to the role.

Seeking the Role of Defender of the Faith in the International System

In addition to the goal of security as expressed in the nonaligned role, Ben-Gurion's grand strategy contained two other goals, according to Sandler (1993: 100–102). The most important goal was *aliyah* and *kibbutz galuyot* (Teveth 1985: 9; Brecher 1972: 258; Aronson 1978: 11).[19] The commitment to bringing the Jewish people "home" to Israel expresses itself in the role of defender of the faith. This role has been described in the US case with regard to ideological commitments and value systems like democracy and capitalism. In the Israeli case, defending the "faith" is more literal. Israel saw itself as the defender of the Jewish people and religion, especially after the close of World War II and the full disclosure of the Holocaust.

The *aliyah* also had strategic importance. The state of Israel had to be peopled in order to persist in a region with such hostile neighbors. Israel's foreign policy officials repeatedly stressed the need for mass *aliyah* from Eastern Europe in order to create and preserve the state of Israel in their discussion with Soviet officials. Israel felt that the Soviets and their Eastern bloc allies would continue to help the *aliyah* as they had prior to independence. The Soviets were not forthcoming with emigration. Israel raised the issue consistently between 1948 and 1951, when the Soviets explicitly rejected the request for increased Jewish emigration. Israel put aside the issue of *aliyah* for fear of reprisals against Jews in the Soviet Union (Bialer 1990: 68–77). Emigration from Eastern Europe proceeded at a slower pace, aided by bribes or "lubricating expenses" to governmental officials at all levels (Bialer 1990: 79).

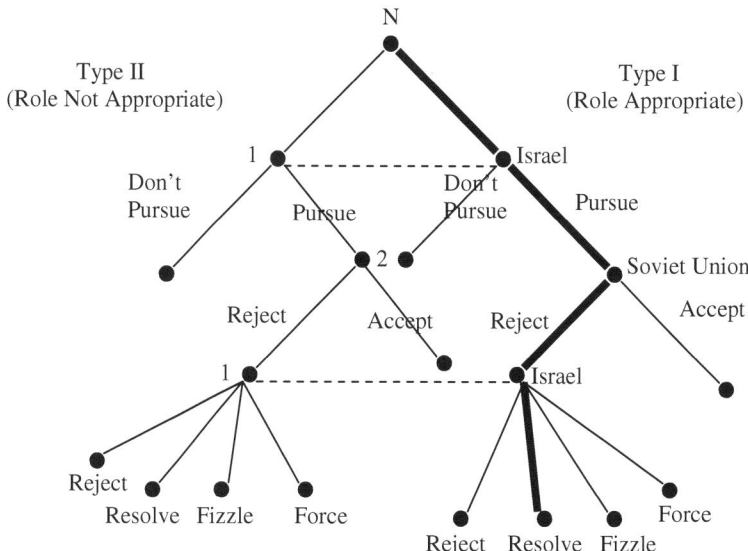

Figure 5.3 The Socialization Game for the Role of Defender of the Faith

In terms of the socialization game that models the role location process, it would appear at the outset that the international structure (Player N) was in favor of *aliyah* (see Figure 5.3). The United States had made efforts before Israeli independence to secure additional Jewish immigration to Palestine. Certainly, public opinion in the United States after World War II was favorable to a Jewish refuge in Palestine (Sheffer and Hofnung 1987: 15). The Soviets had also enabled the emigration of thousands of Jews from Eastern and Central Europe prior to independence. However, when Israel (Player 1) attempts to pursue this role, the Soviets (Player 2) reject it, by refusing to allow the emigration of approximately two million Russian Jews. Israel (Player 1) pursues the role with resolve certain that at some point the Soviets will be secure enough to discuss the future of their Jewish citizens. Israel also secures the emigration of some additional 200,000 Jews from Eastern Europe in exchange for dropping the subject of Russian Jews (Bialer 1990: 76).

Seeking the Internal Development Role, Act I

The third goal of Ben-Gurion's grand strategy was the creation of a Hebrew labor force (*avodah ivrit*) to settle the land and make the desert bloom. This goal is expressed through the internal development role. This role, according to Holsti (1970: 269), has little reference to any task or function in the international system. The main emphasis of this role is that the state's efforts should be directed toward problems of internal development, such as transforming the Jewish immigrants into settlers and the desert into a garden.

While this role has no international system referent, it may implicate other states in its region. This role brought Israel into a crisis with Syria over the Hula Valley in the Demilitarized Zone between them in early 1951.[20] The origins of this dispute lay in the continuing disagreement over control of the sources of the Jordan River. Israel planned to drain a lake and surrounding marshes in the DMZ, eradicate malaria in the area, reclaim about 15,000 acres of land for agriculture, and use the water to irrigate other parts of Israel. Syria claimed that the project violated the 1949 armistice agreement, which proclaimed the DMZ, and it appealed to the UN Security Council to force a halt to the project. Syria probably feared an increase in Israeli economic capabilities if the DMZ became productive under Israeli control.

Israel refused to halt work on the project, leading to an escalation of tensions as Syrian and Israeli civilians and military personnel exchanged fire over several weeks, leading to many casualties on both sides. The Security Council called for a ceasefire on May 8, and the withdrawal of military forces from the DMZ. The UN Mixed Armistice Commission (MAC) succeeded in getting the Israelis to agree to stop work in the area on May 30, except on Jewish-owned land. This compromise was not approved by Syria, so the issue simply lay dormant until the Jordan Waters issue resurfaced again in 1953.[21]

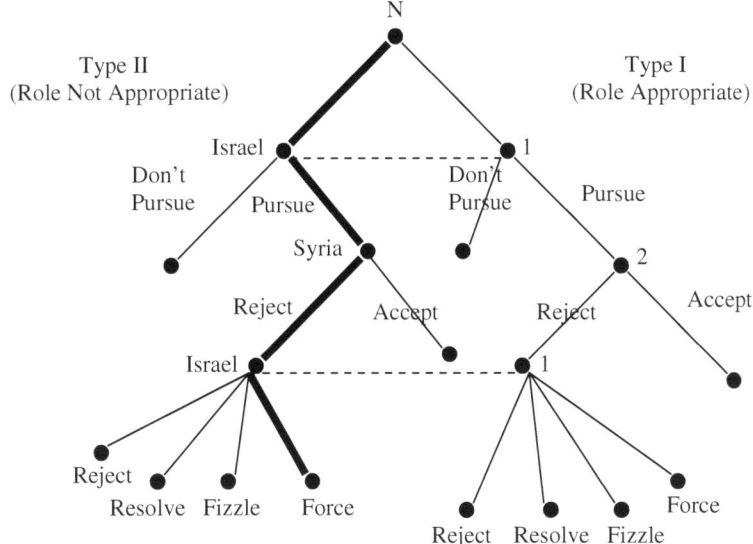

Figure 5.4 The Socialization Game for the Internal Development Role

In terms of the socialization game, the regional structure (Player N) was probably predisposed against the internal development role for Israel (see Figure 5.4). Any further development of Israeli productive capacities could disrupt the balance of power in the region. Israel (Player 1) chooses to pursue the role in the Hula Valley anyway. Syria (Player 2), acting as a peer socializer, rejects the Israeli role. Israel (Player 1) chooses to force the role, despite the impact that its internal development role had on its relations with its neighbors. Israel is able to force this role through the "compromise" the MAC accepted on Syria's behalf, which essentially allowed Israel to continue a modified version of the project.

Seeking the Role of Ally with the United States, Act I

Despite the resumption of diplomatic ties with the Soviets in mid-1953, Israel sought closer ties with the West, and in particular, the United States. Initially, Israel pursued a policy of "facts without pacts," to obtain economic and military support from the West (Bialer 1990: 247). Little support was forthcoming from the United States under this policy despite repeated requests for arms, so in late 1954, Ben-Gurion and Sharett agreed to pursue a security guarantee from the United States.[22] This was a clear signal that Israel had abandoned the nonidentification role. Ben-Gurion saw the main advantage of such a guarantee in the arms it would be able to procure from the United States. Such a guarantee would give Israel access to the types of weapons needed to counter those supplied by the Soviets, British, and French to the surrounding Arab states. Ben-Gurion also feared that a security guarantee would limit Israel's ability to act independently and even result in an American "quasi-mandate" over Israel.

It became clear in 1954, when the United States began providing military aid to Iraq, that the United States' main interest in the region was to win the support of the Arab states. It was also clear that the United States did not believe Israel had anything to offer in terms of defending the region against Soviet aggression. The United States offered several proposals for a regional defense organization that patently excluded Israeli participation. In July 1954, Israel offered its participation in a regional defense plan and was rebuffed by the United States. In September 1954, Ambassador Eban presented an Israeli request for a security guarantee to Secretary of State Dulles, while stating that he was not making a formal application. In October, Dulles informed Eban that the Israeli request had been rejected.

Sharett did not give up on hopes for a US security guarantee. On April 12, 1955, Sharett (1955) sent a telegram to Dulles requesting "a defense treaty between the United States and ourselves, such as would guarantee the territorial integrity of Israel and assure us an arms supply corresponding to that offered the Arab states." Dulles responded by noting that the United States had never entered into a security treaty outside of the Western Hemisphere, unless it was directed against communism. Further, Dulles thought Senate approval was unlikely unless a peace settlement in the region was achieved.

The arms deal that Nasser had worked out with the Soviets through Czechoslovakia, which was made public in September 1955, shocked Israel and threatened to disrupt the balance of power in the region. Ben-Gurion initiated plans for a preventive strike on Egypt. Dulles was aware that this was a possible Israeli response but was still determined not to give Israel a security guarantee. Sharett met with Dulles twice at the end of October 1955 to request an unconditional security guarantee from the United States. Dulles again rejected the security guarantee, as well as a request for arms, only suggesting that the United States would not permit the destruction of Israel.

During this time period, tensions with Israel's neighbors were mounting. Israel mounted a number of retaliatory raids against Egypt and Syria. These raids generally brought condemnation from the United States, France, and Britain. After the Kinneret raid in December 1955, these three states placed an arms embargo on Israel. However, on January 16, 1956, Foreign Minister Sharett again requested arms from Dulles, assuring that they would only be used for defensive purposes. Further, Sharett made it clear that Israel was no longer seeking a security guarantee from the United States, only arms. No answer was forthcoming from the United States. On February 29, Ben-Gurion appealed directly to Eisenhower for arms. Eisenhower believed that the Israeli's wanted arms in order to turn the United States into a "virtual ally," and rejected the request on April 30. Sharett resigned as Foreign Minister in light of this failure, and Ben-Gurion ordered an end to further arms procurement efforts from the United States. Dulles urged the

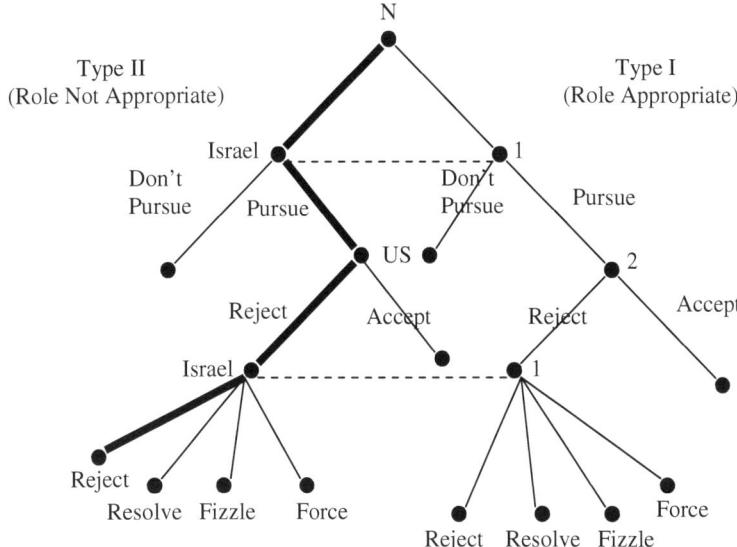

Figure 5.5 The Socialization Game for the Role of Ally to the United States

French and Italians to provide arms to Israel in May 1956. Israel had already switched its arms procurement efforts to France by that time.[23]

In terms of the socialization game, the structure of the international system (Player N) was probably predisposed against the role of ally with the United States. The United States would not commit to such an alliance if it meant driving the Arab states into the Soviet sphere of influence. The Soviets were apparently uninterested in Israel after 1950, having switched their influence attempts to the Arab states as well. The addition of Israel to either side of the global balance of power was viewed as fairly insignificant. However, Israel (Player 1) chooses to pursue the role. The United States (Player 2) rejects the role. Israel (Player 1) pursues the role with resolve. This version of the socialization game went through numerous iterations, before Israel was finally rejected in mid-1956 (see Figure 5.5). The United States socialized Israel out of this role conception over a period of about a year and a half. The failure of the United States to enact the allied role with Israel would have immediate consequences for Israeli foreign policy and alignment.

The Suez Crisis of 1956: The Role of Regional Collaborator?

The rejection of the allied role with the United States led Israel to pursue its security through a relationship with France.[24] In June 1956, Israel and France signed their first major arms deal, providing Israel with a number of modern jets and tanks. The French Defense Ministry was pleased with this transaction and pushed for closer relations with Israel. France and Israel began sharing intelligence on Egypt after Nasser nationalized the Suez Canal on July 26, 1956.[25] During September 1956, the French initiated discussions with Israel concerning possible Israeli participation in a joint Anglo-French operation against Egypt. The Israel Defense Forces (IDF) under Dayan had already begun the planning for a solo preemptive strike against Egypt in 1955, and the added support of the British and the French were welcomed in a conflict that seemed inevitable to Ben-Gurion. Further, Ben-Gurion was convinced that refusing the French proposal might endanger the flow of arms (Dayan 1966; Brecher 1975: 229–231, 258–259).

On October 22–23, 1956, at Sevres, France, Britain and Israel created a temporary military alliance. Israel's objectives were the capture of Sharm el-Sheikh at the tip of the Sinai Peninsula on the Strait of Tiran; the removal of the military threat posed by modern Soviet arms in Egypt; and the removal of the threat posed by the *Fedayeen*, who operated against Israel from the Gaza Strip. Israel invaded the Sinai on October 29, 1956. This attack provided the pretense for Britain and France to issue an ultimatum to Israel and Egypt to cease hostilities. Further, British and French troops would be deployed along the canal to ensure freedom of navigation. Egypt rejected the ultimatum as planned. Britain and France began their aerial assault of Egypt two days later.

On November 1, the United States initiated action in which the UN General Assembly voted to demand Israel to withdraw its forces from the Sinai and that Britain and France cease their air attack on Egypt. By November 2, Israel had succeeded in capturing the Gaza Strip, and by November 3, it had defeated the Egyptian army in the Sinai Peninsula. By November 5, the Israelis achieved their objective by occupying Sharm el-Sheikh. Also on November 5, Britain and France landed troops at Port Said and Port Faud in Egypt. However, on the same day, the Soviets cabled Britain, France, Israel, and the United States to warn that they would retaliate with missile attacks if the situation were not rectified.[26] Britain and France agreed to a ceasefire on November 6. Lacking French support, Israel announced on November 8 that it would evacuate the Sinai once arrangements for an international peacekeeping force were finalized.

The Suez Crisis marked a turning point in the Middle Eastern subsystem. British and French influence in the region declined after this point. It became clear to subsystem members that the dominant powers in the regional subsystem, as well as in the international system, were the United States and the Soviet Union. Both the United States and the Soviet Union rejected the Anglo-French and Israeli action in the Suez. Britain and France would not be allowed to act as great powers engaged in regional socialization after this point. Britain and France did not accomplish their goals of retaking the canal or of removing Nasser from Egypt; thus their socialization attempts upon Egypt failed. Further, the role of regional collaborator that France had altercast to Israel was also rejected by the United States and the Soviet Union.

The rejection of the regional collaborator role also demonstrates the influence that the international system began to exercise over the regional system. The regional role assigned to Israel was not acceptable when it attempted to achieve it in the international system. This role spilled over into the international system in the same way that Israel's internal development role spilled over into the regional system. France, Britain, and Israel did not anticipate the incompatibility of the regional collaborator role with the international system because they kept their plans secret. Role theory tells us that socializing activities can occur only if the novice's behavior is public and open to observation. If the United States and the Soviet Union had been aware of the plan, they may have attempted to deter the invasion; the deleterious impact on the French and British role conceptions may have been lessened; and Israel may have been encouraged to maintain its isolation.[27]

The socialization game proceeds at two levels. First, at the level of the regional system, the structure is disposed against the role of regional collaborator for Israel. France altercasts Israel in the role of regional collaborator, which Israel accepts. At the level of the international system, the structure of the system (Player N) is disposed against the role of regional collaborator (see Figure 5.6). Secretary Dulles had made it clear in late 1955 that an Israeli preemptive attack on Egypt would damage US-Israeli relations. The Soviets clearly supported Egypt. Israel (Player 1) chooses to pursue the role by invading the Sinai. The United States (Player 2) rejects the role by organizing UN action calling for a ceasefire in the Sinai. Israel (Player 1) ultimately rejects the role by agreeing to suspend the operation and withdraw its forces from the Sinai and Gaza.

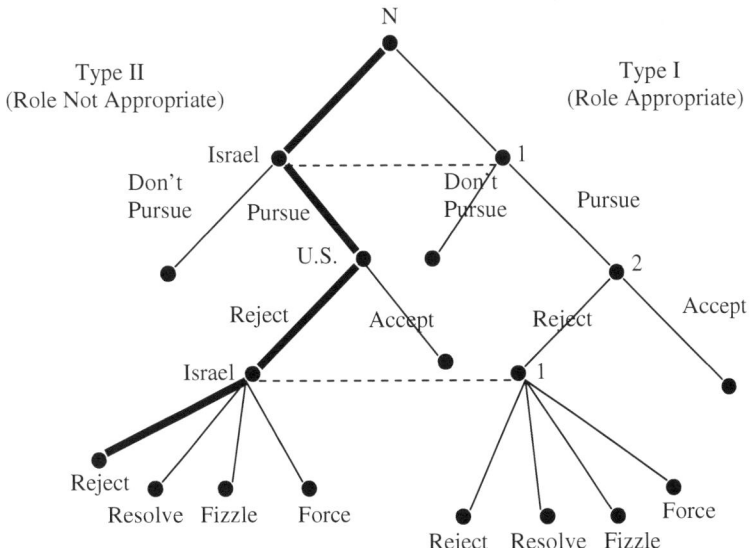

Figure 5.6   The Socialization Game for the Achieved Role of Regional Collaborator

After 1956, the regional subsystem became crucial to the Cold War between the United States and the Soviet Union. President Eisenhower asked the US Congress on January 5, 1957, to authorize the "employment of the armed forces of the United States to secure and protect the territorial integrity and political independence of such nations, requesting such aid, against overt armed aggression from any nation controlled by International Communism" (Einsenhower 1957). The short-lived Eisenhower Doctrine provided some hope to Israel that it would now be treated as an equal to the Arab states by the United States. The Suez Crisis also marked the first war fought by Israel since its independence. Once again, Israel demonstrated that its military capabilities were more than a match for Egypt.

This war is often described in terms of a preventive war designed to redress an imbalance in capabilities (Sandler 1993: 123–129). Indeed, the war addressed the capabilities issue. But further, the Israeli involvement in the Suez Crisis also demonstrates Israel's search for an appropriate regional and international role. It marks the transition to the small member state status for Israel in the international system because it has shed the nonidentification role from its early years of independence.

SMALL MEMBER STATE STATUS, 1956–1967

Theoretically, we expect that small states will have moderate capabilities. They will begin to have a greater number of roles in the regional and international systems. These roles will include a mix of ascribed and achieved roles. Small states will also be subject to socializing pressures at the regional and international level.

Enacting the US Roles of Bipolarity for the Middle East?

After the pronouncement of the Eisenhower Doctrine in January 1957, considerable debate arose in Israel about an appropriate response.[28] After Congress approved the Doctrine, as well as associated economic and military assistance amounting to $200 million, on March 9, Israel expected that it might receive some of the monies. The Israelis were already receiving approximately $20–$25 million for the fiscal year 1957 from the United States, but there was some expectation that the Doctrine's funds might contribute another $5–$10 million if Israel came out in support of the Doctrine. However, the US State Department informed Israel that it would receive none of the $200 million, and future aid would be given only for the fight against communism.

At the same time that the United States told Israel it would not receive any additional funds, it also demanded to know if Israel would accept the Eisenhower Doctrine. The main concern about supporting the Doctrine was the fate of immigration for the Jews remaining in Eastern Europe and the Soviet

Union—Israel had a strong commitment to its defender of the faith role. However, Israel also feared that remaining outside of the Doctrine would give the Arab States an advantage in the region. Israel pressed the United States for a joint statement, which would avoid the anticommunist emphasis of the Doctrine. The United States would not acquiesce to the demand, and Israel eventually issued a separate statement stating that Israel "opposed aggression against the territorial integrity and political independence of any country" (Levey 1997: 88).

This watered-down response to the Eisenhower Doctrine was viewed as a refusal by Israel to play its part in the US role enactment of bloc leader, liberator, and defender of the faith in the Middle East (see Chapter 4). Israel was probably justified in refusing to enact these roles, as the United States would not apply the Eisenhower Doctrine to Syria in 1957, which gave rise in Israel to fears of Soviet-backed Syrian aggression. Israeli leaders believed that the United States would not use force to back the Doctrine. Thus, full commitment to enacting the roles of bipolarity would bring little in added security to Israel and would risk alienating the Soviets, who controlled the future of *aliyah*.

Seeking the Role of Ally with the United States, Act II

Israeli concerns for security in light of a perceived growing Soviet threat in the Middle East prompted overtures toward NATO in late 1957 (Levey 1997: 90–94). Ben-Gurion was somewhat reluctant to pursue this course of action, yet the benefits in terms of arms procurement convinced him to allow it to proceed. Israel planned to rely on a concept within NATO's Declaration of Common Purpose, which suggested that Western states pool their resources and establish ties between NATO and other friendly governments. Israel wanted the United States to present its case before the upcoming December NATO convention. This would include arms sales to Israel and training to raise the IDF to the quality of European armies. However, the United States refused additional requests for arms, refused to guarantee Israel's security, and refused to seek Israeli membership in NATO. The socialization game that models this attempt at the allied role is the same as that presented in Figure 5.5.

Seeking the Internal Development Role, Act II

The ongoing dispute over the use of the Jordan River waters that first flared up in 1951 again became an issue in December 1963.[29] Since the Hula Valley crisis in 1951, several plans had been drawn up to share the resources of the Jordan between Israel and its Arab neighbors. Unfortunately, none of these plans were ever accepted by all parties. In 1959, Israel began the National Water Carrier plan for transporting water from Lake Tiberias to the Negev. Arab states felt that this water scheme would endanger their security because Israel would be able to settle more immigrants in the Negev, thus augmenting potential Israeli capabilities. Israel announced in December 1963 that the plan would be implemented despite Arab objections.

Nasser called a summit under the auspices of the Arab League in January 1964. It was decided that instead of going to war with Israel over the issue, the Arab states would divert the three tributaries of the Jordan.[30] However, under pressure from the United Nations, the United States, and the Soviet Union, the Arabs allowed Israel's plan to commence. The socialization game follows the model described in Figure 5.4 for the original internal development role. Once again, Israel was able to force this internal role (with external repercussions) despite the objections of the Arab states. Those external repercussions were great indeed. As Bailey (1990: 189) notes, Odd Bull, the head of the UN Truce Organization suggested that "the result was the 1967 war, a war for the control of water resources . . . The war did not come as a surprise."

The Six-Day War of 1967: Enacting the Sovereign State Role by Force, Act I

Tensions along the Israeli-Syrian border had been increasing since the increase in Palestinian guerrilla attacks in late 1966.[31] On April 7, 1967, Israel downed six Syrian MIG fighters in a battle near the border. The Soviets passed phony information regarding a massing of Israeli troops on its northern border to Egypt and Syria. On May 14, Nasser announced that Egyptian forces were on maximum alert, and he sent combat units into the Sinai. Nasser ordered the UN Emergency Force out of the Sinai. Syria, Jordan, and Iraq also began to mobilize their armies. On May 22, Egypt ordered a blockade of Israel in the Gulf of Aqaba. Nasser stated publicly that Palestine must be liberated and Israel destroyed.

The UN Security Council met in emergency session, but its efforts were met with the Soviet veto. President Johnson urged the Israelis not to engage in a preemptive strike but offered little additional support. On May 30, Jordan signed a defense pact with Egypt, which allowed Iraqi troops to enter Jordanian territory in the event of hostilities, and placed its troops under Egyptian military authority.

Israel launched a preventive strike on June 5, 1967. The Israeli air force destroyed virtually all of Egypt's planes on the ground, as well as those of the other Arab states. Israeli ground troops defeated the Egyptian army and seized the Gaza Strip and the entire Sinai Peninsula. Israel had asked Jordan to stay out of the war, yet due to misleading information fed to it by Egypt, Jordan joined the war it thought Egypt was winning. Israel then seized the Old City of Jerusalem and the entire West Bank. Israel also waged an intense battle to capture the Golan Heights from Syria. By June 10, 1967, the war was over.

Israel tripled the size of its territory from the 1949 borders. Certainly, this victory brought a sense of security and "strategic depth" to Israel. It also brought a sense of self-confidence and a transition to major member status. UN Resolution 242 brought a diplomatic end to the war in November 1967. The Resolution called on Israel to return occupied territories and declared that states in the region had the right to exist in peace within secure and recognized borders. The Resolution also discussed freedom of passage through international waterways and a solution to the Palestinian refugee problem.

The Resolution was accepted by Israel, Egypt, and Jordan, but not by Syria. This marked the first implicit acceptance of Israel's existence and the possibility for a negotiated settlement to the Israeli-Arab conflict. However, as a result of the war, the Soviet Union, Bulgaria, Hungary, Czechoslovakia, Poland, and Yugoslavia severed relations with Israel. This meant that the goal of *aliyah* (and the role of defender of the faith) would be difficult to enact in the near term.

In terms of the socialization game, Israel sought to maintain the role of the sovereign state. The structure of the international system (Player N) is predisposed in favor of this role, despite the Soviet's nudging of Nasser into action against Israel (see Figure 5.7). Israel (Player 1) seeks to pursue this role with a preemptive strike against Egypt. Egypt (Player 2) rejects the sovereign state role, bringing a coalition of Arab states to bear on Israel. Israel (Player 1) forces the role on Egypt and the rest of the coalition with a decisive victory in the Six-Day War.

Sandler (1993: 129–133) argues that the 1967 war was another case of a preemptive war to redress the balance of power. Egypt's military

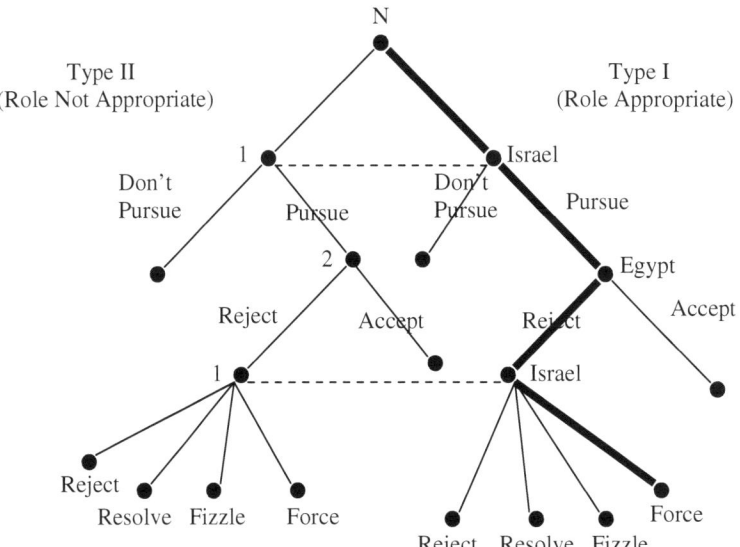

Figure 5.7 The Socialization Game for Enforcing the Role of the Sovereign State

capabilities alone were roughly equal to Israel's at the time, but with the addition of Jordan, Syria, and Iraq in the coalition, they far exceeded Israel. It is difficult to see how the small state of Israel intended to rectify the balance of power in a war with a coalition of vastly greater capabilities. Instead, it makes more sense to view Israel's preemptive strike as the best chance for reducing those capabilities as much as possible in the goal of preserving the state in a war that was inevitable given Nasser's posturing. As a small state, with no alliance partners, Israel had few options in the system—it could not hope to balance the capabilities of the coalition, nor could it hope to hide.[32]

However, Israel's virtual destruction of Egypt's armed forces went beyond maintaining the balance in the region, or even the balance between itself and Egypt. Israel's preemptive strike destroyed the balance of capabilities in the region. As Kerr (1971: 129) describes the situation among the rival Arab states, "[T]here could hardly be a competition for prestige when there was no prestige remaining." Certainly, Israel wanted to prevent an Egyptian drive for regional hegemony accompanied by the bandwagoning of its smaller neighbor states. However, by eliminating Egyptian capabilities, Israel would appear to be making a bid for regional hegemony itself. There is no evidence to suggest that this is the case. Instead, Israel's pursuit of the sovereign state role, and its desire to have this role acknowledged by its Arab neighbors were the impetus behind the Six-Day War.

MAJOR MEMBER STATE STATUS, 1967–PRESENT

According to the theory developed in Chapter 3, we should expect that major member states will have a greater array of well-developed roles, which will on balance include more achieved than ascribed roles. The greater capabilities that major members have is often a function of their natural endowments, but this is not the case with Israel. Israel's capabilities were enhanced by its ability to secure military and economic aid from other major and great powers and by its ability to innovate its internal organization to make the best use of those capabilities.

Major members are responsible for socializing emerging states and small states in their subsystem. However, major members cannot act with impunity, as they are still members of an international system in which great powers exercise the same socializing powers on them that they exercise *vis-à-vis* subsystem members.

After Israel defeated Egypt and Syria, it felt that it had grown into the boundaries required for its security. The IDF had proven itself as a superior fighting force. Israel felt secure in its position in the regional subsystem. That security was accomplished by the defeat of a regional leader—Egypt under Nasser. Under ordinary circumstances, Israel should have assumed the role of regional leader. However, given the "outsider" nature of a Jewish state in a predominantly Arab and Islamic region, that role was not sought. Instead, Israel assumed the role of a major member of the system, with a bias toward the status quo. The enactment of this role varied in terms of its active or passive enactment. Israel defended itself actively along the canal against Egypt during the War of Attrition. However, it was able to turn down a number of proposals to negotiate a peaceful settlement, which had the effect of maintaining the status quo in favor of Israel.[33]

In the aftermath of the 1967 war, balancing became the immediate concern of Egypt, given the overwhelming Israeli victory and increase in strategic territory. The Soviets began to quickly resupply Egypt with equipment and advisors (Rubinstein 1977; McLane 1973). Egypt began bombarding Israeli positions along the canal in late 1968, provoking reprisal from Israel. Soon, the exchange of artillery and air raids developed into the War of Attrition (1969–1970).[34] During this time period, the United States finally began to sell Israel modern weapons, including Phantom jets, and the Soviet Union similarly supplied Egypt, introducing a sophisticated missile air defense system. The United States was able to negotiate a ceasefire based on Secretary of State Rogers's Plan "B" on August 7, 1970.

The plan called upon Israel to withdraw from the occupied territories in return for recognition, a ninety-day ceasefire in the canal zone, and resumption of UN mediator Jarring's mission to secure a negotiated peace. Egypt used the opportunity of the ceasefire to move its surface-to-air missiles into the canal zone, delaying the Jarring talks until December. Before talks resumed in December, Nasser was sidelined with the crisis in Jordan between King Hussein and the Palestinian Liberation Organization (PLO), and he died a few hours after concluding a ceasefire between the two sides on September 27. He was succeeded by Sadat, who proposed his own Initiative for Peace, in which an Israeli withdrawal from the canal would lead to a peace agreement between Egypt and Israel.

Israel refused to withdraw to the 1949 armistice lines as proposed by Jarring. Discussion of a pullback on one or both sides of the canal with its reopening occurred between Israel, Egypt, the UN mediator, and the United States. However, nothing much was accomplished during 1971. Israel probably preferred the status quo at this point. Israel had secure and defensible borders and a steady flow of US arms. However, at a summit meeting in Moscow in May 1972, Nixon and Brezhnev agreed to try and achieve a "military relaxation" in the Middle East, which would essentially freeze the situation.

The freeze was not particularly troublesome to Israel, which currently enjoyed a strategic advantage, but it put Egypt in a difficult position. The US–Soviet détente meant that Egypt was not getting the weapons from the Soviets that Sadat was requesting. In July 1972, Sadat expelled the 21,000 Soviet advisors and personnel in Egypt. However, instead of abandoning Egypt, the Soviets stepped up arms deliveries to both Egypt and Syria after this point, and the United States also continued supplying Israel.

The Yom Kippur War of 1973: Enacting the Sovereign State Role by Force, Act II

Despite a public declaration by Sadat in April 1973 that Egypt was preparing for war, Israel seemed somewhat surprised by the war that was launched on October 6.[35] The Israeli leaders were probably influenced by the notion that they had defensible borders, strategic depth, and military superiority, and that the Arab states had not attempted a first strike since 1948. Vertzberger (1990: 55) argues that the satisfaction with the status quo and the arrogant self-assurance of the Israelis prohibited the search for information that might be inconsistent with their view of the Arab states. Sadat's warnings were underestimated or ignored (Brecher 1980; Perlmutter 1975). When it became clear that Egypt would attack, Secretary of State Kissinger warned Israel not to launch a preemptive attack because it would risk the assistance and goodwill of the United States.

Egypt crossed the canal, and Syria entered the Golan Heights on October 7. The Syrian advance evidently caused the Israeli leadership to adopt the "Sampson Option"—the use of nuclear weapons to protect the coastal plain. Israel was able to turn the tide of the battle against Syria by October 10, advancing into Syrian territory. Israel's nuclear weapons were returned to storage on October 14. On the same day, Israel defeated Egypt in a tank battle. On October 16, Israel crossed the canal. On October 22, both sides accepted a ceasefire, which was subsequently violated by both sides. The United States was concerned that the Soviets might intervene militarily, but on October 26, a US-Soviet Security Council resolution calling for a ceasefire was accepted by all parties.

The socialization game for maintaining the role of the sovereign state is the same pattern as found in Figure 5.7 for the 1967 war. The structure of the international system (Player N) is still disposed favorably toward the role, with the Soviets and the United States arming both sides prior to the 1973 war. Israel (Player 1) pursues the sovereign state role by defending itself during the War of Attrition and ensuing stalemate. Egypt (Player 2) breaks the stalemate by rejecting Israel as a sovereign state and leading Syria into a war to destroy the state. Israel (Player 1) forces the role on Egypt and Syria by repelling the invaders.

Israel nearly lost this war and suffered high casualties and losses of military equipment. Arab losses in manpower and equipment were even higher. The 1973 war shook the sense of invulnerability Israel had attained as a result of the 1967 war. Vertzberger (1990: 293) argues that the status attributed to Israel after the Six-Day War was higher than its deserved status, based on capabilities. After the Six-Day War, Israel adopted the attributed status as a reflection of its real power and position. Vertzberger calls this a case of status self-ascription. As such, it led to an inflated sense of security and self-assurance.

However, Israel was not dislodged from this status, whether self-ascribed or not, during either the War of Attrition or the Yom Kippur War. But in order to maintain the capability dimension of the major member status, Israel became more dependent upon the United States in terms of military and economic aid, especially in light of the Oil Embargo. During the war, Nixon ordered an airlift of approximately $825 million worth of supplies for Israel. This assistance was part of a $2.2 billion appropriation approved by Nixon to cover the costs of the airlift and provide subsequent military aid to Israel. This amount was one and a half times greater than the total amount of aid the United States had given Israel since its emergence (Gazit 1987: 111).

Seeking the Role of Ally with the United States, Act III

Nixon's airlift and subsequent assistance amounted to the security guarantee from the United States that Israel had long been seeking. The actual security guarantee came during the Ford Administration in 1974, when a joint memorandum of agreement was issued by Kissinger and Israeli Foreign Minister Allon. In the memorandum the United States pledged to be "fully responsive . . . on an ongoing and long-term basis to Israel's military equipment and other defense requirements, to its energy requirements and to its economic needs" (Gazit 1987: 114). Further, Israel was placed at the top of the list of foreign countries in the supply of US arms by President Ford. The IDF grew rapidly in quality and quantity during the Ford Administration.

The allied role—though not a formal military alliance—was a long time in coming to Israel. The United States guaranteed weapons and security to Israel as a result of the direct impact of bipolarity on the region. Despite the Nixon Doctrine's overall policy of retrenchment, aid to Israel was expanded dramatically during his presidency. Israel did fulfill Nixon's requirement that a state threatened by communism provide the manpower for its defense. In effect, the War of Attrition and the 1973 war were like so many other proxy wars between the United States and the Soviet Union. The United States and the Soviet Union were not actively engaged in fighting, yet they provided both sides with the arms necessary to continue the struggle.

Israel had been trying to achieve the allied role since the mid-1950s. Both Presidents Truman and Eisenhower had turned them down flatly because of the desire to maintain friendly relations with the Arab states of the region. Kennedy and Johnson both increased arms sales to Israel but were preoccupied with the Soviet threat in Latin America and Southeast Asia. It was not until the United States began to pull out of Vietnam that Nixon could focus on the Soviet threat in the Middle East. Only then, would the United States agree to enact the allied role with Israel. This basic policy, forged during the global turmoil caused by the 1973 war, would remain constant through succeeding US administrations.

In terms of social identity, the allied role with the United States became a large part of Israeli identity. In terms of involvement, Israel had spent a great deal of time and effort attempting to secure this role from the United

States since it abandoned the nonidentification role. The status dimension of the allied role elevated Israel to a place of importance among the members of the regional and international systems. This role was not valued highly among the other Arab states of the region. However, it did not particularly damage US relations with the Arab states. In fact, the United States would remain committed to brokering a peace between Israel and the Arab states, as evidenced by the Camp David Accords sponsored by President Carter.

Seeking the Internal Development Role, Act III

In peace talks with Egypt in 1977, control of the West Bank was an important issue. Begin's proposal was to allow the Arab population cultural autonomy and self-rule under Israeli control.[36] Begin had envisioned Jewish settlements in the West Bank for quite some time. Begin had supported the Gush Emunim efforts to settle in Judea and Samaria against the wishes of Rabin's government in 1975. Gush Emunim was quite successful and created twenty-one communal settlements in these areas in a period of four years. Begin had agreed to halt settlements in his talks with Carter and Sadat, but, just prior to the signing of the treaty, Begin announced that he intended only a three-month moratorium on settlements. Despite the objections of Carter and Sadat, the peace treaty was signed in 1979.

Minister of Agriculture Sharon began to seek the creation of settlements just outside of the major Israeli urban areas. The bedroom communities he created allowed Israelis to build homes for the price of an apartment in the

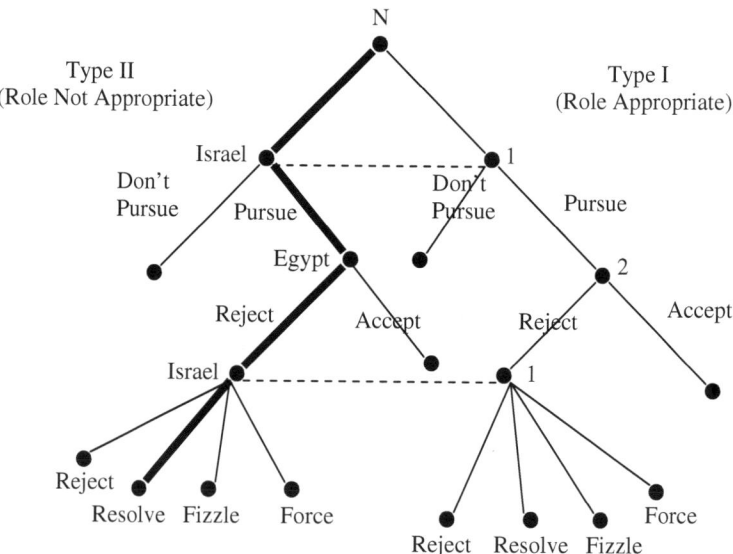

Figure 5.8   The Socialization Game for the Internal Development Role III

city and served to create "facts" on the ground in the West Bank. Whereas the number of Jewish settlements in the West Bank stood at twenty-seven in 1967, with the majority in the Jordan Valley, overall settlement numbers reached 118 by 1986, with the majority in Judea and Samaria.

Thus, the internal development role has external consequences for the regional and international systems. Ben-Gurion's original goal of settlement to make the desert bloom was realized by Begin and Sharon's actions. However, the settlements also served the political goal of retaining control over the West Bank during this time period.

According to the socialization game, the structure of the international system (Player N) is disposed against the internal development role (see Figure 5.8). The United States under Carter was worried that the settlement drive in the West Bank might derail the peace process. Israel (Player 1) pursues the role by expanding the settlements. Egypt (Player 2) rejects the role by objecting to Begin's false promise to halt settlements. Israel (Player 1) pursues the role with resolve by maintaining settlements in the West Bank.

Seeking the Role of Regional Protector, Act I

Israel began to assert itself as a major power in the subsystem after the 1973 war. Israel sought the role of regional protector in response to a French-built nuclear reactor in Iraq.[37] Saddam Hussein secured a French commitment to build a large nuclear reactor for "research" in 1975, just as they had done for the Israelis at Dimona in 1957 (Levey 1997: 124–126). Israel attempted to derail the project from 1976 to 1979 by exerting diplomatic pressure on France. In 1979, a reactor built for Iraq was damaged in a bomb attack at the Marseilles harbor. Prime Minister Begin expressed many times that a nuclear weapon in the hands of any Arab state posed a threat to Israel's existence.

In January 1981, France announced that the Osirak reactor would be fully operational by July 14. The Israeli Air Force destroyed the Osirak reactor on June 7, 1981. Israel's action amounted to the adoption of a regional protector role. The regional protector role implies special leadership responsibilities on a regional or issue-specific area (Holsti 1970: 261–262). Israel placed itself in the role of determining the nuclear status of states in the Middle Eastern region. The regional protector role is often adopted primarily for the state's own security. The United States adopted the regional protector role in Latin America because it felt that European encroachment in the area would eventually threaten its security. Israel similarly felt that the possession of nuclear weapons by other states in the region would threaten its security, in addition to the overall balance of power in area.

In terms of the socialization game, the structure of the international system (Player 1) is against the Israeli role (see Figure 5.9). Israel (Player 1) pursues the role through diplomatic means. France (Player 2) rejects the role. Israel (Player 2) forces the role by destroying the reactor. The reaction

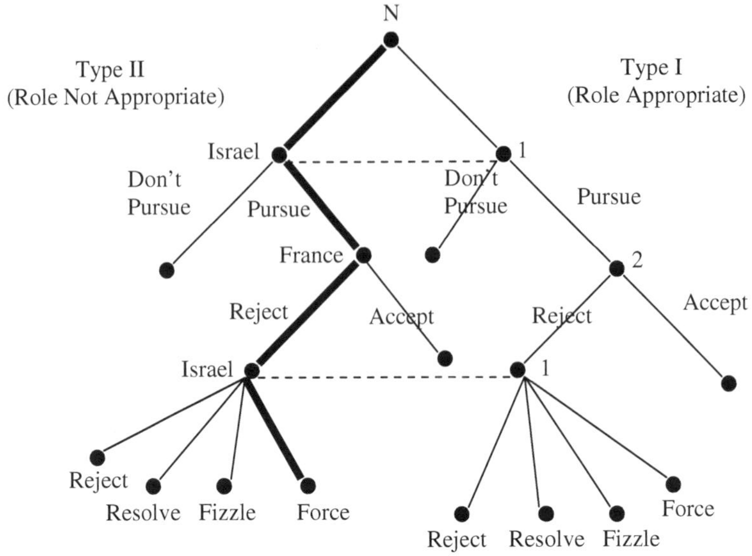

Figure 5.9   The Socialization Game for Role of Regional Protector

by the audience of interested states was overwhelmingly negative. The United States, the Soviet Union, France, the United Nations, and others all condemned Israel for this preemptive strike on the following day. The United States even delayed delivery of F-16s to Israel, and approved sending AWACS aircraft to Saudi Arabia. It would not be until the Gulf War that these same states would reverse their judgment about Israel's destruction of Iraq's nuclear reactor.

In December 1981, Defense Minister Sharon issued a national security doctrine that named Israel's strategic threats and outlined strategies to deal with them.[38] According to Sharon, the three main enemies that threatened Israel's existence were the PLO, the radical Arab states, and the Soviet Union. This was the first instance in which the PLO was accorded the status of a strategic threat, despite the fact that the PLO's intentions had always been taken seriously.

This was also the first time that the Soviet Union had been labeled a strategic threat to Israel's existence. Sharon's comments on the Soviet Union were prompted by the recent invasion of Afghanistan and increased Soviet activity in Africa. Sharon's anti-Soviet stance echoed the recent "American-Israeli Memorandum of Understanding," which clearly allied the United States and Israel against further Soviet penetration of the region.

Sharon's strategies for dealing with these threats included a technological and qualitative superiority in conventional forces *vis-à-vis* its neighbors. It also required Israel to maintain "the ability to prevent the disruption of the territorial military status in neighboring countries" (Sandler 1993: 215).

Sharon's strategy also included the prevention of its neighbors from acquiring nuclear capabilities.

The threats and strategies for dealing with them clearly indicated that Israel had adopted the role of regional protector. Israel intended to enact this role unilaterally, just as the United States enacted its role of regional protector in Latin America. As we have seen, Israel had already employed this role in its decision to destroy the Osirak reactor in Iraq. Israel would then justify its intervention in Lebanon based on the strategic threat of the PLO.

The War in Lebanon: Seeking the Role of Regional Protector, Act II

Israel invaded Lebanon on June 5, 1982, purportedly in response to a terrorist attack on the Israeli Ambassador in London.[39] However, the "Peace for Galilee" operation had been planned for quite some time. The stated aims of the intervention in Lebanon were the removal of PLO artillery and the destruction of its military infrastructure along the Israeli border. Thus, the intervention was justified according to Sharon's doctrine. However, Israel's true aim was to promote to power a Maronite government friendly to Israel. This goal would facilitate the political and military destruction of the PLO, with a subsequent decline in its influence in the West Bank. It would also facilitate the signing of a peace treaty between Lebanon and Israel—the second such treaty with an Arab state.

Israel planned its invasion in concert with Maronite Christians in Lebanon, including Bashir Jemayel. When Jemayel's Maronites failed to conquer West Beirut by June 13 as planned, the IDF held Beirut under siege. The presidential elections took place on August 23, two days after the PLO had agreed to evacuate Beirut. President Jemayel refused Begin's demand to sign a peace treaty, explaining that it would cause division within Lebanon and alienate it from its Arab neighbors. After Jemayel was assassinated, Sharon ordered the conquest of Beirut and the destruction of the remaining PLO elements in the capital. This tactic succeeded in persuading President Amin Jemayel to sign a peace treaty with Israel in May 1983. However, Jemayel later canceled it in March 1984 under pressure from Syria and Saudi Arabia.

After the multinational force that replaced Israel in Beirut withdrew, the IDF came under renewed attack from the PLO and the pro-Syrian Druse and Shiites. Prime Minister Peres, who came to power in 1984, decided to withdraw after establishing a security zone in southern Lebanon. This war marked the second occasion in which Israel attempted to assert its role as regional protector. It sought to increase its own security by eliminating the PLO threat and installing a friendly regime in a neighboring Arab state.

How was this role location process received by the relevant audience? The socialization game proceeds in two stages. First, the structure of the regional system (Player N) is disposed against Israeli intervention (as modeled in Figure 5.9). Israel (Player 1) pursues its regional role by invading Lebanon. Syria (Player 2) rejects the role by engaging in a costly air battle

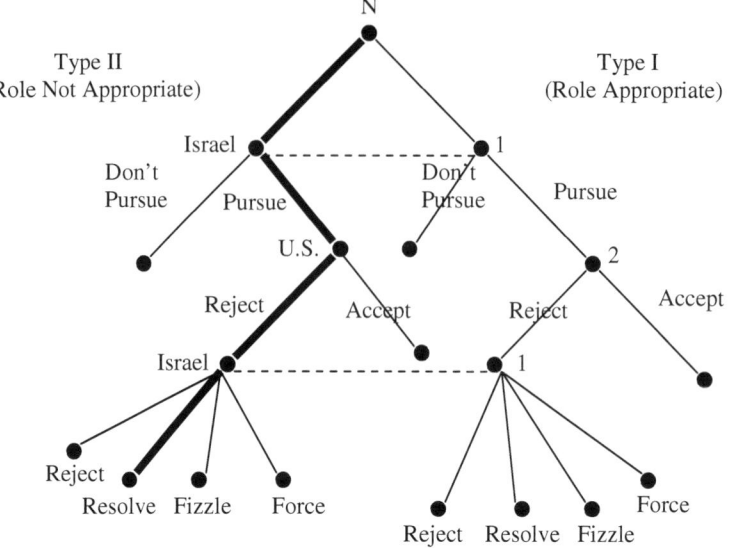

Figure 5.10   The Socialization Game for Role of Regional Protector II

with Israel soon after the IDF entered Lebanon. Israel (Player 1) forces the role on Syria by remaining in Lebanon and pursuing its war aims.

The structure of the international system (Player N) is also disposed against the Israeli intervention (see Figure 5.10). The United States, the Soviet Union, and the United Nations all condemned the Israeli action. The United States quickly became involved by negotiating the ceasefire with Syria on June 11, 1982. The United States suspended military aid to Israel on July 19. The Soviet Union sent military aid to Syria to replace its losses in the fighting. However, Israel (Player 1) pursues its role. The United States (Player 2) rejects the role by heading a multinational force that occupies Beirut and facilitates the withdrawal of PLO forces. Israel (Player 1) pursues its role with resolve. The multination force soon left Beirut due to heavy casualties (such as bombing of the US Marine barracks). Israel occupied Beirut, forced the signing of a peace treaty, and then withdrew to its security zone due to mounting casualties and domestic calls for an end to the war.

Seeking the Defender of the Faith Role, Act II

In the spirit of the New World Order that President Bush announced in light of the Gulf War, Gorbachev reestablished diplomatic relations with Israel in October 1991. As early as 1990, Gorbachev had started to accelerate Jewish emigration to Israel. Between 1990 and 1995, approximately 650,000 Soviet Jews arrived in Israel. The impact upon an Israeli population of only four million was enormous. Many Israelis saw this situation as a renewal of Israel's historic goal of *aliyah*. Others saw the immense financial drain that would be caused by absorbing the new arrivals. The Israeli government chose to pursue the defender of the faith role. In May 1991, Israel launched "Operation Solomon" to airlift 15,000 Ethiopian Jews (Bickerton and Klausner 1998: 249).

In terms of the socialization game, the structure of the international system is disposed in favor of the role (Player N), despite Palestinian fears that increased immigration would threaten the status of their future homeland. Both the United States and the Soviets considered slowing the pace of emigration to Israel at the Bush-Gorbachev summit in 1990. However, Shamir authorized two more Jewish settlements in the occupied territories to assert that Israeli citizens would live where they pleased. Israel (Player 1) pursues the role, and the Soviet Union (Player 2) accepts the role by continuing the flow of immigrants.

Enacting the Sovereign State Role with Nonstate Actors

Any discussion of Israeli foreign policy would be remiss without mentioning its relations with the PLO. The main reason that the PLO and the Palestinians have not been mentioned much so far is that this research is concerned primarily with interstate interaction. However, the PLO, as a nonstate actor, has influenced the course of interstate interaction in the Middle Eastern subsystem. Much of the interaction with the PLO has challenged Israel's role as a sovereign state. I will examine Israeli-PLO interaction through this lens.

One result of Israel's War of Independence was the displacement of approximately 700,000 Palestinian Arabs from their homes.[40] The Palestinians were dispersed into Israel's Arab neighbors, with the majority going to the West Bank and Jordan. Approximately, 150,000 Palestinians remained in Israeli territory. The PLO was founded in May 1964. It did not really exert independence from its host governments until after Israel captured the West Bank, the Sinai, and the Gaza Strip in the 1967 war, when approximately 1.3 million Palestinians were under Israeli control.

In 1968, the PLO revised its covenant. The new covenant maintained the principle that negated Israel's right to exist and supported the armed struggle for the liberation of Palestine. The revised covenant also named the *Fedayeen* as the nucleus of the armed struggle, rather than relying on integration into Arab armies. The Al-Fatah group emerged as the most important group with the PLO, and in 1969, its leader, Yasser Arafat, became the leader of the PLO. The PLO became an important independent force in Jordan. King Hussein, the PLO, and Syria became involved in a struggle for the control of Jordan in 1970. Israel threatened to intervene at the request of the United States Syria withdrew, and the PLO was expelled from Jordan. Most of the PLO went to Lebanon, where they actively participated in that country's civil war in 1975, eliciting Syrian intervention.

Israel, Syria, and Lebanon were drawn into a number of crises during the sixteen years of civil war in Lebanon. Many of these crises, such as the Litani

Operation of 1978, were prompted by Israeli reaction to PLO raids across the Lebanese border. Israel's 1982 invasion of Lebanon was also a response to the continuing PLO raids. Others were prompted by rocket attacks by the Iranian-backed Hezbollah (1993 and 1996) from Lebanon. Israel was continuously called upon to force the enactment of the sovereign state role upon these nonstate actors, as well as the states that supported and harbored them. Further, after the Intifada began in December 1987, Israel had to deal with increased violence from within its borders.

ISRAELI FOREIGN POLICY ROLES

Israel has had a difficult time in its effort toward become a functioning member of the regional and international systems since its emergence in 1948. It emerged not long after several of its Arab neighbors formed states. Even without an Israel, these new states probably would have had a difficult time being integrated into the system because they all emerged at the same time. Existing regional powers, such as Egypt and Iraq, would have their hands full socializing these smaller Arab states into the system. However, the Jewish state of Israel, presented an additional identity-based challenge to socialization in the region. In fact, the challenge was too great, and the solution was the immediate attempt to eliminate the emerging Israeli state. After that initial failure, it was unlikely that regional Arab states would be able to socialize Israel into the region.

As a novice, Israel initially pursued the nonidentification role—a form of neutrality that may be common to emerging states. The United States also adopted a neutral role when it first emerged into the system. Israel also adopted several other roles that would be recurrent themes in Israeli foreign policy—such as the defender of the faith role and the internal development role. Initially, these roles may not have been intended to generate regional or international externalities, but they did. After Israel allowed the non-identification role to fizzle, it pursued an allied role with the United States. The allied role would also be a recurrent theme in Israel's history. Finally, Israel closed its novice years with a bid from France and Britain to serve as their regional collaborator in the Suez Canal operation. The United States socialized Israel out of that regional role and effectively socialized France and Britain out of their role conceptions as great powers.

After the Suez Canal Crisis in 1956, Israel began its tenure in the system as a small member state. Despite its recurrent bid for the allied role with the United States, Israel failed to assist the United States in enacting the roles of bipolarity for the Middle East as set forth in the Eisenhower Doctrine. Israel also persisted in its internal development role. The Six-Day War of 1967 caused Israel to enact the sovereign state role with force to maintain its existence.

After the 1967 war, Israel emerged as a major member of the system. The strength and security it derived from its decisive victory over its Arab neighbors allowed it to stand firm in the War of Attrition (1969–1970). However, due to the lack of a negotiated settlement and the continuous hostilities, Israel had to enact the sovereign state role with force again in the Yom Kippur War of 1973. During the war, Israel sought and achieved the allied role with the United States. It also pursued its traditional roles of internal development and defender of the faith. Israel also sought the role of regional protector on two occasions—once in connection with nuclear capabilities and the other during the Lebanon War. On both occasions, it forced the role, despite rejection by members of both the regional and international systems. Finally, Israel had to enforce the sovereign state role against a non-state actor, the PLO, on many occasions.

Socialization of Israel has indeed proceeded at a slow pace. Israel has had to defend its role as a sovereign state throughout its entire history, up to the point at which it occupied major member status in the system. Israel's social status has never quite matched its power status in the system. The United States rightly socialized Israel out of a regional role when it was still a novice on the verge of becoming a small state, but the United States took the same action against the regional role location process when Israel was a major member state. Israel should be occupying the roles of regional leader and regional protector in the Middle East. To the extent that it does occupy one of those roles, it does so by force. The regional leader role is probably out of the question given the identity-based differences between Israel and the region it would provide with leadership.

If Lustick's (1997) argument is correct, then Israel has no chance at seeking a great power master status. Lustick argues that states that were not great powers at the end of the nineteenth century were unlikely to become great powers. After that time, the existing great powers began to interrupt the interaction of war and state building that had elevated them to their status. Further, international norms and institutions designed to prevent such wars also became much more prevalent during the twentieth century. Lustick (1997: 661–662) argues that this has occurred frequently in the Middle East, as great powers have propped up vulnerable regimes against both internal and external challenges and prevented regional hegemons from exercising their capabilities to conquer their neighbors.

Lustick makes his argument based on case studies of Egypt under Muhammad Ali and Nasser, and of Iraq under Saddam Hussein. However, Lustick (1997: 663) also acknowledges that his theory may indeed apply to Israel in its interactions with states over the conquered territories and in the Lebanon War. I would also add the Osirak reactor incident with Iraq. It is true that the great powers—particularly the United States—have intervened at the close of each of Israel's wars to negotiate a return of conquered territory. Indeed, the core of the peace process between Israel and its neighbors has always been "land for peace."

Has the United States prevented Israel from becoming a great power? The United States rejected both of the regional protector roles that Israel attempted to achieve in Iraq and Lebanon. That Israel is not considered a great power, despite its possession of nuclear weapons, is also peculiar. Further, Israel has projected capabilities beyond its region in the raid on Entebbe in 1976 and in the airlift of 15,000 Ethiopian Jews in 1991. It may be the case that Israel's transition to a great power master status will never occur, despite possession of the capabilities that would allow the forceful enactment of that role. However, this would only be a partial enactment because Israel's cultural uniqueness in the region would impede its social acceptance, and thus the willing partners available to enact the role.

6   Conclusion

The research in this book fills a gap in the theoretical literature on inter-state interaction in the international system. It accomplishes this goal by demonstrating how structure constrains agent behavior through the competition and socialization mechanisms. Those mechanisms produce four different kinds of units, rather than the functionally undifferentiated units that inhabit Waltzian neorealism. These four kinds of units are expected to behave in the conduct of foreign policy according to their position. When they do not behave according to expectations, they are subject to socialization attempts to correct their behavior.

Role theory has proven to be an excellent complementary vehicle to developing the social version of neorealism presented in this book. Role theory, like neorealism, views the social world as a highly structured environment. Role theory also has an implicit model of the socialization process in its discussion of role location. However, role theory, like neorealism and systemic theories in general, is somewhat indeterminate when it comes to predicting actual actor behavior. The marriage of role theory with the analytic narrative approach has helped to reduce the range of uncertainty about state behavior.

The resulting model does not yield precise predictions about state behavior, but it does reduce the range of possible outcomes in the role location process. It does so by lending shape to the socialization process through the use of the socialization game. The socialization game is based on insights from role theory and dissonance theory and is applied to the cases at hand as a theoretical searchlight. Such a device helps us to select information that is useful to explaining the process at hand out of an enormous amount of data available to the researcher. But just how useful is the model?

EVALUATING THE MODEL

In Chapter 1, I discussed five criteria developed by Bates et al. (1998: 14–18) for evaluating an analytic narrative. A reexamination of these criteria is in order in light of the data collected in the case studies. First, do the assumptions of the model correspond to what is known? I argued in Chapter 1 that roles figure prominently in both constructivist and rationalist accounts of international politics. I also grounded the model in a systemic version of neorealism, which expected that states would seek foreign policy roles within the constraints of a master role deduced from the interaction of competition and socialization mechanisms. Further, in Chapter 2, I developed a socialization game based on theoretical expectations from role theory and dissonance theory.

Second, do conclusions follow from premises? This involves appraising the logic of the model. The socialization game models the role location process that is at the heart of socialization attempts in the system. Indeed, the adoption of foreign policy roles by states implicated others; a socializer stepped forward from the audience to assess the role; and then, if the role was rejected, the socializee entered a dissonance reduction phase. The completion of the dissonance reduction phase, or the termination of the role location prior to that point, marked the end of the foreign policy crisis, and the socialization episode.

Third, do the model's implications find confirmation in the data? This criterion involves interplay between model building and constructing an explanation from the data. I found that the model could apply equally to an altercast role as well as to an achieved role with some minor modifications in the order of play. Further, I found that the socialization game does not describe the actions of active great powers, at least in the case of a bipolar international system. Thus, in the US case after the abortive Eisenhower Doctrine, the socialization game has little to say about great power socialization.

Fourth, how well does the theory stand up to competing explanations? This is a difficult criterion to meet when the focus is on explaining a process, rather than an outcome. In some cases, such as the early US attempts at neutrality and some of the Israeli wars, a socialization explanation was advanced over standard neorealist balance of power explanations. At times, the socialization explanation seemed to fit well with a balance of threat explanation.

Finally, how generalizable is the explanation? This is obviously a small-N study, which limits my ability to generalize. I have examined seven cases of transitions through master statuses in the international system. Within those seven cases, I have analyzed slightly over two-dozen foreign policy role location processes. I have also limited the cases to instances of states that are members of the "club of nations"—states that appear to be well-adjusted, functioning members of the international system. This also constrains my ability to generalize in terms of prescriptive advice to socializers and socializees. However, I am confident that the socialization game used to model the role location process is applicable to all states in the system. Despite the limitations imposed upon generalizability from these cases, let us review what we have learned from the United States and Israel.

INSIGHTS FROM THE UNITED STATES AND ISRAEL

The United States and Israel are quite similar in their early role location processes. Both the United States and Israel had to force the role of the sovereign state on their socializers, Britain and Egypt, respectively. As novice states, both pursued neutral roles in the international system. These roles were not accepted by their socializers—the United States even ended up fighting a war over its neutral role, but neither Israel nor the United States ever achieved the neutral role.

Israel pursued a much more active conception of the neutral role than did the United States. Rather than attempting to eschew involvement in international politics like the United States, Israel sought to engage both the United States and the Soviet Union without formally allying with either. Israel generally was much more active as a novice than was the United States. It pursued a number of roles, such as defender of the faith and eventually ally with the United States, which were not accepted. It was able to force the internal development role on its peer socializer Syria.

Both the United States and Israel began their tenure as small members of the international system by being altercast into a regional collaborator role. Israel accepted the regional collaborator role in which France attempted to cast it, but it was later socialized out of that role by the United States. The United States was able to reject being altercast in the regional collaborator role by Britain, offering instead its own role of regional protector. This role was largely hollow in that it was not enacted for nearly one-quarter of a century after its pronouncement in the Monroe Doctrine. Further, it was backed by the strength of the British (not the American) navy. Therefore, the regional roles were inappropriate for both states in their small member capacities.

Unfortunately for Israel, it had to force the sovereign state role on its socializer Egypt in the Six-Day War in 1967 to make the transition to major member status. This also parallels the US experience with the sovereign state role, in which it forced the role in 1783 and in 1812 on Britain to make the transition to the small member status. Apparently, emerging states that have to force their statehood may end up defending that role in a subsequent war. Israel fought the Yom Kippur war in 1973 to again force the sovereign state role against Egypt.

Israel sought the allied role with the United States as a novice and as a small member, and finally succeeded as a major member, largely because of the threat to its sovereign state role posed by its Arab neighbors. The United States, on the other hand, sought the allied role only once as an emerging state, with France, to secure its sovereign state role. The United States did its best to stay out of alliances, even offering the inappropriate neutral roles as a great power prior to World War I and World War II. After that it sought allies to enact its self-ascribed role of bloc leader against the Soviet Union.

As major member states, both Israel and the United States sought regional roles as would be expected with their power and social status. The United States was initially unsuccessful in achieving the roles of regional protector and leader due to its socializer Britain's interests in Latin America. However, the United

States continued to enact those roles with the audience of Latin American states and finally succeeded in securing British recognition of these roles in the Venezuelan Crisis of 1895. Israel forced the regional protector role on France and Syria, but could not force the United States to accept the role in the Lebanon War. Regardless, Israel did not abandon the role but held onto it with resolve.

The United States' and Israel's activities at the regional level point to an interesting difference in their emergence and development as states. The United States emerged in an international system but not as a regional system of states. The United States was the only entity organized as a state in North or South America in 1783. Further, it emerged on the fringes of the international system centered on Europe. Both of these factors gave the United States greater flexibility in its development than most states are allowed. Thus, the region that the United States would soon protect and lead was largely a product of its own making. The United States took the lead in recognizing Latin American republics; it "policed" the region and eventually set up interstate organizations such as the Organization of American States and the Rio Pact to ensure forums for its leadership.

Israel, on the other hand, emerged into a regional subsystem that had already begun to take shape prior to its independence. Egypt and Iraq were established states, and the remainder of Israel's Arab neighbors emerged several years prior it. Further, the former colonial powers, such as Britain and France, were still actively involved in the region. And, soon enough, the United States and the Soviet Union would take their place. Israel's interaction was constrained at the regional level by its neighbors and by international socializers. Further, as discussed in Chapter 5, Israel's distinctiveness in this region also posed problems for its acceptance as a member. Thus, Israel's attempts to achieve the regional protector role were strongly resisted by both regional socializers and international socializers, despite the fact that Israel has the capabilities to enact such a role.

Of the role location processes analyzed in this book, Israel's primary socializers included the United States (5 times), Egypt (5 times), the Soviet Union (3 times), France (2 times), Syria (2 times), and Iraq (1 time). By contrast, the United States was subject to socialization efforts from emergence to major member status by Great Britain (6 times) and France (2 times). Not only did Israel face more potential socializers, it also consequently faced many more socialization attempts.

Only the United States makes the transition to great power status in our cases. As a great power in a multipolar system, the United States still faced socialization attempts in its role location process. Britain served as the major socializer and allowed the United States to achieve regional roles in Asia and Latin America. However, during the world wars, Britain and Germany had to socialize the United States out of the neutral role to adopt the belligerent and allied roles demanded of a great power during a systemic war. After World War II, the United States could no longer refuse to enact its role as a great power in a bipolar system.

As a great power in a bipolar system, the United States was not subject to socialization efforts in its foreign policy role location process. The United States and the Soviet Union adopted similar roles—the roles of bipolarity (bloc leader, defender of the faith, and liberation supporter/liberator) due to structural imperatives. The roles of bipolarity were subsequently articulated by every US president in the bipolar era. The techniques and methods adopted to enact these roles may have varied, but the underlying themes remained constant.

The only time the roles of bipolarity did face socialization pressure, that pressure came from tiny Lebanon (with the backing of most of the Middle Eastern member states), which eventually rejected enactment of the US roles, leading the United States to let the roles fizzle. This was a tough and competitive region for both Israel and the United States at the time. In the unipolar system, the United States also appears to have the ability to enact whatever role it chooses, since other states have not chosen to balance against it. The limitations on the great power role, in terms of intervention, have largely come as the result of domestic, rather than systemic, imperatives.

We might also be interested in other characteristics of the roles adopted by Israel and the United States. Holsti (1970: 285–289) rates national role conceptions in terms of their passivity to activity on a scale from 0 to 5. The most active roles include regional leader (5), regional protector (5), liberation supporter/ liberator (4), active independent (e.g., Israel's nonaligned role) (4), balancer (4), defender of the faith (3), and regional collaborator (3). The most passive roles include ally (2), independent (e.g., the US neutral role) (2), example (1), internal development (0). On balance, we find that both the United States and Israel have fairly active national role conceptions that have become increasingly active as they mature in the system. Israel's recurrent internal development role should be considered more active than Holsti imagined it, as internal development always has external repercussions with its Arab neighbors.

Another interesting finding, echoed by Holsti (1970: 291), is that the international system may be subsystem dominant. Roles such as regional leader, regional protector, regional collaborator, and internal development are enacted at the subsystem level. These roles dominate the Israeli and US role location processes up through their major member statuses. Some roles, such as the sovereign state, neutral, allied, and balancer roles may be operative in both the regional and international systems. Only after the United States becomes a great power does it begin to offer roles peculiar to the international system, such as the bloc leader or global leader.

INTERNATIONAL POLITICS AND FOREIGN POLICY

This book began by locating Waltz's propositions about socialization and competition in a system. A systemic perspective requires that we take into account the interaction of the units. In so doing, we move from a theory of international politics to the beginnings of a theory of foreign policy. Walker

(1987) similarly attempted to bridge the gap between Waltz's structural theory and the behavior of the units. As Walker (1987: 67) said of his project, "[T]his task is both more and less than a simple refinement and extension of Waltz's work." I think this is also true of the book at hand.

It is less simple in the sense that I am still offering an account of foreign policy behavior that driven by structural imperatives. Waltz (1979) argues that a theory of international politics is not a theory of foreign policy and that many domestic variables also come into play at the level of foreign policy. However, if states do not adjust to structural imperatives, they will fail to survive. Hence, Elman (1996) and others have argued that neorealism does indeed offer the potential for a theory of foreign policy.

It is also less simple in the sense that I am employing concepts already developed for the study of foreign policy. One could study the foreign policy role location process for states without considering its systemic implications. Or, the role location process might simply be analyzed in terms of standard balance of power propositions, with states rejecting roles that threaten the equilibrium.

The book is also a refinement of Waltzian neorealism. By fleshing out the mechanisms associated with competition and socialization, it adds to the theoretical framework of neorealism. Socialization has long been left out of most neorealist accounts, including Waltz's. Socialization and competition have generally been considered to perform the same function for structure. Since competition fits nicely with the analogy to microeconomics, socialization is largely forgotten. I have demonstrated that it is an important structural feature in its own right.

However, in drawing out the logical implications of socialization, I have also accomplished more than a refinement of neorealism. I have demonstrated that when the mechanisms associated with competition and socialization interact, they produce functionally differentiated units (see Figure 2.2). These units sort into four main categories, or master statuses—novices, small members, major members, and great powers. Although Waltz (1979) himself discusses a special role for great powers and the sorry lot of small states, he still views all states as formal equals, which thus require functional undifferentiation. This aspect of Waltz's theory has been soundly criticized since the beginning, but I have demonstrated a way to incorporate functional differentiation into the theory.

I also incorporate the notion of agency into Waltz's theory by placing structure and agents within a true international system. Structure still works its effects on agents by constraining them into one of the four master statuses. The master statuses constrain the types of auxiliary foreign policy roles that states may attempt to achieve in the international system. Socialization operates at a more specific level in unit interactions that accompany the role location processes in the system. Elements of hierarchy are also present at the system level, as states with higher social status (and capabilities) socialize those with lower status. Auxiliary foreign policy roles must be consistent with a state's master status, or the state will be socialized out of the role. Thus, identity becomes an important determinant of interests.

The unit-level interactions in the system also open up the possibility of transforming the system and elements of the structure (see Figure 2.3). For example, during its tenure as a great power, the United States has seen the system and the distribution of power change from a multipolar, to a bipolar, to a unipolar system. How is that possible? States may be socialized out of the great power master role, or they may stop trying to achieve auxiliary foreign policy roles related to the great power master role (Britain, France, and Germany after World War II). States may never be socialized into the great power master status, even though their capabilities are commensurate with the role (Japan). They may also fail in terms of competition—great powers that are unable to innovate will not remain great powers for long (Soviet Union). These changes, initiated at the system level, may eventually transform the deep structure of the international system. Thus, the "unipolar moment" could turn into a virtual hierarchy, or hegemony.

THE INTERPLAY OF IDENTITY AND INTEREST

The aim of many constructivists has been to show that identities trump interests in the explanation of state behavior (e.g., Bukovansky 1997; Kier 1995). As I have argued in this book, constructivism and rationalism (i.e., neorealism and neoliberalism) should not be seen as mutually exclusive approaches to explanation. Thus, the research question should not be, is it identity *or* interest, but rather, how do identity *and* interest interact to affect state behavior?

I have demonstrated that the structure of a neorealist system produces four master statuses through the interaction of the competition and socialization mechanisms. These identities, in and of themselves, help us to predict a range of possible state actions. For example, we would not expect a novice state to adopt a regional role in a subsystem because its power and social status preclude the enactment of such a role. Even though a novice state's interests might be served by such a role, its identity should constrain it from adopting that role.

If a state chooses to adopt a role and to behave in a manner inconsistent with its master status, then other states should intervene in the role location process to socialize the state out of the inappropriate role. For example, Israel was altercast into the role of regional collaborator during the Suez Canal crisis by France. The United States and the Soviet Union correctly viewed this as a role inconsistent with Israel's status as a novice state. The United States socialized Israel out of this role, in addition to socializing France and Great Britain out of enacting the great power role in the Middle East. Certainly, it was in the interest of Israel to act in concert with France and Great Britain against Egypt. Israel stood to gain strategic territory with the assistance of its temporary allies. And it did use the critical juncture produced by the Suez Crisis to make the transition to the small member state master status. However,

Israel's interest in performing a regional role was not appropriate to its current identity; thus it was socialized out of the role by the United States.

The United States also faced a similar inconsistency between identity and interest when it was a small member state. If you will recall, Britain attempted to altercast the United States into a regional collaborator role in Latin America. This identity was inconsistent with the small state status occupied by the United States, but with the support of the dominant international socializer, it was an acceptable role for the United States to play. It was also consistent with US interests according to past Presidents Jefferson and Madison. However, the United States as a small state rejected the regional collaborator role in favor of its own regional protector role for Latin America. This identity was also inconsistent with the small state master status but was consistent with expanding US commercial and security interests in the region. Because this role also served the interests of the British, it was not challenged. In fact, the United States grew into this role in terms of its power and social status as it made the transition to the major member master role during the critical juncture caused by the Mexican-American War. The regional leader and protector roles became an ingrained feature of US social identity, reflecting long-standing interests and shaping future interests in the region.

As this book has shown, neorealism should not be seen as antithetical to identity-based approaches to international relations. Neorealism is often portrayed as a billiard-ball model of international relations, in which one ball is just as good as another (i.e., sovereign state); some balls move across the table faster than others (i.e., capabilities); and yet all balls share the same interest in winning the game (i.e., survival).[1] However, billiard balls are differently striped and solid-colored, and the eight-ball has a special function; thus even in a game of pool, identity is important—even if it is still at a high level of generalization.

The master statuses deduced from the interaction of competition and socialization are general identities that can be taken on by any state in the system that has the appropriate capabilities to defend them or the social support of other states to enact them. These general identities then constrain and shape the more specific identities that states adopt in the form of auxiliary foreign policy roles. Some of these roles may be specific to the master status, but others may become an integral part of a state's social identity and may move with the state through other master statuses over time. Often the state's interests will foster the adoption of a foreign policy role, but the identity that role implicates may then shape future interests.

AREAS FOR FURTHER RESEARCH

The generalizability of the empirical portion of this book is limited because of the focus on two states that fall into the "club of nations." The United States and Israel have generally attempted to achieve foreign policy roles consistent with their master status. On occasion, they have attempted to achieve roles in anticipation of a transition to the next master status. Israel has been denied a regional role, yet the frustration that this might cause may be alleviated in the peace process.

Other states might react to Israel's situation—a highly structured environment—by failing to conform to socialization efforts. These states are known as rogues, such as present-day Iran and North Korea. An examination of their role location processes may explain how these states moved away from conformity by asserting foreign policy roles that were inconsistent with their master roles. Further, we should also examine the "joiners"— states that are relatively less impacted by structure, yet seem to conform in their choices of foreign policy roles. What do the role location processes of the post-Communist states in Eastern and Central Europe look like? How have Poland, the Czech Republic, and Hungary adapted their foreign policy behavior to make them acceptable partners to the European Union and NATO? And, finally, we could examine the foreign policy role location processes of the quasi-states that populate Africa. However, there simply may not be much to look at, as these states are the least impacted by structure and fail to conform even to the conventions of modern statehood.

This book has focused on socialization into the security sector of the international system. However, socialization into the economic sector of the system is a complementary aspect of a holistic understanding of the socialization process. Such an inquiry poses a number of questions. Do states always fall into the same master status in the economic and security sectors, or can there be slippage? What kinds of foreign economic policies do states adopt? Do they vary across the master statuses, or are they more similar than those found in the security sector? Does socialization into one sector spill over into the other, such that states that might not otherwise be conformist in one sector are because of the other?

Further research should also spend more time on examining the domestic-level determinants of national role conceptions. This book has focused mainly on how role conceptions are formed in response to international and foreign policy crises. Certainly, other national role conceptions are formed and offered by leaders. How are these noncrisis roles dealt with in terms of socialization? What is the relationship between foreign policy roles articulated by a leader and domestic politics? This book has expended some effort on explaining the domestic context of role choices, but more effort is needed to fully understand this part of the role location process.

Ultimately, a full examination of the socialization process may lead us to rethink some of the major theoretical divisions in international relations. Neorealism, neoliberalism, and constructivism are all different approaches to the same puzzle. Socialization should help us to explain this puzzle— namely, why do some elements of state behavior endure due to social structure, while others change in interstate interaction, leading to possible change in the composition of structure? Neorealists may have to accept that the behavior of states in a system may indeed be *social* behavior, as neoliberals and constructivists suggest. Waltz's theory, as it stands, is an asocial theory of international politics; however, as this book suggests, a focus on the socialization process may produce a social theory of international politics based on the same fundamental assumptions. Socialization cuts to the heart of the agent-structure debate, the constructivist-rationalist debate, and the division between world politics and foreign policy analysis. Perhaps the real puzzle is why so few scholars in international relations have heretofore attempted to unravel the socialization process in interstate relations.

Notes

NOTES TO CHAPTER 1

1. The fact that Britain and the United States did not imitate the Prussians indicates to Waltz that they were outside the arena of competition.
2. Waltz (1986: 330–331) argues that selection is of "central importance" to neorealism. As Kahler (1998: 925) notes, Waltz's position on the factor(s) responsible for the sameness effect is uncertain, as is his position on whether or not the units act rationally in pursuit of survival. See Elman (1996: 42–44) for an argument that Waltz relies on a weak form of rationality, as opposed to evolutionary selection or socialization. See also Resende-Santos (1996).
3. See Wendt (1987: 369) and Dessler (1989: 442–444) for arguments that structurationism offers little substantive guidance to the social scientist. Even Giddens (1983: 77) has stated that the theory of structuration "is not a magical key that unlocks the mysteries of empirical research, nor a research programme." Both Wendt and Dessler advocate the adoption of scientific realism in the pursuit of international relations theory building. While Wendt retains the practice of "oscillatory bracketing" peculiar to structurationism, Dessler incorporates the intentional interactions of states as a structural feature of the international system. I treat unit interactions as a systemic feature, rather than a structural feature, as does Waltz (1979: 80). However, I agree with Doty (1997) that any approach based on scientific realism will privilege structure over agency. Indeed, any approach that makes use of the concept of socialization will necessarily privilege structure over agency. See Goddard and Nexon (2005) for an excellent recent review of the possibilities and problems associated with Waltzian neorealism in this regard.
4. See also Dessler (1989: 448–449).
5. See Jervis (1998) for a review of this literature.
6. As an illustration of this last point regarding numerous levels of analysis, see Buzan et al.'s (1993: 79) final depiction of the levels of analysis in their version of structural realism. The structural level is broken down into the "deep" structure (organizing principle and functional differentiation of the units) versus the distributional structure, which is not as deep. The unit level is broken down into unit behavior, explained in terms of unit attributes and a level of process formations. Process formations refer to action-reaction relations between units. It is not clear why Buzan et al. separate action-reaction relations from the forms of interactions they posit to occur in their interaction level of analysis. The result is that Buzan et al. produce five levels of analysis for their study of international relations, whereas a systems theory could make do with only three (unit, system, and structure). A systems-level

approach is much more parsimonious and is still able to incorporate the interaction processes Waltz loses with his two levels of analysis.

7. See Dessler (1989: 448–451) for a similar analysis of what he calls Waltz's "positional" model of international structure.

8. Gulick (1955) and Kaplan (1957) offer versions of balance of power theory that require the internalization of rules on the part of states and their leaders. The most fundamental rule of both versions is that of self-restraint and the denial of immediate self-interest. If states are not socialized to adhere to these rules, the balance is destroyed, and the system changes.

9. See Thies (2001) for a more elaborate discussion of the use of these mechanisms with an eye toward the development of a social psychological theory of enduring rivalry. For a different approach to using roles to understand rivalry, see Kowert and Thies (forthcoming). Material in this section is reproduced with permission from Thies (2001).

10. March and Olsen (1998: 964–966) discuss the problem of competency traps. Competency traps occur when "the exploitation and refinement of known technologies, practices, and rules tend to drive out the exploration of possible new ones." As an organization falls into a competency trap, the likelihood that it will retain its competence or gain a competitive advantage decreases. March and Olsen offer no guidelines to predicting how or when an organization becomes subject to the competency trap.

11. Kier (1995, 1996, 1997) and Johnston (1995, 1996) challenge the primacy of external factors in determining military doctrine in France and China, respectively, by focusing on aspects of strategic culture within those societies.

12. See Mercer (1995) for a review.

13. Finnemore and Sikkink (1998) apply the notion of tipping points to their model of the norm life cycle.

14. By focusing on crises to examine foreign policy roles, I continue Waltz's practice of viewing socialization as conditioning behavior, rather than preferences—which may be difficult to judge from behavior (Morrow 1988). However, my approach does not preclude examining identity or the interests of the relevant actors, as Wendt (1992: 403) seems to imply. Role theory allows us to examine behavior, interests, and identity as states undergo socialization.

NOTES TO CHAPTER 2

1. Material in this section is reproduced from Thies (2010b) with permission.

2. Waltz continues to insist that neorealism is not a theory of foreign policy, despite the efforts of other scholars to deduce foreign policy propositions from it (Elman 1996). Role theory offers a way to link neorealism as a theory of international politics to the foreign policy behavior of states.

3. See Thies (2010a) for an expanded version of this discussion. Material in this section is reproduced from Thies (2010a) with permission.

4. Anticipatory socialization refers to the vicarious learning of appropriate behavior through role taking. Essentially, the individual imagines being the other in order to "try out" or practice the role without actually enacting it (Stryker and Statham 1985: 324–325, 335). Anticipatory socialization is not a focus of this study, since vicarious learning experiences tend to have less impact on an individual than experiential learning (Levy 1994; Reiter 1996: 34–40).

5. The socialization game and its description are reproduced from Thies (2012) with permission.

6. See Thies (2010a) for a discussion of the use of role theory as a theory of social identity. Material in this section is reproduced with permission.

NOTES TO CHAPTER 3

1. This discussion is based on several good overviews of the field of diplomatic history, including Hogan and Paterson (1991), Combs (1983), and DeConde (1976).
2. See McMahon (1991) and Rosenberg (1991) for a review of the criticisms leveled against the field of diplomatic history.
3. See Gaddis (1987) and Pelz (1988) for approaches that outline how diplomatic historians can incorporate theoretical constructs from international relations and political science. For a review of the commonalities, differences, and benefits of synthesizing the work of diplomatic historians and international relations specialists, see contributions by Levy, Haber, Kennedy, Krasner, Ingram, Schroeder, and Gaddis, in the *International Security* Symposium on History and Theory, edited by Colin Elman and Miriam Fendius Elman (1997).
4. For a review, see Holsti (1991) and Immerman (1991).
5. I acknowledge that ethnocentrism and parochialism are undoubtedly the source of much of this literature.
6. See Hunt (1992).
7. It is not uncommon for historians to have overlapping periods. Varg (1990) does the same thing with the periods 1890–1917 as the era of developing a new ideology of foreign policy, and 1898–1917 as implementation of the new ideology. This makes sense, as developing and implementing a new ideological basis for foreign policy may work in tandem. However, the political scientist's sensibilities are generally offended if periods or categories overlap.
8. Historical source material for the period 1776–1783 is found in Bailey (1980), Bartlett (1963), DeConde (1978), Pratt et al. (1980), and Rappaport (1975). Brune (1985, 1991) also provides analysis-free, chronological accounts of events in US diplomatic history.
9. The phrase "small international system" denotes the relatively small number of sovereign states in existence at this time and their geographic concentration in the European region.
10. See Thompson (1988: 104–108) for a review of the literature on the identification of systemic wars.
11. See Chapter 6 in Bemis (1942) for an extensive discussion of the Armed Neutrality.
12. See Walt (1996) for an argument that existing states will balance against the perceived threat posed by a revolutionary regime, often resulting in war. See pages 269–287 for a discussion of the American Revolution.
13. The apparent contradiction between the statement that a novice state will be subject to the most intense socialization pressure and at the same time be less subject to normative control due to its occupation of few roles in the system is also found in Waltz's (1979) treatment of small states. Elman (1995: 175) points out that Waltz (1979: 184–185, 195) argues that small state behavior will be dependent upon structural constraints due to their "narrow margin for error" in pursuing survival. However, Waltz (1979: 72–73) also argues that the smaller the state, the less likely it is to seriously have any effect on the international system. As such, great powers will focus little attention on small states since they pose no security threat. Therefore, small states face fewer external constraints on their behavior. I think that both statements are true. When a small state's primary socializer is a great power, we should expect strong external constraints on that state's behavior. However, at the same time, the small state may resist normative control (as opposed to force) if it is not well integrated into the system.

14. Historical source material for the time period 1783–1815 is found in Bailey (1980), Bartlett (1963), DeConde (1978), Ferrell (1975), and Pratt et al. (1980). Material in this section is reproduced with permission from Thies (2010b).
15. See Perkins (1993), Chapters 4 and 5, DeConde (1956: 31–65), and Varg (1963: 73–80). See Hatzenbuehler (1981: 23–25) for a summary of the literature that disputes the functioning of these groups as organized, national parties.
16. Armstrong (1993: 68–78) argues that Hamilton's approach to foreign policy attempted to bring about the socialization of the United States within the prevailing international society, while Jefferson stood for the opposite. Armstrong traces the beginnings of the notion of enlightened universalism, in which the United States would promote its own standards of diplomacy and international governance by example if possible, and by force if necessary. He further argues that this tendency was evident in the rhetoric of later presidents such as Wilson, Truman, Kennedy, and Reagan.
17. The neutral role is similar to Holsti's (1970: 262–263) "active independent" role. This role conception is a statement of an independent foreign policy that is free of military commitments to any of the great powers. This role generally eschews permanent military or ideological commitments and emphasizes activity to extend diplomatic and commercial relations to many states. See Bemis (1962a), Chapter 10, for an extensive discussion of the independent foreign policy enunciated in Washington's Farewell Address.
18. In addition to the source material previously cited, see Ellis (1951), Chapter 6, for an overview of neutrality during this time period.
19. See DeConde (1966) and Stinchcombe (1980) for more information on the Quasi-War.
20. Material in this section is reproduced with permission from Thies (2010b).
21. For additional information on the embargo and nonimportation, see Perkins (1963: 239–253) and Stagg (1983: 54–57).
22. Historical source material for this period may be found in Bailey (1980), Cole (1974), DeConde (1978), Perkins (1993), and Pratt et al. (1980), in addition to materials cited in the text.
23. Holsti (1970: 265–266) describes the regional-subsystem collaborator role as an active, far-reaching commitment to cooperate to build a wider community in a subsystem.
24. Armstrong (1993: 70) quotes Jefferson as advising Monroe that the United States should have "a system of her own, separate and apart from that of Europe" encompassing North and South America.
25. The liberation supporter role conception does not indicate formal responsibilities for organizing liberation movements abroad, yet it implies diffuse support for such indigenous efforts (Holsti 1970: 263). The anti-imperialist agent role conception involves viewing the state as an agent of struggle against outside imperial powers (Holsti 1970: 264).
26. According to Holsti (1970: 270), the role of the isolate demands a minimum of external contact. This role reveals a fear of any kind of external involvement and emphasizes self-reliance.
27. According to Holsti (1970: 269), the internal development has no referent in the international system. Most of the efforts of the government should be directed toward problems of internal development. This role tends to express a general inclination to stay uninvolved in international affairs, yet its enactment does not preclude international cooperation, particularly in economic matters.

28. Holsti (1970: 261) suggests that the themes for the role of regional leader involve special duties or responsibilities that a state perceives for itself in relation to other states in the region.

29. Historical source material for the period 1848–1898 may be found in Bailey (1980), Cole (1974), DeConde (1978), LaFeber (1993), Perkins (1993), and Pratt et al. (1980).

NOTES TO CHAPTER 4

1. For a general overview of the Open Door policy, see Cohen (1971), Crabb (1982), Dulles (1946), and Fairbank (1974).

2. For an explanation of the US involvement in the treaty system established in China, see Fairbank (1974: 83–101).

3. Bemis (1942: 482–484) reports that the British actually suggested the Open Door policy to the United States; however, Hay rejected a joint Anglo-American declaration because he felt US policy would be viewed as subservient to Britain. Despite Hay's concern for a close relationship with Great Britain, he believed that as a newly emerged great power, the United States should not play second-fiddle to Britain (Dulles 1961: 28–33).

4. Kennan (1951) argues that Hay's conduct during the Open Door notes was a flagrant example of how diplomacy should not be done.

5. The balancer role involves the state actively seeking equilibrium, peace, and stability in a system or subsystem (Holsti 1970: 248).

6. The mediator-integrator role is adopted by a state that perceives itself as responsible for reconciling conflict between states or groups of states (Holsti 1970: 265).

7. Pratt (1955: 434) argues that the United States acquired the Philippines solely for the purpose of protecting its interests in China.

8. It is no coincidence that Bailey (1948: 285) declared the Open Door Policy to be the least fundamental of all of the historic US foreign policy doctrines.

9. Historical overviews of the Roosevelt Corollary may be found in Bailey (1980), Crabb (1982), Gerassi (1965), LaFeber (1993), and Perkins (1955). For an overview of contending interpretations of Roosevelt's motives and goals, see Coletta (1981).

10. For other analytical approaches that employ metaphor, see Khong (1992) and Doty (1996).

11. For arguments that these defense pacts ultimately multilateralized the Monroe Doctrine, see Bailey (1980) and Welles (1944).

12. For general discussions of the politics of neutrality, see Chapters 38 and 39 in Bailey (1980), Chapter 2 in Iriye (1993), and Chapter 4 in Schulzinger (1984).

13. According to Holsti (1970: 265), the mediator role involves a state's perception that it is capable of, or responsible for, undertaking special tasks to reconcile conflicts between adversaries.

14. This was the standard interpretation of Wilson's decision to enter the war as exemplified by his biographer, Ray Stannard Baker (1919). However, revisionists writing after the war, such as Barnes (1926), Tansill (1938), Grattan (1929), and Tunnel (1922), shifted attention away from violations of the neutral role as the source of the war to the economic interests of US investment bankers and corporations in protecting their investments in British securities. Later realist interpretations would suggest that Wilson fought the right war for the wrong reasons (Lippmann 1943; Kennan 1951; Morgenthau 1951; Osgood 1952). Others, including Link (1974) and Devlin

(1975) argued that Wilson's decision to enter the war was based upon his desire to create a reformed postwar order grounded in principles of justice. For more on contending historiographical interpretations see James (1981).

15. The peace builder and catalyst roles are Chotard's own terminology.

16. The peace organizer role is similar to Holsti's (1970: 272) defender of the peace role, which indicates a universal commitment to defend against any aggression or threat to peace in the international system.

17. Chotard (1997: 54) argues that Cabot Lodge was satisfied with the balancer role for the United States, which he thought would allow the interposition of US power on a less frequent basis than the peace organizer role. The balancer role would be enacted again as the United States abandoned neutrality in favor of belligerency during World War II.

18. See Walker (1992) for a discussion of the relationship between role strain and role transition.

19. For a discussion of the active-passive continuum of roles, see Holsti (1970: 283–289).

20. This discussion of the Neutrality Acts relies upon Bailey (1980: 700–716) and Schulzinger (1984: 158–161).

21. Holsti (1970: 255) describes a state in the role of bloc leader as protecting bloc members and encouraging bloc cohesion through opposition to the other bloc(s).

22. After Eisenhower become president the number of bilateral and multilateral security treaties increased even more with the addition of SEATO in 1954, and separate pacts with South Korea (1954), Formosa (1954), and Pakistan (1954).

23. According to Holsti (1970: 264), a state in the role of defender of the faith views its foreign policy objectives in terms of defending value systems, rather than specific territories. The state undertakes special responsibilities to guarantee the ideological purity for a group of states. This role, in combination with the bloc leader role, committed the United States to defend the territory and democratic value systems of the free states against totalitarianism through the policy of containment.

24. Chotard (1997: 64) also interprets Truman as enunciating the role of example to the free peoples around the world that look up to the United States.

25. See Holsti (1970: 301–304) for a discussion of incompatible role conceptions.

26. See Jervis (1993) for additional arguments on why the United States should not seek international primacy.

NOTES TO CHAPTER 5

1. Some of the material in this chapter is reprinted with permission from Thies (2012).

2. This notion of system membership is also found in Bull (1977), Buzan (1991), and Buzan et al. (1993).

3. For discussions on the potential of pan-Arabism, see Kerr and Yassin (1982), Luciani and Salame (1988), and Waterbury and el Mallakh (1978). For discussions on the failures, see Ajami (1992), Azzam (1993), and Brown (1984).

4. Telhami (1990, 1996) argues that Israel has always pursued separate, but inevitably overlapping, and sometimes contradictory, strategies in the regional and international systems.

5. The term "new history" is not related to the term as it is used in the United States or France in reference to the Annales School. Morris (1988a) coined the term to describe recent trends in Israeli historiography.

6. Finkelstein includes among the new historians Morris (1988b, 1990), Flapan (1987), Pappe (1988), Shlaim (1988), and Palumbo (1987). See Karsh (1997) for a forceful rebuttal of these claims.

7. Klingberg's (1983) dates actually mark lagged responses to wars, such as the War of 1812, the US Civil War, World War I, and World War II.

8. For general historical information on the Mandate period and Israel's War of Independence, see Bailey (1990), Bickerton and Klausner (1998), Peretz (1996), Safran (1969), and Tessler (1994).

9. The *Yishuv* refers to the Jewish community in Palestine prior to the establishment of Israel. The *Haganah* was a Jewish paramilitary organization formed during the British Mandate in Palestine.

10. The Arab Liberation Army was a force of armed guerrilla fighters created by the Arab League in December 1947. This force was organized, armed, and trained by Syria.

11. Secretary of State Marshall also feared Soviet participation in a UN force to implement partition because Soviet troops might not leave the area once the mission was complete. This would give the Soviets access to Greece, Turkey, and the oil fields of the Middle East.

12. *Aliyah* means "ascent." It is the Zionist term for immigration to Israel.

13. The vote on partition was thirty-three to thirteen, with eleven abstentions. Thus, the international system is still fairly small at this point with only fifty-seven recognized members.

14. In fact, Egypt had to appeal to the British, who sent Israel an ultimatum to withdraw from the Sinai. Israel eventually shot down five British airplanes during the ensuing crisis. Israel did not withdraw from the Sinai at this point, but did when the UN Security Council called for a ceasefire on January 7, 1949 (Brecher and Wilkenfeld 1997: 271).

15. See the discussion of early US history in Chapter 3 for an explanation of this apparent contradiction.

16. The nonidentification role is similar to Holsti's (1970: 262) "active independent" role. The active independent role confirms that a state will make policy decisions based on its own interests rather than in support of the interests of other states. Further, in addition to shunning permanent military commitments, the role involves efforts to cultivate relations with as many states as possible with occasional involvement in bloc conflicts.

17. Britain, however, continued to supply arms to Egypt, Jordan, and Iraq during this period in compliance with arms treaties still in force. On May 25, 1950, the United States, Britain, and France issued the Tripartite Declaration, which stated that these governments would not supply arms to states in the region intending to use them for aggressive purposes against any other state in the region. This essentially eliminated these three states as a source of arms for Israel (Gazit 1987: 85–89).

18. The Soviets then supplied about one-third of Israel's oil consumption until the Suez Crisis when deliveries were halted. However, Israel viewed the USSR's motives for selling oil as primarily economic.

19. *Kibbutz galuyot* refers to the ingathering of the exiles.

20. See Brecher and Wilkenfeld (1997: 272–273) and Bar-Yaacov (1967).

21. See Brecher (1975: 173–224) for a discussion of developments concerning water rights surrounding the Jordan River.

22. This discussion is based on Levey (1997: 7–34).

23. See Levey (1997: 58–74).

24. Walt (1987: 61), following Crosbie (1974), argues that Israel and France established a "tacit" alliance by 1954 that would persist for a decade.

25. Historical source material covering the Suez Crisis can be found in Bailey (1990), Brecher (1975), Childers (1962), Levey (1997), Love (1969), Safran (1969), and Troen and Shemesh (1990).
26. The United States responded to the Soviet note by declaring that it would not stand idly by if Paris and London were bombed, but Tel Aviv was not mentioned in this warning.
27. The Israelis might also have been pushed toward unilateral action, although Ben-Gurion had prevented Dayan and the military from launching a preventive war against Egypt in 1955 (Aronson 1978: 13).
28. This discussion relies on Levey (1997: 80–89).
29. For a discussion of the 1963 Jordan Waters Crisis, see Brecher and Wilkenfeld (1997) and Safran (1981).
30. See Kerr (1971) and Dawisha (1976) for more on the summit.
31. Historical sources on the Six-Day War include Bailey (1990), Bickerton and Klausner (1998), Brecher (1980), Dupuy (1978), Laqueur (1968), O'Ballance (1972), and Safran (1969).
32. Rothstein (1968: 26–27) suggests that a strategy of hiding is adopted by a small state that decides its best policy is neither to act against nor with a threatening concentration of power. Small states may feel that their insignificance may grant them some measure of invisibility. Israel could never adopt the strategy of hiding in the Middle East given the obvious differences between it and its Arab neighbors.
33. See Finkelstein (1995: 150–171) for a different approach that still argues that Israel was not actively seeking peace in the aftermath of the 1967 war.
34. For historical sources regarding the War of Attrition and surrounding events, see Aronson, (1978), Bar-Siman-Tov (1980), Brecher (1974), and Peretz (1996).
35. For more information on the 1973 war, see Aronson (1978), Bailey (1990), Bickerton and Klausner (1998), Brecher (1980), and Brecher and Wilkenfeld (1997).
36. This discussion is based on Bickerton and Klausner (1998), Peretz (1996), and Sandler (1993).
37. See Brecher and Wilkenfeld (1997: 292).
38. See Sandler (1993: 213–217).
39. This discussion is based on Rabinovich (1985), Schiff and Yaari (1984), and Yaniv (1987).
40. The following discussion is based on Bickerton and Klausner (1998) and Peretz (1996).

NOTE TO CHAPTER 6

1. Mearsheimer (1994/1995: 48) is a restatement of the argument that realism treats states like billiard balls.

References

Ajami, F. (1992) *The Arab Predicament*, Cambridge: Cambridge University Press.

Ammon, H. (1973) *The Genet Mission*, New York: W.W. Norton.

Armstrong, D. (1993) *Revolution and World Order: The Revolutionary State in International Society*, Oxford: Clarendon Press.

Aronson, S. (1978) *Conflict and Bargaining in the Middle East: An Israeli Perspective*, Baltimore, MD: The Johns Hopkins University Press.

—— (1984) *The Evolution of Cooperation*, New York: Basic Books.

Axelrod, R. (1997) *The Complexity of Cooperation*, Princeton, NJ: Princeton University Press.

Azar, E. E., P. Jureidini, and R. McLaurin (1978) "Protracted Social Conflict: Theory and Practice in the Middle East," *Journal of Palestine Studies* 8: 41–60.

Azzam, M. (1993) "Overarching Regional Cooperation," in Nonneman, G. (ed.) *The Middle East and Europe: The Search for Stability and Integration*, London, UK: Federal Trust for Education and Research.

Bailey, S. D. (1990) *Four Arab-Israeli Wars and the Peace Process*, New York: Macmillan.

Bailey, T. A. (1948) *The Man in the Street: The Impact of American Public Opinion on Foreign Policy*, New York: MacMillan.

—— (1969) *Essays Diplomatic and Undiplomatic*, New York: Appleton Century-Crofts.

Bailey, T. A. (1980) *A Diplomatic History of the American People*, Englewood Cliffs, NJ: Prentice-Hall.

Baker, R. S. (1919) *Woodrow Wilson*, New York: Macmillan.

Baldwin, D., ed. (1993) *Neorealism and Neoliberalism*, New York: Columbia University Press.

Bar-On, M. (1998) "Historiography as an Educational Project: The Historians' Debate in Israel and the Middle East Peace Process," in Peleg, I. (ed.) *The Middle East Peace Process: Interdisciplinary Perspectives*, Albany: State University of New York Press.

Bar-Siman-Tov, Y. (1980) *The Israeli-Egyptian War of Attrition, 1969–70*, New York: Columbia University Press.

Bar-Yaacov, N. (1967) *The Israel-Syrian Armistice: Problems of Implementation, 1949–1966*, Jerusalem: Magnes Press.

Barnes, H. E. (1926) *Genesis of the World War: An Introduction to the Problem of War Guilt*, New York: A.A. Knopf.

Barnett, M. N. (1993) "Institutions, Roles, and Disorder: The Case of the Arab States System," *International Studies Quarterly* 37(3): 271–296.

—— (1995) "The New United Nations Politics of Peace: From Juridical Sovereignty to Empirical Sovereignty," *Global Governance* 1: 79–97.

Barnett, M. N. (1996) "The Politics of Uniqueness: The Status of the Israeli Case," in Barnett, M. N. (ed.) *Israel in Comparative Perspective: Challenging the Conventional Wisdom,* Albany: State University of New York Press.

—— (1997) "Bringing in the New World Order: Liberalism, Legitimacy, and the United Nations," *World Politics* 49: 526–551.

—— (1998) *Dialogues in Arab Politics: Negotiations in Regional Order.* New York: Columbia University Press.

Bartlett, R. (1963) *Policy and Power: Two Centuries of American Foreign Relations,* New York: Hill & Wang.

Bates, R. H., A. Greif, M. Levi, J. Rosenthal, and B. Weingast (1998) *Analytic Narratives,* Princeton, NJ: Princeton University Press.

Beard, C. A. and M. R. Beard (1921) *History of the United States,* New York: Macmillan.

Bemis, S. F. (1942) *A Diplomatic History of the United States,* rev. ed., New York: Henry Holt.

—— (1962a) *American Foreign Policy and the Blessings of Liberty,* New Haven, CT: Yale University Press.

—— (1962b) *Jay's Treaty: A Study in Commerce and Diplomacy,* New Haven, CT: Yale University Press.

—— (1969) *John Quincy Adams and the Foundations of American Foreign Policy,* New York: Alfred A. Knopf.

Bennett, S. (1998) "Integrating and Testing Models of Rivalry Termination," *American Journal of Political Science* 42: 256–270.

Bialer, U. (1990) *Between East and West: Israel's Foreign Policy Orientation, 1948–1956,* Cambridge: Cambridge University Press.

Bickerton, I. J. and C. L. Klausner (1998) *A Concise History of the Arab-Israeli Conflict,* 3rd ed., Upper Saddle River, NJ: Prentice Hall.

Biddle, B. J. (1986) "Recent Developments in Role Theory," *American Review of Sociology* 12: 67–92.

Borg, D. (1947) *American Policy and the Chinese Revolution, 1925–1928,* New York: MacMillan.

Brecher, M. (1972) *The Foreign Policy System of Israel,* London, UK: Oxford University Press.

—— (1974) *Decisions in Israel's Foreign Policy,* London: Oxford University Press.

—— (1975) *Decisions in Israel's Foreign Policy,* New Haven, CT: Yale University Press.

—— (1980) *Decisions in Crisis: Israel, 1967 and 1973,* Berkeley: University of California Press.

—— (1984) "International Crises and Protracted Conflicts," *International Interactions* 11: 237–297.

—— (1993) *Crisis in World Politics: Theory and Reality,* Oxford, UK: Pergamon Press.

Brecher, M., and J. Wilkenfeld (1997) *A Study of Crisis,* Ann Arbor: University of Michigan Press.

Brown, W. R. (1984) "The Dying Arab Nation," *Foreign Policy* 54: 27–43.

Brune, L. H. (1985) *Chronological History of United States Foreign Relations, 1776–January 20, 1981: Volumes I and II,* New York: Garland Publishing.

Brune, L. H. (1991) *Chronological History of United States Foreign Relations, January 21, 1981 to January 20, 1989: Volume III, The Reagan Years,* New York: Garland Publishing.

Bukovansky, M. (1997) "American Identity and Neutral Rights from Independence to the War of 1812," *International Organization* 51: 209–243.

Bull, H. (1977) *The Anarchical Society: A Study of Order in World Politics,* New York: Columbia University Press.

Buzan, B. (1991) *People, States and Fear,* 2nd ed., Boulder, CO: Lynne Rienner.

Buzan, B., C. Jones, and R. Little (1993) *The Logic of Anarchy,* New York: Columbia University Press.

Campbell, J. L. (1995) "State Building and Postcommunist Budget Deficits," *American Behavioral Scientist* 38: 760–787.

——— (1996) "An Institutional Analysis of Fiscal Reform in Postcommunist Europe," *Theory and Society* 25: 45–84.

Cashman, G. (1993) *What Causes War? An Introduction to Theories of International Conflict,* New York: Lexington Books.

Cederman, L. (1997) *Emergent Actors in World Politics: How States and Nations Develop and Dissolve,* Princeton, NJ: Princeton University Press.

Checkel, J. T. (1997) "International Norms and Domestic Politics: Bridging the Rationalist Constructivist Divide," *European Journal of International Relations* 3: 473–495.

——— (1998) "The Constructivist Turn in International Relations Theory," *World Politics* 50: 424–348.

Checkel, J. T. (2005) "International Institutions and Socialization in Europe: Introduction and Framework," *International Organization* 59(4): 801–826.

Childers, E. B. (1962) *The Road to Suez,* London: MacGibbon and Kee.

Chotard, J. (1997) "Articulating the New International Role of the United States during Previous Transitions, 1916–1919, 1943–1947," in Le Prestre, P. G. (ed.) *Role Quests in the Post–Cold War Era,* Montreal: McGill-Queen's University Press.

Cialdini, R. (1984) *Influence: The Psychology of Persuasion,* New York: Quill.

Cohen, W. I. (1971) *America's Response to China: An Interpretive History of Sino-American Relations,* New York: John Wiley and Sons.

Cole, W. S. (1974) *An Interpretive History of American Foreign Relations,* Homewood, IL: The Dorsey Press.

Coleman, J. (1964) *Introduction to Mathematical Sociology,* New York: The Free Press.

——— (1986) "Social Theory, Social Research and a Theory of Action," *American Journal of Sociology* 9: 1309–1335.

Coletta, P. E. (1981) "The Diplomacy of Theodore Roosevelt and William Howard Taft," in Haines, G. K., and J. S. Walker (eds.) *American Foreign Relations: A Historiographical Overview,* Westport, CT: Greenwood Press.

Collier, R. B. and D. Collier. (1991) *Shaping the Political Arena: Critical Junctures, the Labor Movement, and Regime Dynamics in Latin America,* Princeton, NJ: Princeton University Press.

Combs, J. (1970) *The Jay Treaty: Political Battleground of the Founding Fathers,* Berkeley: University of California Press.

Combs, J. A. (1983) *American Diplomatic History: Two Centuries of Changing Interpretations,* Berkeley: University of California Press.

Crabb, C. V. (1982) *The Doctrines of American Foreign Policy: Their Meaning, Role and Future,* Baton Rouge: Louisiana State University Press.

Crosbie, S. K. (1974) *A Tacit Alliance: France and Israel from Suez to the Six Day War,* Princeton, NJ: Princeton University Press.

Dawisha, A. (1976) *Egypt and the Arab World,* London: Macmillan.

Dayan, M. (1966) *Diary of the Sinai Campaign,* New York: Shocken Press.

DeConde, A. (1956) *Entangling Alliance: Politics and Diplomacy under George Washington,* Durham, NC: Duke University Press.

——— (1966) *The Quasi-War: The Politics and Diplomacy of the Undeclared War with France, 1979–1801,* New York: Scribner's.

——— (1976) *American Diplomatic History in Transformation,* Washington, DC: American Historical Association.

——— (1978) *A History of American Foreign Policy,* New York: Charles Scribner's Sons.

Dessler, D. (1989) "What's At Stake in the Agent-Structure Debate?" *International Organization* 43: 441–473.

Devlin, P. (1975) *Too Proud to Fight: Woodrow Wilson's Neutrality*, New York: Oxford University Press.

DiMaggio, P. J. and W. W. Powell (1991) *The New Institutionalism in Organizational Analysis*, Chicago, IL: University of Chicago Press.

Doty, R. L. (1996) *Imperial Encounters: The Politics of Representation in North-South Relations*, Minneapolis: University of Minnesota Press.

—— (1997) "Aporia: A Critical Exploration of the Agent-Structure Problematique in International Relations Theory," *European Journal of International Relations* 3: 365–392.

Dull, J. R. (1981) "American Foreign Relations Before the Constitution: A Historiographical Wasteland," in Haines, G. K. and J. S. Walker (eds.) *American Foreign Relations: A Historiographical Overview*, Westport, CT: Greenwood Press.

Dulles, F. R. (1946) *China and America: The Story of their Relations Since 1784*, Princeton, NJ: Princeton University Press.

—— (1961) "John Hay," in Graebner, N. A. (ed.) *An Uncertain Tradition: American Secretaries of State in the Twentieth Century*, New York: McGraw Hill.

Dupuy, T. N. (1978) *Elusive Victory, The Arab-Israeli Wars, 1947–74*, New York: Harper & Row.

Earle, W. (1986) "International Relations and the Psychology of Control: Alternative Control Strategies and Their Consequences," *Political Psychology* 7: 369–375.

Eisenhower, D. (1957) "The Eisenhower Doctrine on the Middle East, a Message to Congress, January 5, 1957." *The Department of State Bulletin* 36(917): 83–87.

Ellis, L. E. (1951) *A Short History of American Diplomacy*, New York: Harper and Brothers.

Elman, C. (1996) "Horses for Courses: Why Not Neorealist Theories of Foreign Policy?" *Security Studies* 6: 7–53.

Elman, C. and M. Elman, eds. (1997) "Symposium: History and Theory," *International Security* 22: 5–85.

Elman, M. F. (1995) "The Foreign Policies of Small States: Challenging Neorealism in Its Own Backyard," *British Journal of Political Science* 25: 171–217.

Elster, J. (1998) "A Plea for Mechanisms," in Hedstrom, P. and R. Swedborg (eds.) *Social Mechanisms: An Analytical Approach to Social Theory*, Cambridge: Cambridge University Press.

Engelbrecht, H. C. and F. C. Hanighen (1934) *Merchants of Death: A Study of the International Armament Industry*, New York: Dodd, Mead and Company.

Fairbank, J. K. (1974) *China Perceived: Images and Policies in Chinese-American Relations*, New York: Alfred A. Knopf.

Fearon, J. D. (1998) "Domestic Politics, Foreign Policy, and Theories of International Relations," *Annual Review of Political Science* 1: 289–313.

Ferrell, R. H. (1975) *American Diplomacy: A History*, New York: W.W. Norton and Company.

Festinger, L. (1957) *A Theory of Cognitive Dissonance*, Stanford, CA: Stanford University Press.

Finkelstein, N. G. (1995) *Image and Reality of the Israel-Palestine Conflict*, London: Verso.

Finnemore, M. (1996a) *National Interests in International Society*, Ithaca, NY: Cornell University Press.

—— (1996b) "Constructing Norms of Humanitarian Intervention," in Katzenstein, P. J. (ed.) *The Culture of National Security: Norms and Identity in World Politics*, New York: Columbia University Press.

—— (1996c) "Norms, Culture, and World Politics: Insights from Sociology's Institutionalism," *International Organization* 50: 325–347.

Finnemore, M. and K. Sikkink (1998) "International Norms and Political Change," *International Organization* 52(4): 887–917.

Flapan, S. (1987) *The Birth of Israel: Myths and Realities,* New York: Pantheon Books.

Flockhart, T. (2006) "'Complex Socialization': A Framework for the Study of State Socialization," *European Journal of International Relations* 12(1): 89–118.

Gaddis, J. L. (1983) "The Emerging Post-revisionist Synthesis on the Origins of the Cold War," *Diplomatic History* 7: 171–190.

—— (1987) "Expanding the Data Base: Historians, Political Scientists, and the Enrichment of Security Studies," *International Security* 12: 3–21.

—— (1990) "New Conceptual Approaches to the Study of American Foreign Relations: Interdisciplinary Perspectives," *Diplomatic History* 14: 403–425.

Gambetta, D. (1998) "Concatenations of Mechanisms," in Hedstrom, P. and R. Swedberg (eds.) *Social Mechanisms: An Analytical Approach to Social Theory,* Cambridge: Cambridge University Press.

Gantenbein, J. W. (1950) *The Evolution of Our Latin American Policy: A Documentary Record,* New York: Columbia University Press.

Gause, F. G. (1999) "Systemic Approaches to Middle East International Relations," *International Studies Review* 1: 11–31.

Gazit, M. (1987) "Israeli Military Procurement from the United States," in Sheffer, G. (ed.) *Dynamics of Dependence: U.S.-Israeli Relations,* Boulder, CO: Westview Press.

George, A. L., and A. Bennett (2004) *Case Studies and Theory Development in the Social Sciences,* Cambridge, MA: MIT Press.

George, A. L. and T. J. McKeown (1985) "Case Studies and Theories of Organizational Decision Making," *Advances in Information Processing in Organizations* 2: 21–58.

Gerassi, J. (1965) *The Great Fear in Latin America,* New York: Collier Books.

Giddens, A. (1983) "Comments on the Theory of Structuration," *Journal for the Theory of Social Behaviour* 13: 75–96.

Gilpin, R. (1981) *War and Change in World Politics,* New York: Cambridge University Press.

Goddard, S. E. and D. H. Nexon (2005) "Paradigm Lost: Reassessing Theory of International Politics," *European Journal of International Relations* 11(1): 9–61.

Goertz, G. and P. F. Diehl (1992) "The Empirical Importance of Enduring Rivalries," *International Interactions* 18: 151–163.

—— (1993) "Enduring Rivalries: Theoretical Constructs and Empirical Patterns," *International Studies Quarterly* 37: 147–171.

Goldstein, J. and R. O. Keohane (1993) *Ideas and Foreign Policy: Beliefs, Institutions and Political Change,* Ithaca, NY: Cornell University Press.

Goode, W. J. (1960) "A Theory of Role Strain," *American Sociological Review* 25: 483–496.

Granovetter, M. (1978) "Threshold Models of Collective Behavior," *American Journal of Sociology* 83: 1420–1443.

Grattan, C. H. (1929) *Why We Fought,* New York: The Vanguard Press.

Gulick, E. (1955) *Europe's Classical Balance of Power,* New York: Norton.

Hall, D. T. (1972) "A Model of Coping with Conflict: The Role of College Educated Women," *Administrative Science Quarterly* 4: 471–486.

Hall, P. and R. Taylor (1996) "Political Science and the Three New Institutionalisms," *Political Studies* 44: 936–957.

Harnisch, S., C. Frank, and H. W. Maull, eds. (2011) *Role Theory in International Relations,* London: Routledge.

Harris, J. R. (1998) *The Nurture Assumption: Why Children Turn Out the Way They Do,* New York: Free Press.

Hatzenbuehler, R. L. (1981) "The Early National Period, 1789–1815: The Need for Redefinition," in Haines, G. K. and J. S. Walker (eds.) *American Foreign Relations: A Historiographical Overview,* Westport, CT: Greenwood Press.

Hestrom, P. (1998) "Rational Imitation," in Hedstrom, P. and R. Swedberg (eds.) *Social Mechanisms: An Analytical Approach to Social Theory,* Cambridge: Cambridge University Press.

Hedstrom, P. and R. Swedberg (1998) "Social Mechanisms: An Introductory Essay," in Hedstrom, P. and R. Swedberg (eds.) *Social Mechanisms: An Analytical Approach to Social Theory,* Cambridge: Cambridge University Press.

Hermann, C. F., ed. (1972) *International Crises: Insights from Behavioral Research,* New York: The Free Press.

Herzl, Theodor (1896) *Der Judenstaat,* Leipzig: M. Breitenstein's Verlags-Buchhandlung.

Hoffman, S. (1977) "An American Social Science: International Relations," *Daedalus* 106: 41–60.

Hogan, M. J. and T. G. Paterson (1991) "Introduction," in Hogan, M. J. and T. G. Paterson (eds.) *Explaining the History of American Foreign Relations,* Cambridge: Cambridge University Press.

Holsti, K. J. (1970) "National Role Conceptions in the Study of Foreign Policy," *International Studies Quarterly* 14(3): 233–309.

Holsti, O. R. (1991) "International Relations Models," in Hogan, M. J. and T. G. Paterson (eds.) *Explaining the History of American Foreign Relations,* Cambridge: Cambridge University Press.

Hse, I.C.Y. (1975) *The Rise of Modern China,* 2nd ed., New York: Oxford University Press.

Hunt, M. H. (1992) "The Long Crisis in U.S. Diplomatic History: Coming to Closure," *Diplomatic History* 16: 360–385.

Ikenberry, G. J. (1988) "Conclusion: An Institutional Approach to American Foreign Economic Policy," *International Organization* 42(1): 219–243.

Ikenberry, G. J., and C. A. Kupchan (1990) "Socialization and Hegemonic Power," *International Organization* 44: 283–315.

Immerman, R. H. (1991) "Psychology," in Hogan, M. J. and T. G. Paterson (eds.) *Explaining the History of American Foreign Relations,* Cambridge: Cambridge University Press.

Iriye, A. (1993) *The Globalizing of America, 1913–1945,* Cambridge: Cambridge University Press.

Jackson, R. H. (1990) *Quasi-States: Sovereignty, International Relations, and the Third World,* Cambridge: Cambridge University Press.

James, E. (1981) "Wilsonian Wartime Diplomacy: The Sense of the Seventies," in Haines, G. K. and J. S. Walker (eds.) *American Foreign Relations: A Historiographical Overview,* Westport, CT: Greenwood Press.

Jepperson, R. L., A. Wendt, and P. J. Katzenstein (1996) "Norms, Identity, and Culture in National Security," in Katzenstein, P. J. (ed.) *The Culture of National Security: Norms and Identity in World Politics,* New York: Columbia University Press.

Jervis, R. (1976) *Perception and Misperception in International Politics,* Princeton, NJ: Princeton University Press.

—— (1993) "International Primacy: Is the Game Worth the Candle?" *International Security* 17: 52–67.

Jervis, R. (1998) *System Effects: Complexity in Political and Social Life,* Princeton, NJ: Princeton University Press.

Johnston, A. I. (1995) *Cultural Realism: Strategic Culture and Grand Strategy in Chinese History,* Princeton, NJ: Princeton University Press.

—— (1996) "Cultural Realism and Strategy in Maoist China," in Katzenstein, P. J. (ed.) *The Culture of National Security: Norms and Identity in World Politics,* New York: Columbia University Press.

Kahler, M. (1998) "Rationality in International Relations," *International Organization* 52(4): 919–941.

Kaplan, M. (1957) *System and Process in International Politics*, New York: Wiley.

Karsh, E. (1997) *Fabricating Israeli History: The "New Historians,"* London: Frank Cass & Co.

Katzenstein, P. J. (1996) "Introduction: Alternative Perspectives on National Security," in Katzenstein, P. J. (ed.) *The Culture of National Security: Norms and Identity in World Politics*, New York: Columbia University Press.

Katzenstein, P. J., R. O. Keohane, and S. D. Krasner (1998) "'International Organization' and the Study of World Politics," *International Organization* 52: 645–685.

Kegley, C. (1995) *Controversies in International Relations Theory: Realism and the Neoliberal Challenge*, New York: St. Martin's Press.

Kennan, G. F. (1951) *American Diplomacy, 1900–1950*, Chicago, IL: University of Chicago Press.

Keohane, R. (1984) *After Hegemony*, Princeton, NJ: Princeton University Press.

Kerr, M. H. (1971) *The Arab Cold War: Gamal Abdel Nasser and His Rivals*, London: Oxford University Press.

Kerr, M. H., and E. S. Yassin, eds. (1982) *Rich and Poor States in the Middle East: Egypt and the New Arab Order*, Boulder, CO: Westview Press.

Khong, Y. F. (1992) *Analogies at War: Korea, Munich, Dien Bien Phu, and the Vietnam Decisions of 1965*, Princeton, NJ: Princeton University Press.

Kier, E. (1995) "Culture and Military Doctrine: France Between the Wars," *International Security* 19: 65–93.

—— (1996) "Culture and French Military Doctrine Before World War II," in Katzenstein, P. J. (ed.) *The Culture of National Security: Norms and Identity in World Politics*, New York: Columbia University Press.

—— (1997) *Imagining War: French and British Military Doctrine Between the Wars*, Princeton, NJ: Princeton University Press.

King, G., R. O. Keohane, and S. Verba (1994) *Designing Social Inquiry: Scientific Inference in Qualitative Research*, Princeton, NJ: Princeton University Press.

Klapp, O. E. (1962) *Heroes, Villains and Fools*, Englewood Cliffs, NJ: Prentice-Hall.

Klingberg, F. L. (1983) *Cyclical Trends in American Foreign Policy Moods: The Unfolding of America's World Role*, Lanham, MD: University Press of America.

—— (1996) *Positive Expectations of America's World Role: Historical Cycles of Realistic Idealism*, Lanham, MD: University Press of America.

Kowert, P. and J. Legro (1996) "Norms, Identity, and their Limits," in Katzenstein, P. J. (ed.) *The Culture of National Security: Norms and Identity in World Politics*, New York: Columbia University Press.

Kowert, P. A., and C. G. Thies (forthcoming) "(Babylonian) Lions, (Asian) Tigers, and (Russian) Bears: A Statistical Test of Three Rivalrous Paths to Conflict," *Journal of International Relations and Development*.

Kranser, S. D., ed. (1983) *International Regimes*, Ithaca, NY: Cornell University Press.

—— (1988) "Sovereignty: An Institutional Perspective," *Comparative Political Studies* 21(1): 66–94.

Kuhn, T. S. (1970) *The Structure of Scientific Revolutions*, 2nd ed., Chicago, IL: University of Chicago Press.

Kuran, T. (1998) "Social Mechanisms of Dissonance Reduction," in Hedstrom, P. and R. Swedberg (eds.) *Social Mechanisms: An Analytical Approach to Social Theory*, Cambridge: Cambridge University Press.

LaFeber, W. (1963) *The New Empire: An Interpretation of American Expansion, 1860–1898*, Ithaca, NY: Cornell University Press.

—— (1981) "Responses to Charles S. Maier's 'Marking Time: The Historiography of International Relations,'" *Diplomatic History* 5: 60–72.

—— (1993) *The American Search for Opportunity, 1865–1913,* Cambridge: Cambridge University Press.

Laqueur, W. (1968) *The Road to Jerusalem: The Origins of the Arab-Israeli Conflict, 1967,* New York: Macmillan.

Layne, C. (1993) "The Unipolar Illusion: Why New Great Powers Will Rise," *International Security* 17: 5–51.

Le Prestre, P. G. (1997a) "Author! Author! Defining Foreign Policy Roles after the Cold War," in Le Prestre, P. G. (ed.) *Role Quests in the Post–Cold War Era,* Montreal: McGill-Queen's University Press.

—— (1997b) "The United States: An Elusive Role Quest after the Cold War," in Le Prestre, P. G. (ed.) *Role Quests in the Post-Cold War Era,* Montreal McGill-Queen's University Press.

Levey, Z. (1997) *Israel and the Western Powers, 1952–1960,* Chapel Hill: University of North Carolina Press.

Levy, J. S. (1994) "Learning and Foreign Policy: Sweeping a Conceptual Minefield," *International Organization* 48: 279–312.

—— (1997) "Too Important to Leave to the Other: History and Political Science in the Study of International Relations," *International Security* 22: 22–33.

Liebman, C. S. and E. Don-Yehiya (1983) *Civil Religion in Israel,* Berkeley: University of California Press.

Lieuwen, E. (1965) *U.S. Policy in Latin America: A Short History,* New York: Praeger.

Link, A. (1974) *Wilson the Diplomatist: A Look at His Major Foreign Policies,* New York: New Viewpoints.

Lippman, W. (1943) *American Foreign Policy: Shield of the Republic,* New York: Macmillan.

Little, D. (1991) *Varieties of Social Explanation: An Introduction to the Philosophy of Social Science,* Boulder, CO: Westview Press.

Love, K. (1969) *Suez: The Twice Fought War,* New York: McGraw-Hill.

Luciani, G., and G. Salame (1988) *The Politics of Arab Integration,* London: Croom Helms.

Lustick, I. S. (1996) "History, Historiography, and Political Science: Multiple Historical Records and the Problem of Selection Bias," *American Political Science Review* 90: 605–618.

—— (1997) "The Absence of Middle Eastern Great Powers: Political 'Backwardness' in Historical Perspective," *International Organization* 51: 653–683.

Maoz, Z. (1989) "Joining the Club of Nations: Political Development and International Conflict, 1816–1976," *International Studies Quarterly* 33: 199–231.

March, J. G. and J. P. Olsen (1984) "The New Institutionalism: Organizational Factors in Political Life," *American Political Science Review* 78: 734–749.

—— (1989) *Rediscovering Institutions: The Organizational Basis of Politics,* New York: Free Press.

—— (1995) *Democratic Governance,* New York: Free Press.

—— (1998) "The Institutional Dynamics of International Political Orders," *International Organization* 52: 943–969.

Martin, L. L. and B. A. Simmons (1998) "Theories and Empirical Studies of International Institutions," *International Organization* 52(4): 729–757.

Mastanduno, M. (1997) "Preserving the Unipolar Moment: Realist Theories and U.S. Grand Strategy after the Cold War," *International Security* 21: 49–88.

Mearsheimer, J. J. (1990) "Back to the Future: Instability in Europe After the Cold War," *International Security* 15: 5–56.

—— (1994/1995) "The False Promise of International Institutions," *International Security* 19: 5–49.

Mercer, J. (1995) "Anarchy and Identity," *International Organization* 49(2): 229–252.

Meyer, J. W. (1980) "The World Polity and the Authority of the Nation-State," in Bergesen, A. (ed.) *Studies of the Modern World-System*, New York: Academic Press.

Meyer, J. W., J. Boli, G. M. Thomas, and F. O. Ramirez (1997) "World Society and the Nation State," *American Journal of Sociology* 103: 144–181.

McCoy, C. A. (1960) *Polk and the Presidency*, Austin: University of Texas Press.

McLane, C. (1973) *Soviet-Middle East Relations*, London: Central Asian Research Centre.

McMahon, R. J. (1991) "The Study of American Foreign Relations: National History or International History?" in Hogan, M. J. and T. G. Paterson (eds.) *Explaining the History of American Foreign Relations*, Cambridge: Cambridge University Press.

McNeely, C. L. (1995) *Constructing the Nation-State: International Organization and Prescriptive Action*, Westport, CT: Greenwood Press.

Milner, H. (1991) "The Assumption of Anarchy in International Relations Theory: A Critique," *Review of International Studies* 17: 67–85.

Modelski, G. (1987) *Long Cycles in World Politics*, Seattle: University of Washington Press.

Moravcsik, A. (1993) "Preferences and Power in the European Community: A Liberal Intergovernmentalist Approach," *Journal of Common Market Studies* 31: 473–524.

Moreland, R. L. (1985) "Social Categorization and the Assimilation of 'New' Group Members," *Journal of Personality and Social Psychology* 48: 1173–1190.

Morgenthau, H. J. (1951) *In Defense of the National Interest*, New York: Alfred A. Knopf.

Morris, B. (1988a) "The New Historiography: Israel and its Past," *Tikkun* 3: 26–44.

—— (1988b) *The Birth of the Palestinian Refugee Problem, 1948–1949*, New York: Cambridge University Press.

—— (1990) *1948 and After*, Oxford: Oxford University Press.

Morrow, J. D. (1988) "Social Choice and System Structure in World Politics," *World Politics* 56: 75–97.

Nathan, J. A. and J. K Oliver (1985) *United States Foreign Policy and World Order*, 3rd ed., Boston, MA: Little, Brown and Company.

Neu, C. E. (1975) *The Troubled Encounter: The United States and Japan*, New York: John Wiley and Sons.

O'Ballance, E. (1972) *The Third Arab-Israeli War*, London: Faber and Faber.

Osgood, R. E. (1952) *Ideals and Self-Interest in American Foreign Relations*, Chicago, IL: University of Chicago Press.

Oye, K., ed. (1986) *Cooperation Under Anarchy*, Princeton, NJ: Princeton University Press.

Palumbo, M. (1987) *The Palestinian Catastrophe*, London: Faber.

Pappe, I. (1988) *Britain and the Arab-Israeli Conflict, 1948–51*, New York: Macmillan.

—— (1992) *The Making of the Arab-Israeli Conflict, 1948–51*, London: I. B. Tauris.

Paterson, T. G. (1991) "Defining and Doing the History of American Foreign Relations: A Primer," in Hogan, M. J. and T. G. Paterson (eds.) *Explaining the History of American Foreign Relations*, Cambridge: Cambridge University Press.

Pelz, S. E. (1988) "A Taxonomy for American Diplomatic History," *Journal of Interdisciplinary History* 19: 259–276.

Peretz, D. (1996) *The Arab-Israel Dispute*, New York: Facts On File, Inc.

Perkins, B. (1963) *Prologue to War: England and the United States, 1805–1812*, Berkeley: University of California Press.

—— (1984) "'The Tragedy of American Diplomacy': Twenty-five Years After," *Reviews in American History* 12: 1–18.

—— (1993) *The Creation of a Republican Empire, 1776–1865*, Cambridge: Cambridge University Press.

Perkins, D. (1927) *The Monroe Doctrine, 1823–1826*, Cambridge: Cambridge University Press.

—— (1955) *A History of the Monroe Doctrine*, Boston, MA: Little, Brown.

Perlmutter, A. (1975) "Israel's Fourth War, October 1973: Political and Military Misperceptions," *Orbis* 19: 434–460.

Pierson, P. (1996) "The Path to European Integration: A Historical Institutionalist Analysis," *Comparative Political Studies* 29(2): 123–163.

Pratt, J. W. (1955) *A History of United States Foreign Policy*, Englewood Cliffs, NJ: Prentice-Hall.

Pratt, J. W., V. P. De Santos, and J. M. Siracusa (1980) *A History of United States Foreign Policy*, 4th ed., Englewood Cliffs, NJ: Prentice-Hall.

Putnam, R. (1988) "Diplomacy and Domestic Politics: The Logic of Two-Level Games," *International Organization* 42: 427–461.

Rabinovich, I. (1985) *The War for Lebanon, 1970–1985*, Ithaca, NY: Cornell University Press.

Rappaport, A. (1975) *A History of American Diplomacy*, New York: MacMillan Company.

Reiter, D. (1996) *Crucible of Beliefs: Learning, Alliances and World Wars*, Ithaca, NY: Cornell University Press.

Resende-Santos, J. (1996) "Anarchy and the Emulation of Military Systems: Military Organization and Technology in South America, 1870–1930," *Security Studies* 5: 193–260.

Risse, T., S. C. Ropp, and K. Sikkink (1999) *The Power of Human Rights: International Norms and Domestic Change*, Cambridge: Cambridge University Press.

Ro'i, Y. (1980) *Soviet Decision-Making in Practice: The U.S.S.R. and Israel, 1947–1954*, New Brunswick, NJ: Transaction.

Rosecrance, R. N. (1963) *Action and Reaction in World Politics: International Systems in Perspective*, Boston, MA: Little, Brown.

Rosenau, J. N. (1990) *Turbulence in World Politics: A Theory of Change and Continuity*, Princeton, NJ: Princeton University Press.

Rosenberg, E. S. (1991) "Walking the Borders," in Hogan, M. J. and T. G. Paterson (eds.) *Explaining the History of American Foreign Relations*, Cambridge, MA: Cambridge University Press.

Rothstein, R. L. (1968) *Alliances and Small Powers*, New York: Columbia University Press.

Rubinstein, A. Z. (1977) *Red Star on the Nile: The Soviet-Egyptian Influence Relationship Since the June War*, Princeton, NJ: Princeton University Press.

Ruggie, J. G. (1986) "Continuity and Transformation in the World Polity: Toward a Neorealist Synthesis," in Keohane, R. O. (ed.) *Neorealism and Its Critics*, New York: Columbia University Press.

—— (1998a) "What Makes the World Hang Together? Neo-utilitarianism and the Social Constructivist Challenge," *International Organization* 52: 855–885.

—— (1998b) *Constructing the World Polity*, London: Routledge.

Safran, N. (1969) *From War to War: The Arab-Israeli Confrontation, 1968–1967*, Indianapolis, IN: The Bobbs-Merrill Company.

—— (1981) *Israel: The Embattled Ally*, Cambridge, MA: Harvard University Press.

Sampson, M. W. and S. G. Walker (1987) "Cultural Norms and National Roles: A Comparison of Japan and France," in Walker, S. G. (ed.) *Role Theory and Foreign Policy Analysis*, Durham, NC: Duke University Press.

Sandler, S. (1993) *The State of Israel, the Land of Israel: The Statist and Ethnonational Dimensions of Foreign Policy*, Westport, CT: Greenwood Press.

Sarbin, T. R. and V. L. Allen (1968) "Role Theory," in Lindzey, G. and E. Aronson (eds.) *Handbook of Social Psychology,* 2nd ed., Reading, MA: Addison-Wesley Publishing Company.

Schelling, T. C. (1978) *Micromotives and Macrobehavior,* New York: W. W. Norton.

Schiff, Z. and E. Yaari (1984) *A War of Deception,* Tel Aviv, Israel: Schocken.

Schimmelfennig, F. (2000) "International Socialization in the New Europe: Rational Action in an Institutional Environment," *European Journal of International Relations* 6(1): 109–139.

Schulzinger, R. D. (1984) *American Diplomacy in the Twentieth Century,* Oxford: Oxford University Press.

Schweller, R. L. (1996) "Neorealism's Status-Quo Bias," *Security Studies* 5: 90–121.

Sharett, M. (1955) "Telegram from the Embassy in Israel to the Department of State," *Foreign Relations of the United States, 1955–1957,* Vol. 14, Arab-Israeli Dispute, 1955, Document 73.

Sheffer, G., and M. Hofnung (1987) "Israel's Image," in Sheffer, G. (ed.) *Dynamics of Dependence: U.S.-Israeli Relations,* Boulder, CO: Westview Press.

Shlaim, A. (1988) *Collusion Across the Jordan: King Abdullah, the Zionist Movement and the Partition of Palestine,* Oxford: Clarendon Press.

Spanier, J. W. (1992) *American Foreign Policy Since World War II,* 12th ed., Washington, DC: Congressional Quarterly Press.

Spruyt, H. (1994) *The Sovereign State and Its Competitors,* Princeton, NJ: Princeton University Press.

Spyckman, N. J. (1941) *America's Strategy in World Politics: The United States and the Balance of Power,* New York: Harcourt, Brace and Company.

Stagg, J. C. A. (1983) *Mr. Madison's War: Politics, Diplomacy, and Warfare in the Early American Republic, 1783–1830,* Princeton, NJ: Princeton University Press.

Stein, A. A. (1990) *Why Nations Cooperate: Circumstance and Choice in International Relations,* Ithaca, NY: Cornell University Press.

Steinmo, S., K. Thelen and F. Longstreth (1992) *Structuring Politics: Historical Institutionalism in Comparative Analysis,* Cambridge: Cambridge University Press.

Stinchcombe, A. (1991) "The Conditions of Fruitfulness of Theorizing about Mechanisms in Social Science," *Philosophy of the Social Sciences* 21: 367–388.

—— (1998) "Monopolistic Competition as a Mechanism: Corporations, Universities and Nation-States in Competitive Fields," in Hedstrom, P. and R. Swedberg (eds.) *Social Mechanisms: An Analytical Approach to Social Theory,* Cambridge: Cambridge University Press.

Stinchcombe, W. (1980) *The XYZ Affair,* Westport, CT: Greenwood Press.

Stokes, R., and J. P. Hewitt (1976) "Aligning Actions," *American Sociological Review* 41: 838–849.

Stryker, S. and A. Statham (1985) "Symbolic Interaction and Role Theory," in Lindzey, G. and E. Aronson (eds.) *Handbook of Social Psychology,* 3rd ed., New York: Random House.

Tansill, C. (1938) *America Goes to War,* Boston, MA: Little, Brown and Company.

Telhami, S. (1990) *Power and Leadership in International Bargaining: The Path to the Camp David Accords,* New York: Columbia University Press.

—— (1996) "Israel's Foreign Policy: A Realist Ideal-Type or a Breed of Its Own?" in Barnett, M. N. (ed.) *Israel in Comparative Perspective,* Albany: State University of New York Press.

Tessler, M. (1994) *A History of the Israeli-Palestinian Conflict,* Bloomington: Indiana University Press.

Teveth, S. (1985) *Ben-Gurion and the Arabs of Palestine,* New York: Oxford University Press.

—— (1990) "The Palestine Arab Refugee Problem and its Origins," *Middle Eastern Studies* 26: 214–249.

Thies, C. G. (2001) "A Social Psychological Approach to Enduring Rivalries," *Political Psychology* 22(4): 693–725.

—— (2002) "A Pragmatic Guide to Qualitative Historical Analysis in the Study of International Relations," *International Studies Perspectives* 3(4): 351–372.

—— (2003) "Sense and Sensibility in the Study of State Socialization: A Reply to Kai Alderson," *Review of International Studies* 29(4): 543–550.

—— (2010a) "Role Theory and Foreign Policy," in Denemark, R. A. (ed.) *The International Studies Encyclopedia*, West Sussex, UK: Wiley-Blackwell.

—— (2010b) "State Socialization and Structural Realism," *Security Studies* 19(4): 689–717.

—— (2012) "International Socialization Processes v. Israeli National Role Conceptions: Can Role Theory Integrate IR Theory and Foreign Policy Analysis?" *Foreign Policy Analysis* 8(1): 25–46.

Thies, C. G. (forthcoming) "The Roles of Bipolarity: A Role Theoretic Understanding of the Effects of Ideas and Material Factors on the Cold War," *International Studies Perspectives*.

Thies, C. G., and M. Breuning (2012) "Integrating Foreign Policy Analysis and International Relations through Role Theory," *Foreign Policy Analysis* 8(1): 1–4.

Thomas, G. M., J. W. Meyer, F. O. Ramirez, and J. Boli, eds. (1987) *Institutional Structure: Constituting State, Society, and Individual*, Newbury Park, CA: Sage Publications.

Thompson, W. (1988) *On Global War*, Columbia: University of South Carolina Press.

Troen, S. I. and M. Shemesh, eds. (1990) *The Suez-Sinai Crisis 1956: Retrospective and Reappraisal*, London: Frank Cass.

Tucker, R. W. and D.C. Hendrickson (1990) *Empire of Liberty: The Statecraft of Thomas Jefferson*, New York: Oxford University Press.

Tunnel, J. K. (1922) *Shall It Be Again?* New York: Macmillan.

Varg, P. A. (1963) *Foreign Policies of the Founding Fathers*, East Lansing: Michigan State University Press.

—— (1990) *America, from Client State to World Power: Six Major Transitions in United States Foreign Relations*, Norman: University of Oklahoma Press.

Vertzberger, Y. (1990) *The World in Their Minds: Information Processing, Cognition, and Perception in Foreign Policy Decision Making*, Stanford, CA: Stanford University Press.

Vinson, J. C. (1961) "Charles Evans Hughes," in Graebner, N. A. (ed.) *An Uncertain Tradition: American Secretaries of State in the Twentieth Century*, New York: McGraw-Hill.

Walker, S. G. (1979) "National Role Conceptions and Systemic Outcomes," in Falkowski, L. (ed.) *Psychological Models in International Politics*, Boulder, CO: Westview Press.

—— (1987) "Role Theory and the International System: A Postscript to Waltz's Theory of International Politics?" in Walker, S. G. (ed.) *Role Theory and Foreign Policy Analysis*, Durham, NC: Duke University Press.

—— (1992) "Symbolic Interactionism and International Politics: Role Theory's Contribution to International Organization," in Cottam, M. and C. Shih (eds.) *Contending Dramas: A Cognitive Approach to International Organizations*, New York: Praeger.

Walt, S. M. (1987) *The Origin of Alliances*, Ithaca, NY: Cornell University Press.

—— (1996) *Revolution and War*, Ithaca, NY: Cornell University Press.

Waltz, K. N. (1979) *Theory of International Politics*, New York: McGraw-Hill.

—— (1986) "Reflections on 'Theory of International Politics': A Response to My Critics," in Keohane, R. O. (ed.) *Neorealism and Its Critics*, New York: Columbia University Press.

—— (1990) "The Emerging Structure of International Politics," in *Relations in a Multipolar World,* U.S. Senate, Committee on Foreign Relations, 101st Congress, 2nd Session.

—— (1993) "The Emerging Structure of International Politics," *International Security* 18: 44–79.

Waterbury, J., and R. el Mallakh (1978) *The Middle East in the Coming Decade: From Wellhead to Well-Being?* New York: McGraw-Hill.

Weinstein, E. and P. Deutschberger (1963) "Some Dimensions of Altercasting," *Sociometry* 26: 454–466.

Welles, S. (1944) *The Time for Decision,* New York: Harper and Row.

Wendt, A. (1987) "The Agent-Structure Problem in International Relations Theory," *International Organization* 41: 335–370.

—— (1992) "Anarchy is What States Make of It: The Social Construction of Power Politics," *International Organization* 46: 391–425.

—— (1994) "Collective Identity Formation and the International State," *American Political Science Review* 88: 384–396.

—— (1999) *Social Theory of International Politics,* Cambridge: Cambridge University Press.

Wentworth, W. M. (1980) *Context and Understanding: An Inquiry into Socialization Theory,* New York: Elsevier.

Whitaker, A. P. (1941) *The United States and the Independence of Latin America, 1800–1830,* Baltimore, MD: Johns Hopkins University Press.

Whitcomb, R. S. (1998) *The American Approach to Foreign Affairs: An Uncertain Tradition,* Westport, CT: Praeger Publishers.

Williams, W. A. (1959) *The Tragedy of American Diplomacy,* New York: Dell Publishing Co.

Wish, N. B. (1987) "National Attributes as Sources of National Role Conceptions: A Capability-Motivation Model," in Walker, S. G. (ed.) *Role Theory and Foreign Policy Analysis,* Durham, NC: Duke University Press.

Yaniv, A. (1987) *Dilemmas of Security: Politics, Strategy, and the Israeli Experience in Lebanon,* London: Oxford University Press

Index

An environmentally friendly book printed and bound in England by www.printondemand-worldwide.com

PEFC Certified

This product is
from sustainably
managed forests
and controlled
sources

www.pefc.org

PEFC/16-33-415

This book is made entirely of sustainable materials; FSC paper for the cover and PEFC paper for the text pages.

#0035 - 050913 - C0 - 229/152/10 [12] - CB